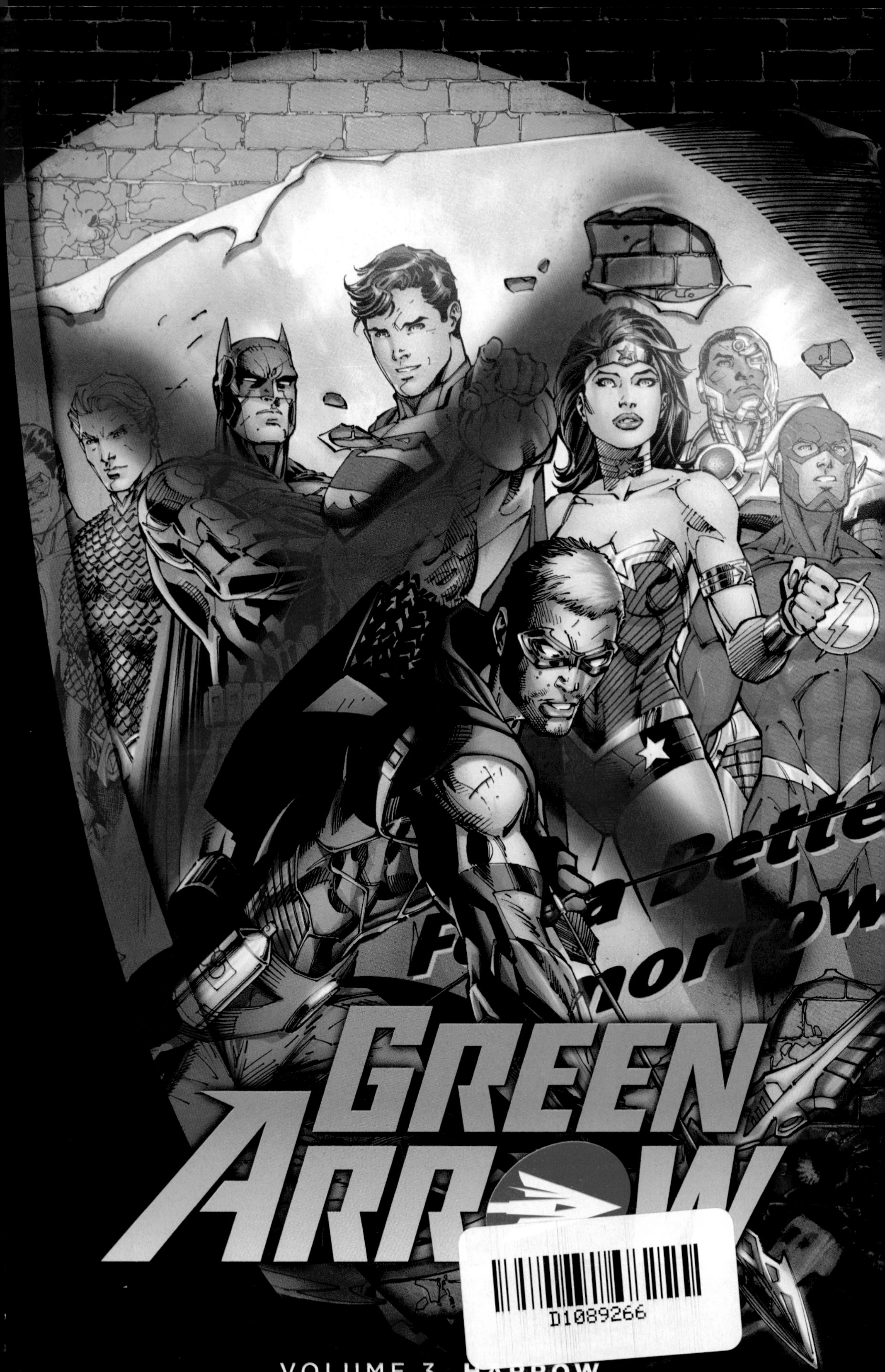

GREEN ARROW

VOLUME 3 HARROW

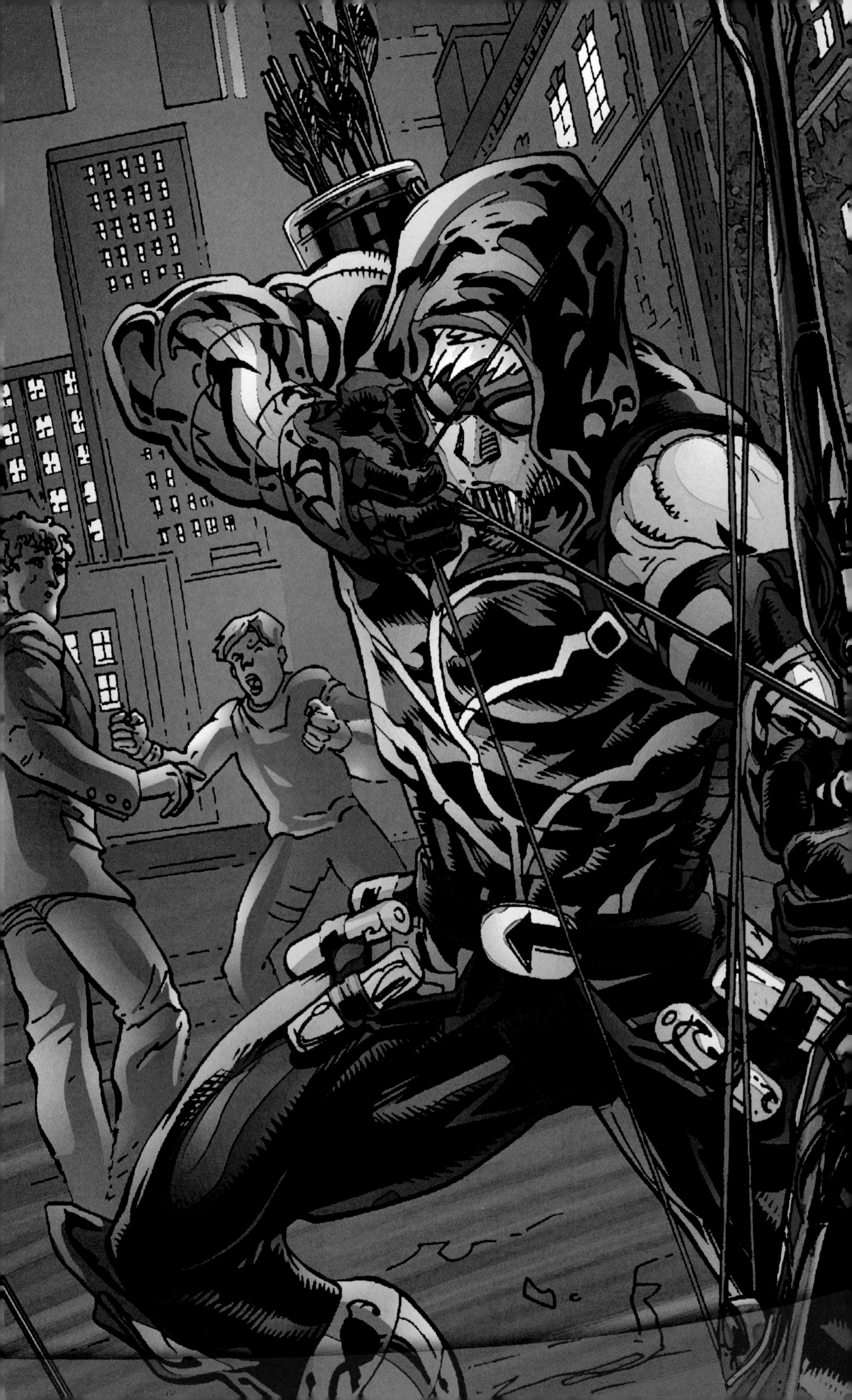

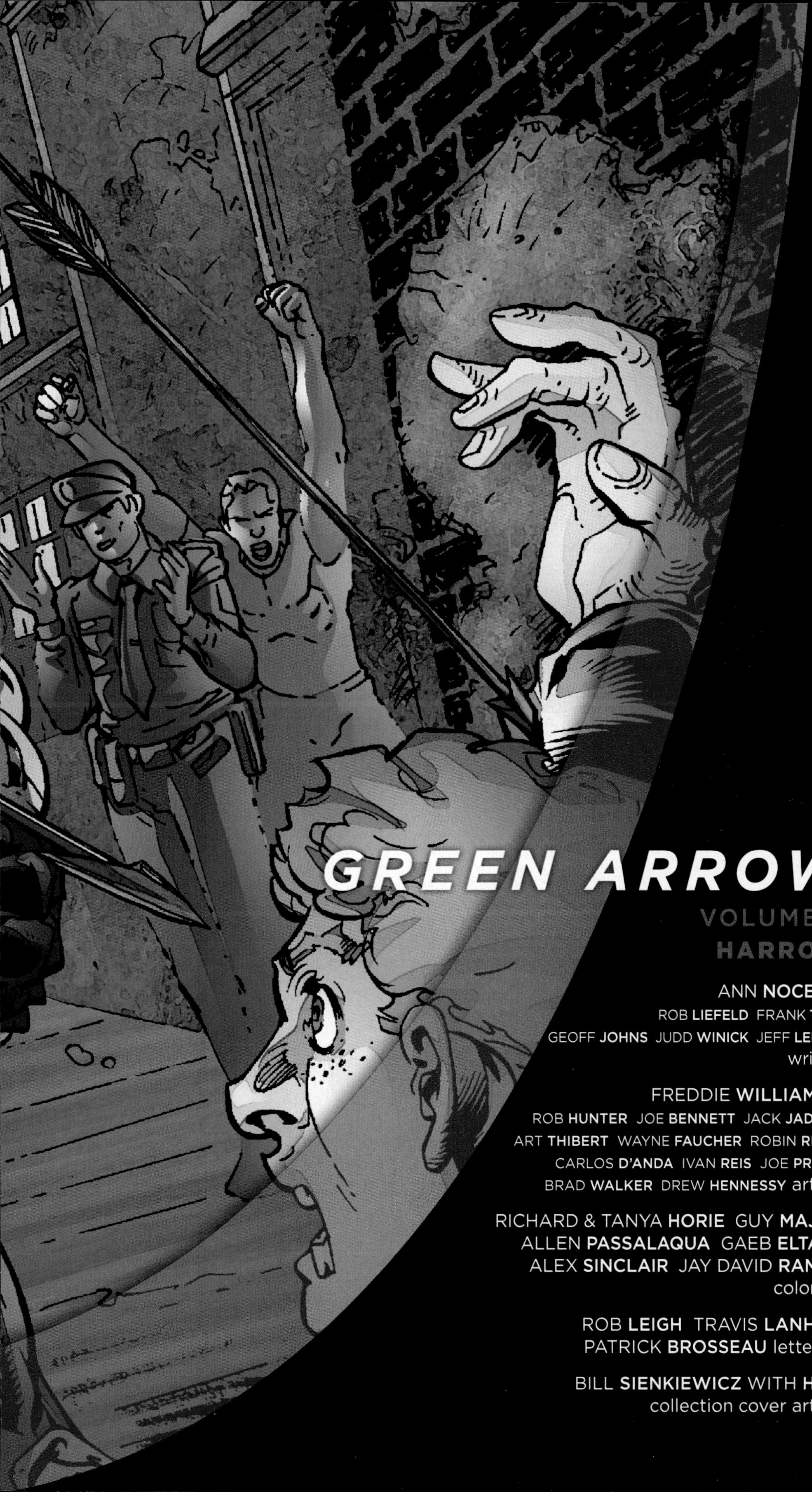

GREEN ARROW

VOLUME 3
HARROW

ANN **NOCENTI**
ROB **LIEFELD** FRANK **TIERI**
GEOFF **JOHNS** JUDD **WINICK** JEFF **LEMIRE**
writers

FREDDIE **WILLIAMS II**
ROB **HUNTER** JOE **BENNETT** JACK **JADSON**
ART **THIBERT** WAYNE **FAUCHER** ROBIN **RIGGS**
CARLOS **D'ANDA** IVAN **REIS** JOE **PRADO**
BRAD **WALKER** DREW **HENNESSY** artists

RICHARD & TANYA **HORIE** GUY **MAJOR**
ALLEN **PASSALAQUA** GAEB **ELTAEB**
ALEX **SINCLAIR** JAY DAVID **RAMOS**
colorists

ROB **LEIGH** TRAVIS **LANHAM**
PATRICK **BROSSEAU** letterers

BILL **SIENKIEWICZ** WITH **HI-FI**
collection cover artists

JOEY CAVALIERI HARVEY RICHARDS BRIAN CUNNINGHAM Editors – Original Series
KATE STEWART DARREN SHAN KATIE KUBERT Assistant Editors – Original Series
ROWENA YOW Editor ROBBIN BROSTERMAN Design Director – Books ROBBIE BIEDERMAN Publication Design

BOB HARRAS Senior VP – Editor-in-Chief, DC Comics

DIANE NELSON President DAN DIDIO and JIM LEE Co-Publishers
GEOFF JOHNS Chief Creative Officer AMIT DESAI Senior VP – Marketing & Franchise Management
AMY GENKINS Senior VP – Business & Legal Affairs NAIRI GARDINER Senior VP – Finance
JEFF BOISON VP – Publishing Planning MARK CHIARELLO VP – Art Direction & Design
JOHN CUNNINGHAM VP – Marketing TERRI CUNNINGHAM VP – Editorial Administration
LARRY GANEM VP – Talent Relations & Services ALISON GILL Senior VP – Manufacturing & Operations
HANK KANALZ Senior VP – Vertigo & Integrated Publishing JAY KOGAN VP – Business & Legal Affairs, Publishing
JACK MAHAN VP – Business Affairs, Talent NICK NAPOLITANO VP – Manufacturing Administration
SUE POHJA VP – Book Sales FRED RUIZ VP – Manufacturing Operations
COURTNEY SIMMONS Senior VP – Publicity BOB WAYNE Senior VP – Sales

GREEN ARROW VOLUME 3: HARROW

DC Comics, 1700 Broadway, New York, NY 10019
A Warner Bros. Entertainment Company.
Printed by RR Donnelley, Owensville, MO, USA. 7/25/14. Second Printing.

ISBN: 978-1-4012-4405-7

SUSTAINABLE FORESTRY INITIATIVE

Certified Chain of Custody
20% Certified Forest Content,
80% Certified Sourcing
www.sfiprogram.org
SFI-01042
APPLIES TO TEXT STOCK ONLY

Library of Congress Cataloging-in-Publication Data

Nocenti, Ann.
Green Arrow. Volume 3, Harrow / Ann Nocenti, Freddie E. Williams II.
pages cm
"Originally published in single magazine form in Green Arrow, 14-16,
Hawkman 14, Justice League 8, 13."
ISBN 978-1-4012-4405-7
1. Graphic novels. I. Williams, Freddie E., 1977- II. Title. III. Title: Harro.
PN6728.G725N65 2013
741.5'973—dc23
                                        2013016907

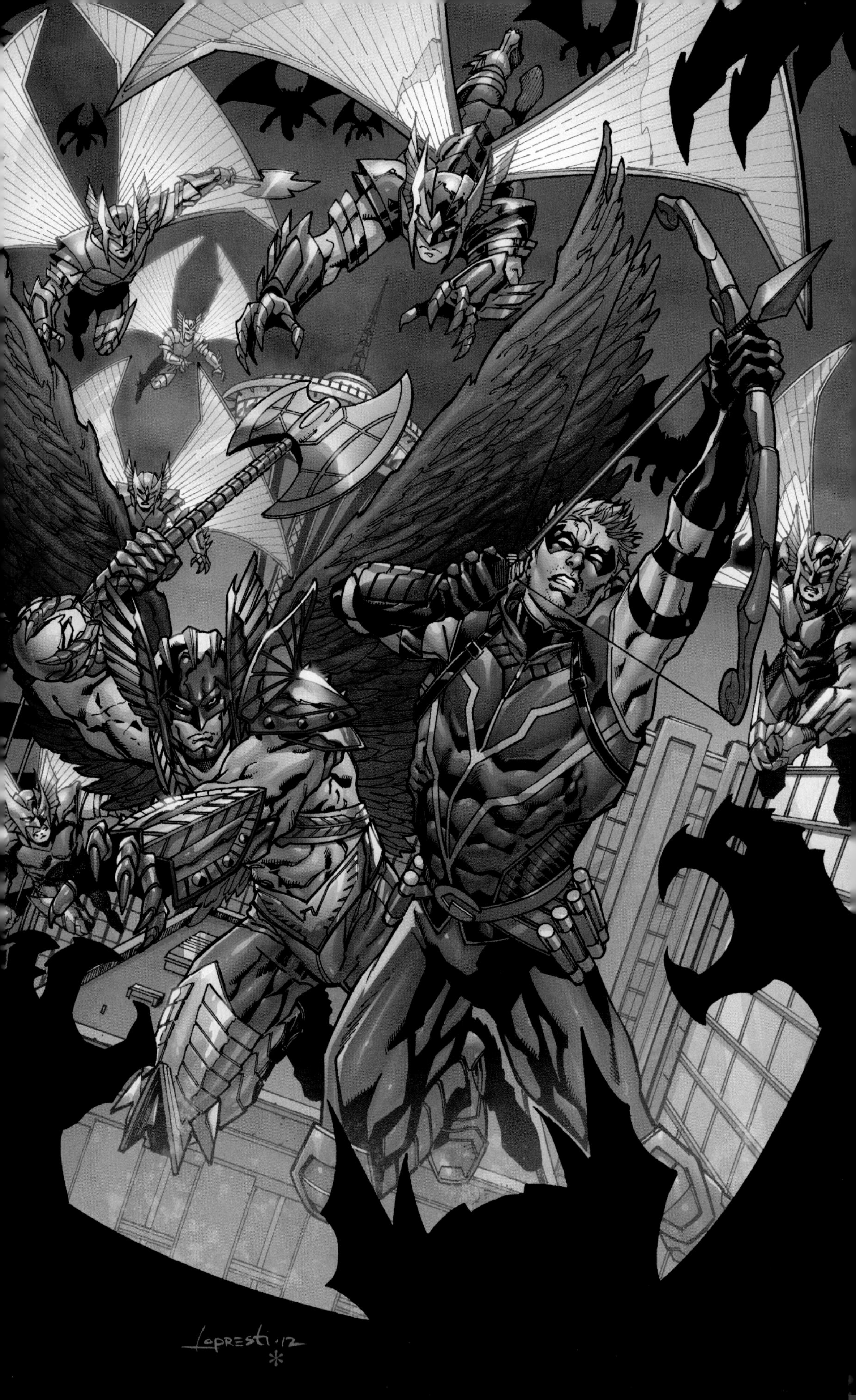
Lopresti·12

SKY WAR

ANN NOCENTI writer **FREDDIE WILLIAMS II** penciller **ROB HUNTER** inker cover by **AARON LOPRESTI** with **HI-FI**

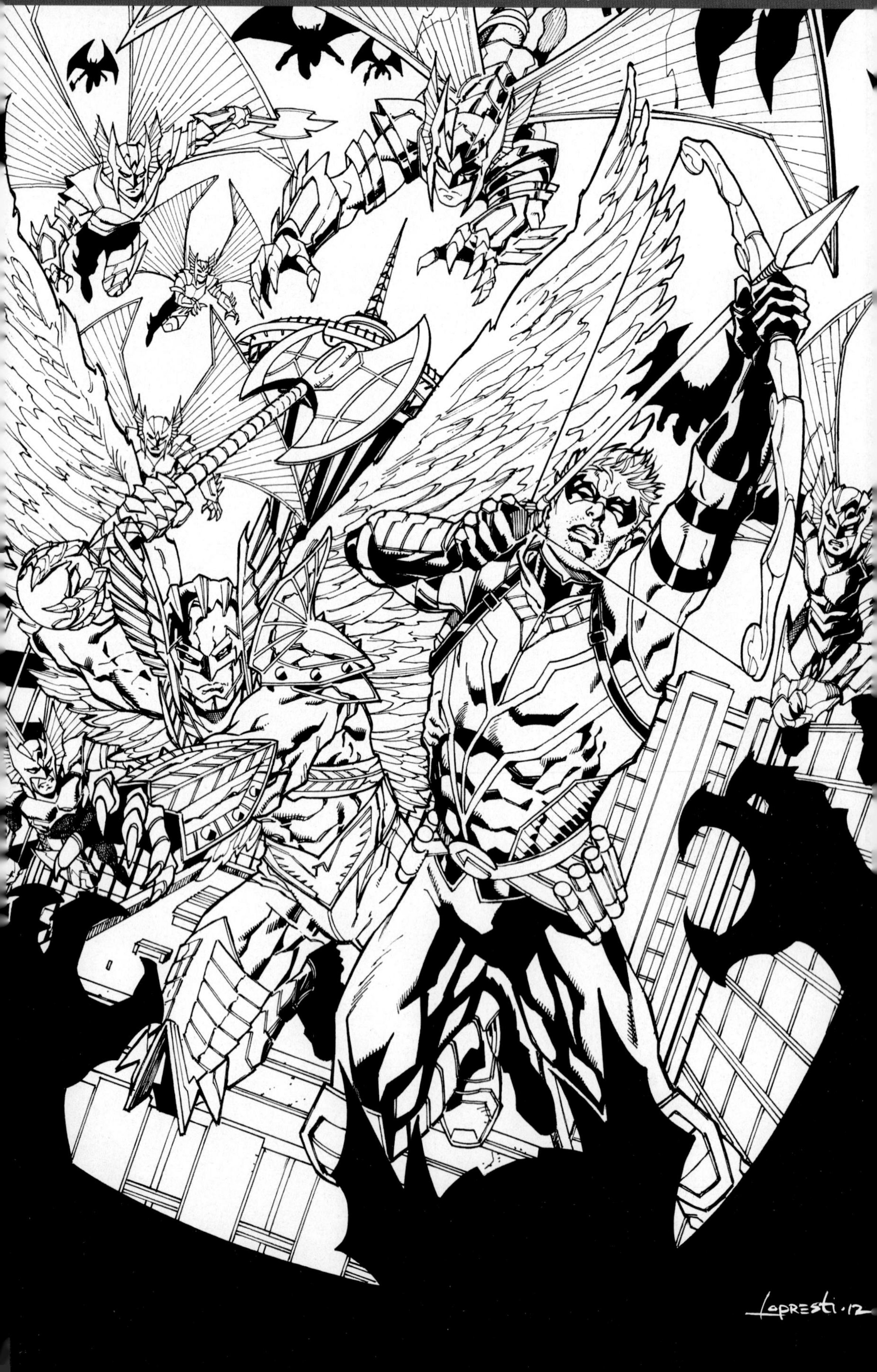
Lopresti.12

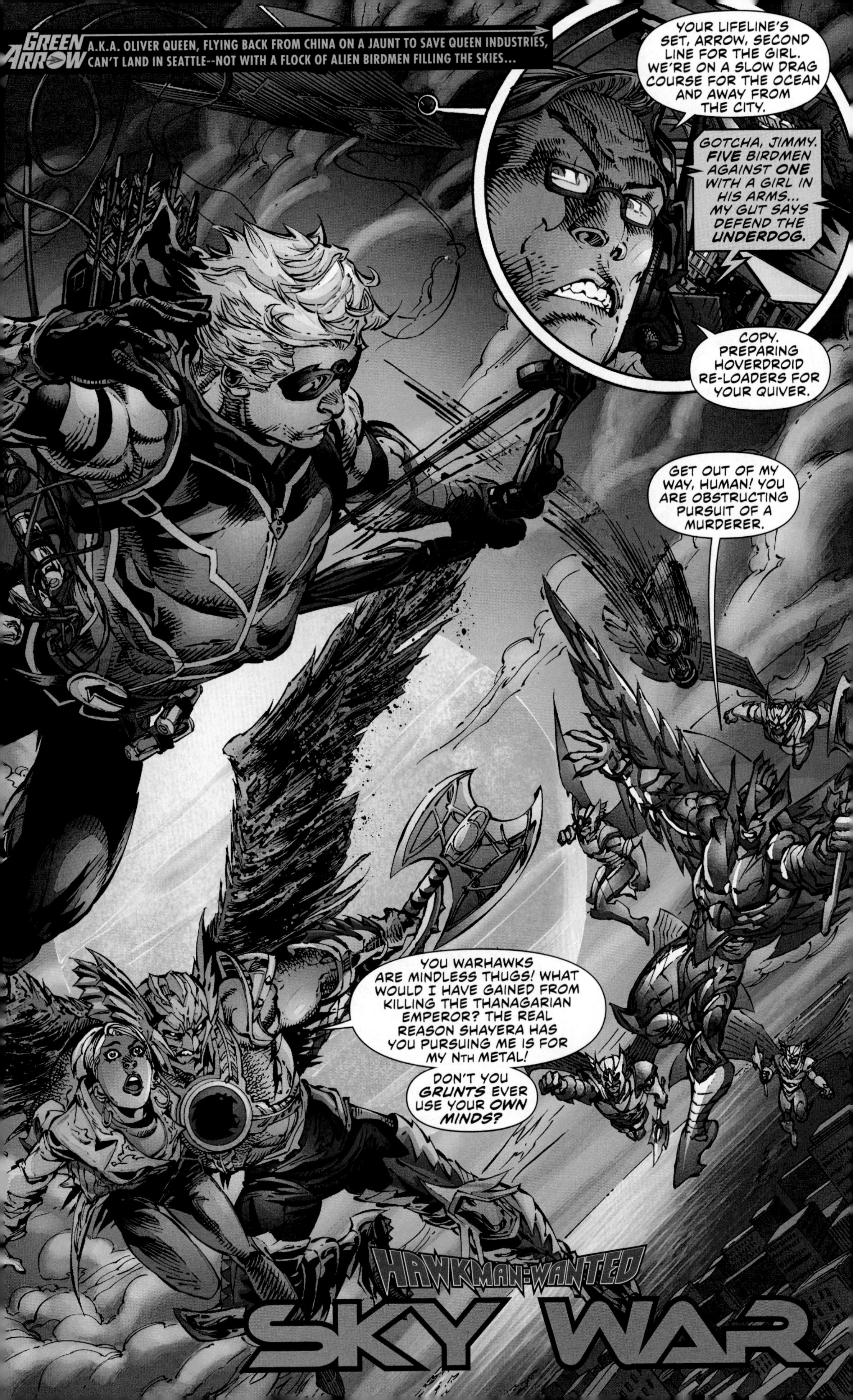GREEN ARROW A.K.A. OLIVER QUEEN, FLYING BACK FROM CHINA ON A JAUNT TO SAVE QUEEN INDUSTRIES, CAN'T LAND IN SEATTLE--NOT WITH A FLOCK OF ALIEN BIRDMEN FILLING THE SKIES...
YOUR LIFELINE'S SET, ARROW, SECOND LINE FOR THE GIRL. WE'RE ON A SLOW DRAG COURSE FOR THE OCEAN AND AWAY FROM THE CITY.
GOTCHA, JIMMY. FIVE BIRDMEN AGAINST ONE WITH A GIRL IN HIS ARMS... MY GUT SAYS DEFEND THE UNDERDOG.
COPY. PREPARING HOVERDROID RE-LOADERS FOR YOUR QUIVER.
GET OUT OF MY WAY, HUMAN! YOU ARE OBSTRUCTING PURSUIT OF A MURDERER.
YOU WARHAWKS ARE MINDLESS THUGS! WHAT WOULD I HAVE GAINED FROM KILLING THE THANAGARIAN EMPEROR? THE REAL REASON SHAYERA HAS YOU PURSUING ME IS FOR MY NTH METAL!
DON'T YOU GRUNTS EVER USE YOUR OWN MINDS?
HAWKMAN: WANTED
SKY WAR

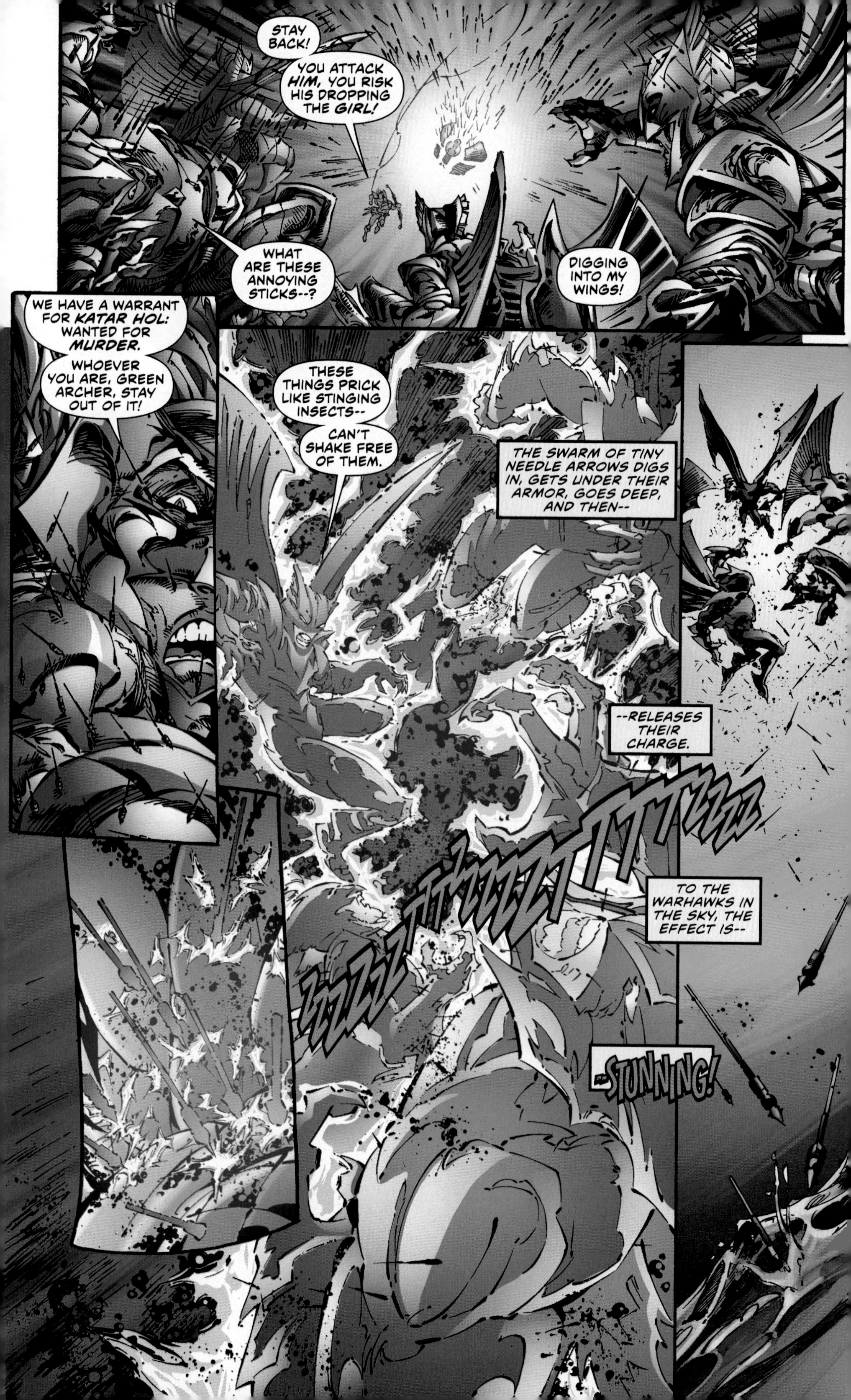
STAY BACK!
YOU ATTACK HIM, YOU RISK HIS DROPPING THE GIRL!
WHAT ARE THESE ANNOYING STICKS--?
DIGGING INTO MY WINGS!
WE HAVE A WARRANT FOR KATAR HOL: WANTED FOR MURDER.
WHOEVER YOU ARE, GREEN ARCHER, STAY OUT OF IT!
THESE THINGS PRICK LIKE STINGING INSECTS--
CAN'T SHAKE FREE OF THEM.
THE SWARM OF TINY NEEDLE ARROWS DIGS IN, GETS UNDER THEIR ARMOR, GOES DEEP, AND THEN--
--RELEASES THEIR CHARGE.
TO THE WARHAWKS IN THE SKY, THE EFFECT IS--
--STUNNING!

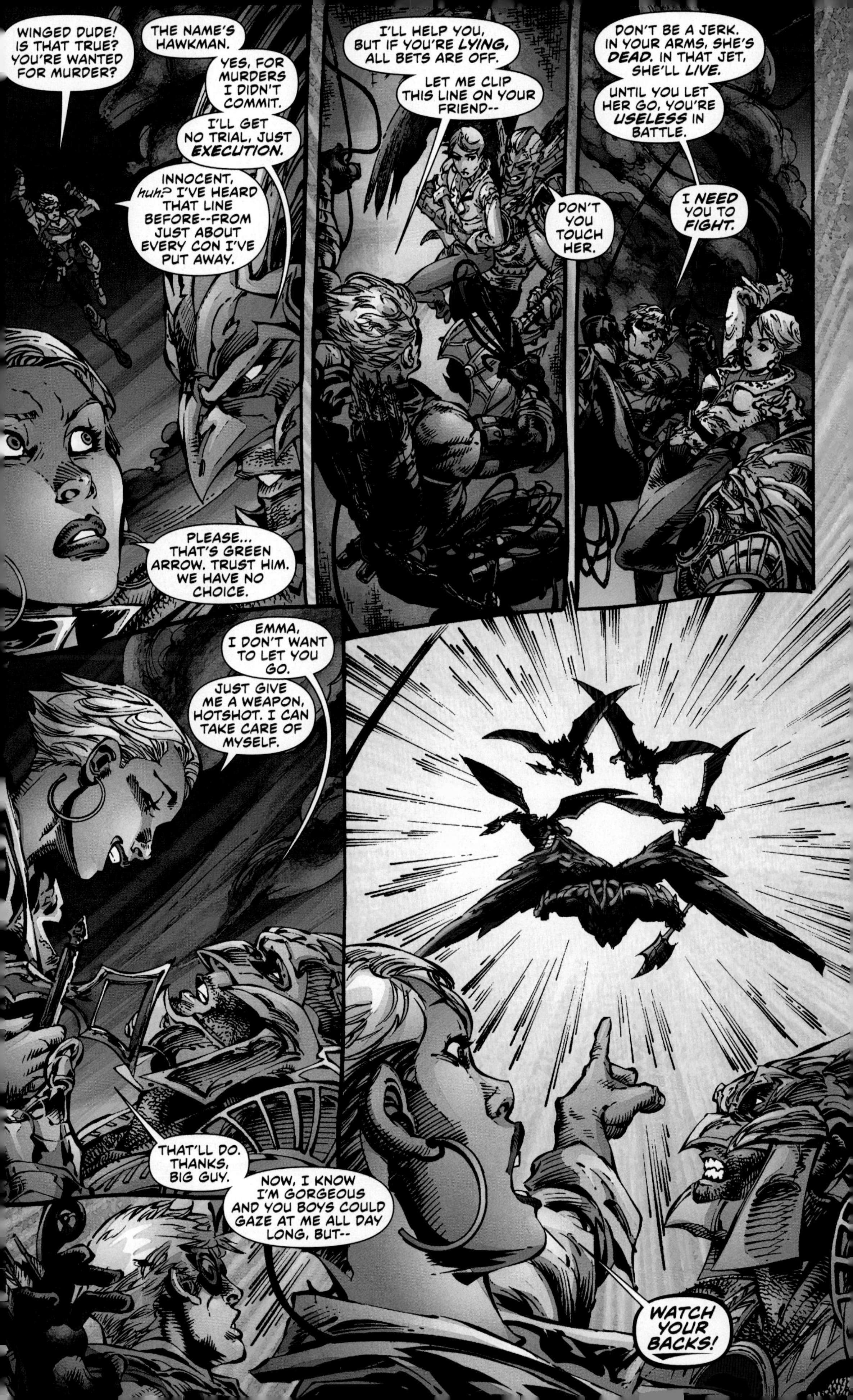

WINGED DUDE! IS THAT TRUE? YOU'RE WANTED FOR MURDER?
THE NAME'S HAWKMAN.
YES, FOR MURDERS I DIDN'T COMMIT.
I'LL GET NO TRIAL, JUST **EXECUTION.**
INNOCENT, *huh?* I'VE HEARD THAT LINE BEFORE--FROM JUST ABOUT EVERY CON I'VE PUT AWAY.
PLEASE... THAT'S GREEN ARROW. TRUST HIM. WE HAVE NO CHOICE.
I'LL HELP YOU, BUT IF YOU'RE ***LYING,*** ALL BETS ARE OFF.
LET ME CLIP THIS LINE ON YOUR FRIEND--
DON'T YOU TOUCH HER.
DON'T BE A JERK. IN YOUR ARMS, SHE'S ***DEAD.*** IN THAT JET, SHE'LL ***LIVE.***
UNTIL YOU LET HER GO, YOU'RE ***USELESS*** IN BATTLE.
I ***NEED*** YOU TO ***FIGHT.***
EMMA, I DON'T WANT TO LET YOU GO.
JUST GIVE ME A WEAPON, HOTSHOT. I CAN TAKE CARE OF MYSELF.
THAT'LL DO. THANKS, BIG GUY.
NOW, I KNOW I'M GORGEOUS AND YOU BOYS COULD GAZE AT ME ALL DAY LONG, BUT--
WATCH YOUR BACKS!

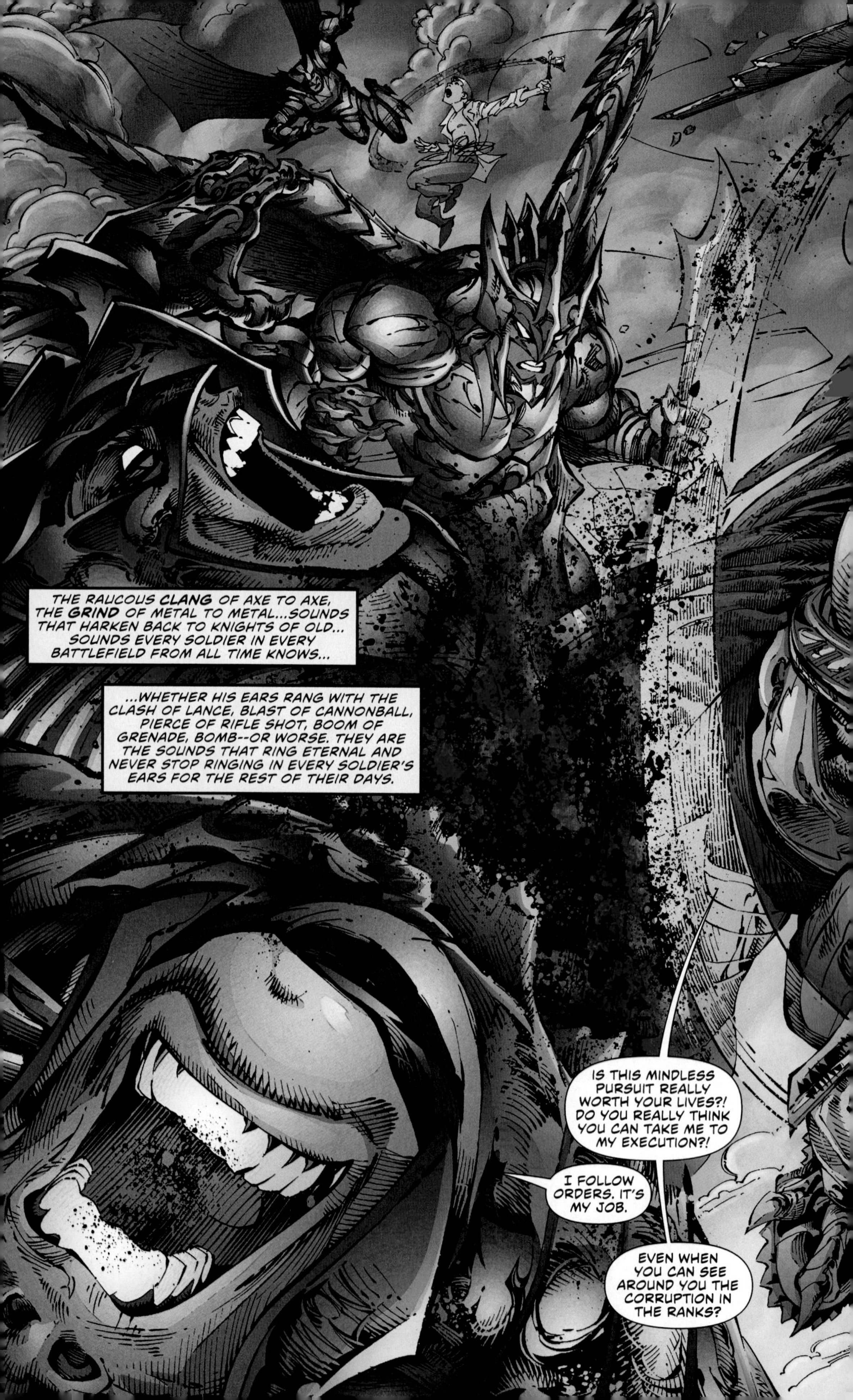
THE RAUCOUS CLANG OF AXE TO AXE, THE GRIND OF METAL TO METAL...SOUNDS THAT HARKEN BACK TO KNIGHTS OF OLD... SOUNDS EVERY SOLDIER IN EVERY BATTLEFIELD FROM ALL TIME KNOWS...
...WHETHER HIS EARS RANG WITH THE CLASH OF LANCE, BLAST OF CANNONBALL, PIERCE OF RIFLE SHOT, BOOM OF GRENADE, BOMB--OR WORSE. THEY ARE THE SOUNDS THAT RING ETERNAL AND NEVER STOP RINGING IN EVERY SOLDIER'S EARS FOR THE REST OF THEIR DAYS.
IS THIS MINDLESS PURSUIT REALLY WORTH YOUR LIVES?! DO YOU REALLY THINK YOU CAN TAKE ME TO MY EXECUTION?!
I FOLLOW ORDERS. IT'S MY JOB.
EVEN WHEN YOU CAN SEE AROUND YOU THE CORRUPTION IN THE RANKS?

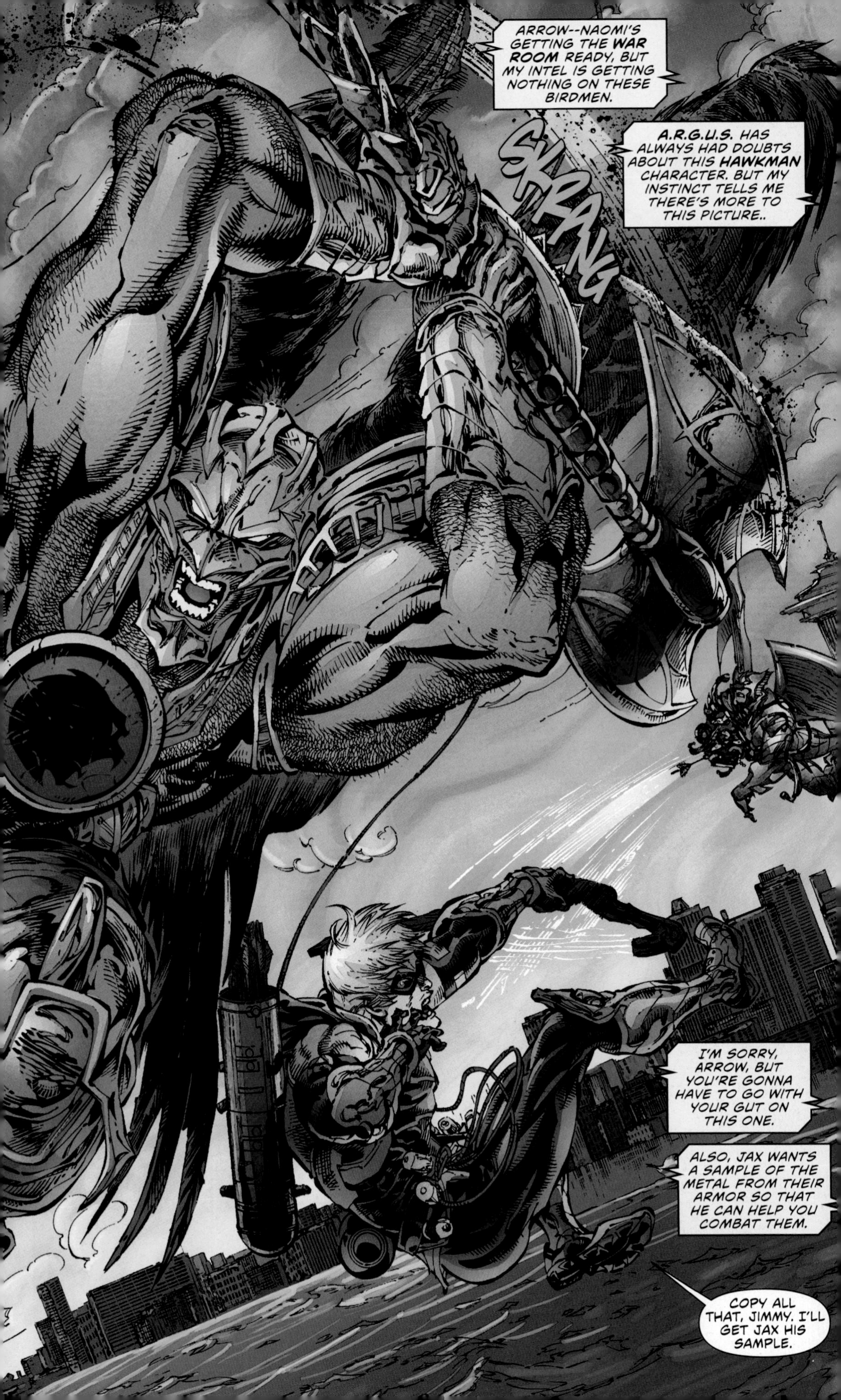
ARROW--NAOMI'S GETTING THE WAR ROOM READY, BUT MY INTEL IS GETTING NOTHING ON THESE BIRDMEN.
A.R.G.U.S. HAS ALWAYS HAD DOUBTS ABOUT THIS HAWKMAN CHARACTER. BUT MY INSTINCT TELLS ME THERE'S MORE TO THIS PICTURE..
SKRANG
I'M SORRY, ARROW, BUT YOU'RE GONNA HAVE TO GO WITH YOUR GUT ON THIS ONE.
ALSO, JAX WANTS A SAMPLE OF THE METAL FROM THEIR ARMOR SO THAT HE CAN HELP YOU COMBAT THEM.
COPY ALL THAT, JIMMY. I'LL GET JAX HIS SAMPLE.

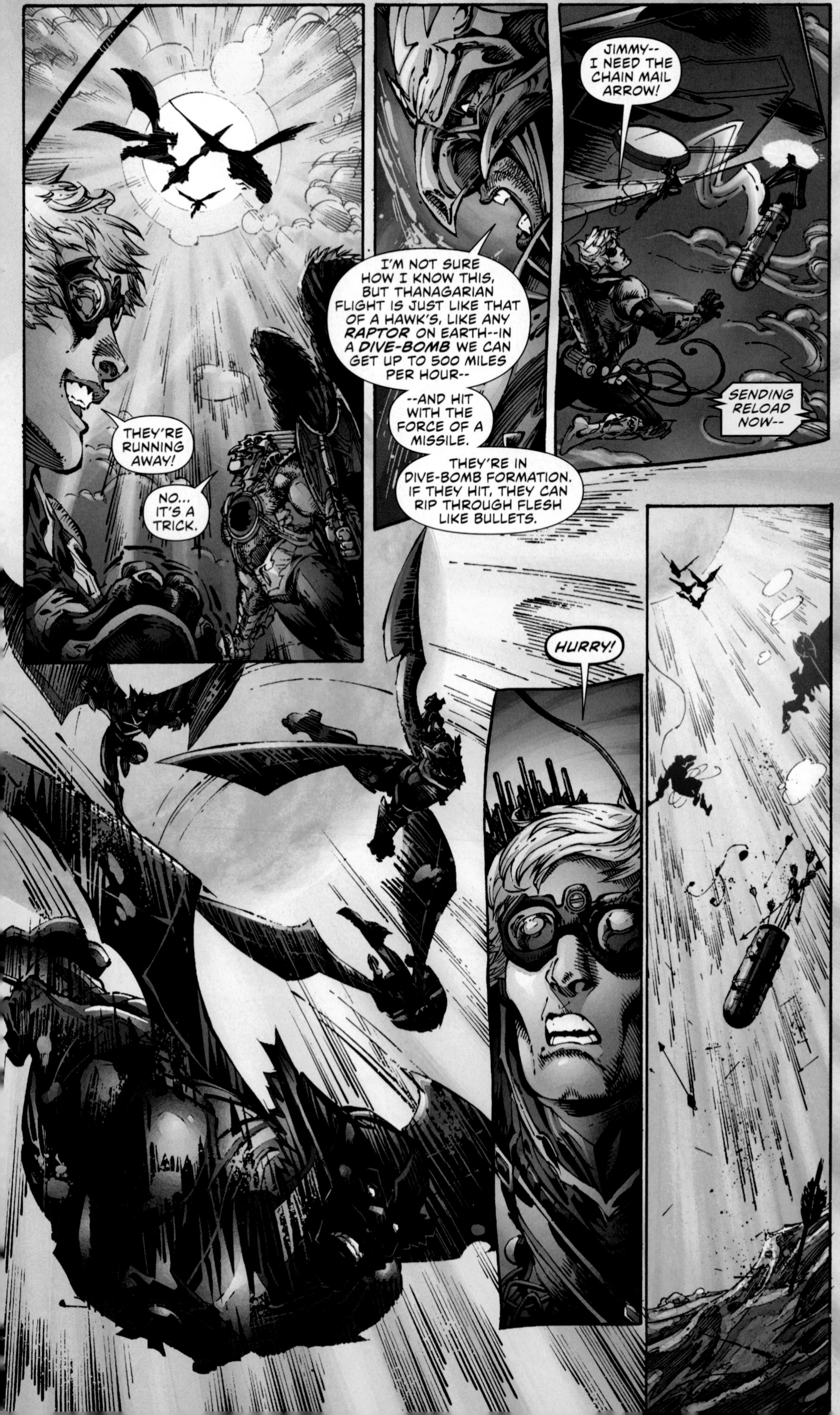
THEY'RE RUNNING AWAY!
NO... IT'S A TRICK.
I'M NOT SURE HOW I KNOW THIS, BUT THANAGARIAN FLIGHT IS JUST LIKE THAT OF A HAWK'S, LIKE ANY RAPTOR ON EARTH--IN A DIVE-BOMB WE CAN GET UP TO 500 MILES PER HOUR--
--AND HIT WITH THE FORCE OF A MISSILE.
THEY'RE IN DIVE-BOMB FORMATION. IF THEY HIT, THEY CAN RIP THROUGH FLESH LIKE BULLETS.
JIMMY-- I NEED THE CHAIN MAIL ARROW!
SENDING RELOAD NOW--
HURRY!

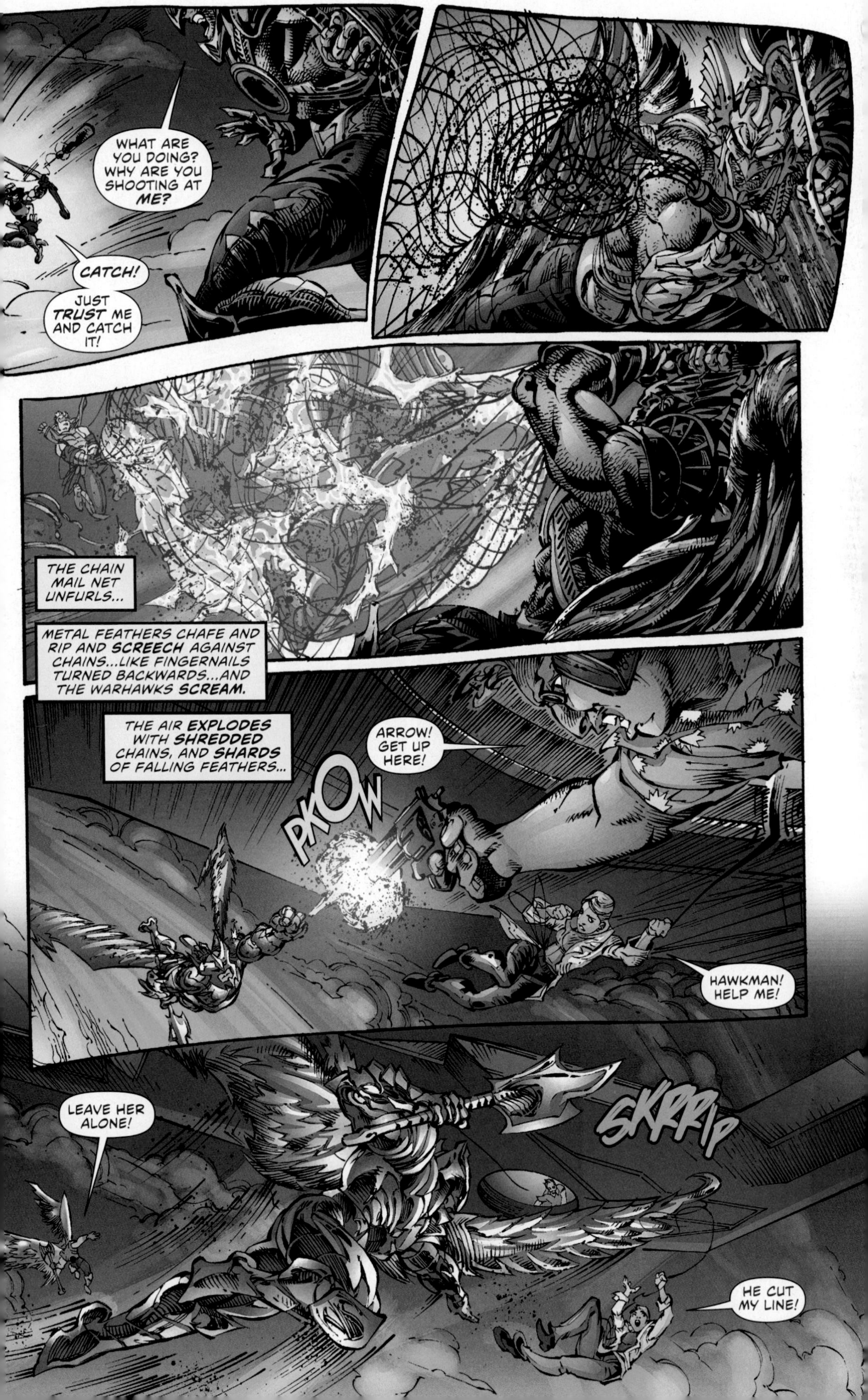
WHAT ARE YOU DOING? WHY ARE YOU SHOOTING AT ME?
CATCH!
JUST TRUST ME AND CATCH IT!
THE CHAIN MAIL NET UNFURLS...
METAL FEATHERS CHAFE AND RIP AND SCREECH AGAINST CHAINS...LIKE FINGERNAILS TURNED BACKWARDS...AND THE WARHAWKS SCREAM.
THE AIR EXPLODES WITH SHREDDED CHAINS, AND SHARDS OF FALLING FEATHERS...
ARROW! GET UP HERE!
PKOW
HAWKMAN! HELP ME!
LEAVE HER ALONE!
SKRRIP
HE CUT MY LINE!

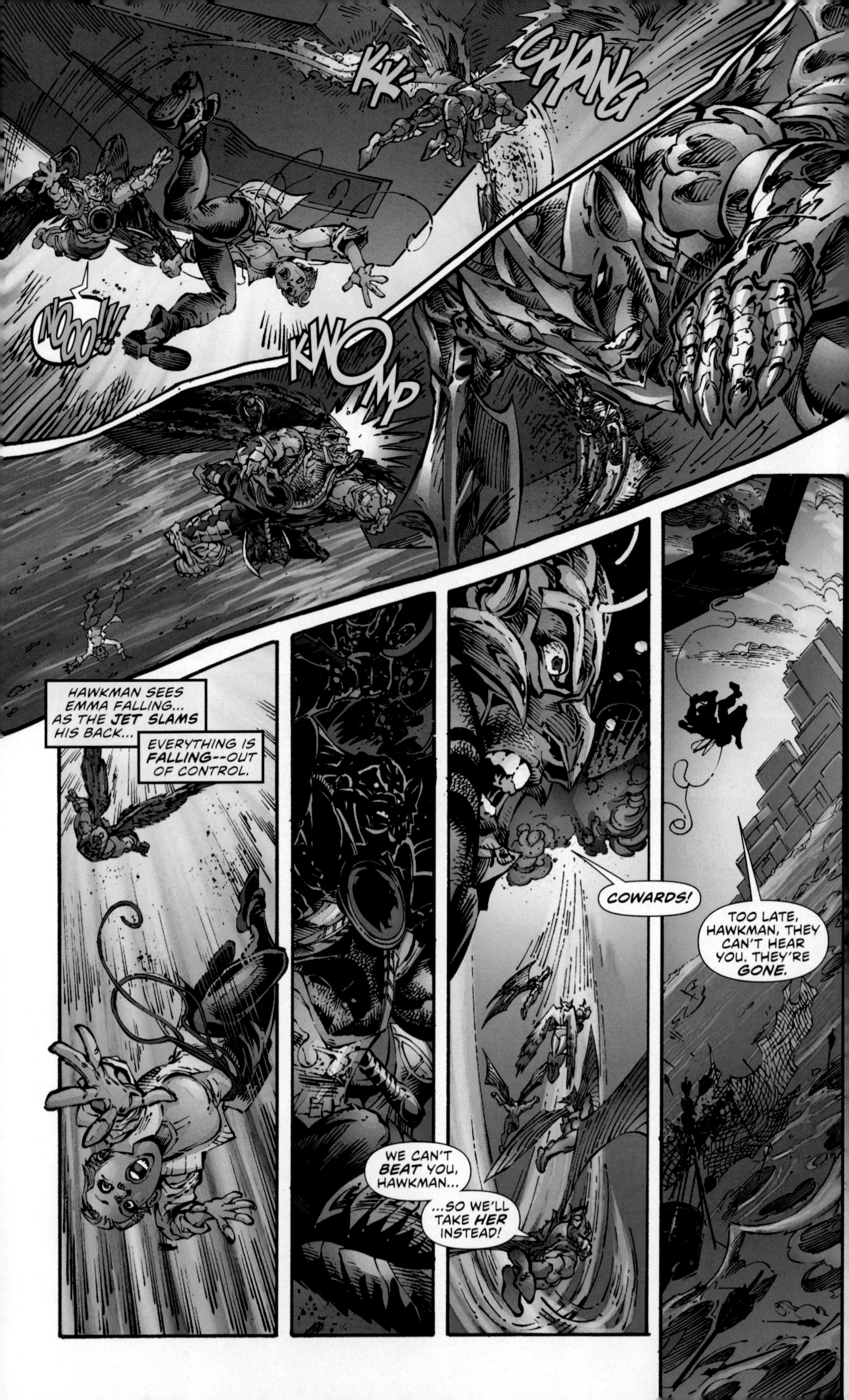
KK
CHANG
NOOO!!!
KWOMP
HAWKMAN SEES EMMA FALLING... AS THE JET SLAMS HIS BACK...
EVERYTHING IS FALLING--OUT OF CONTROL.
WE CAN'T BEAT YOU, HAWKMAN...
...SO WE'LL TAKE HER INSTEAD!
COWARDS!
TOO LATE, HAWKMAN, THEY CAN'T HEAR YOU. THEY'RE GONE.

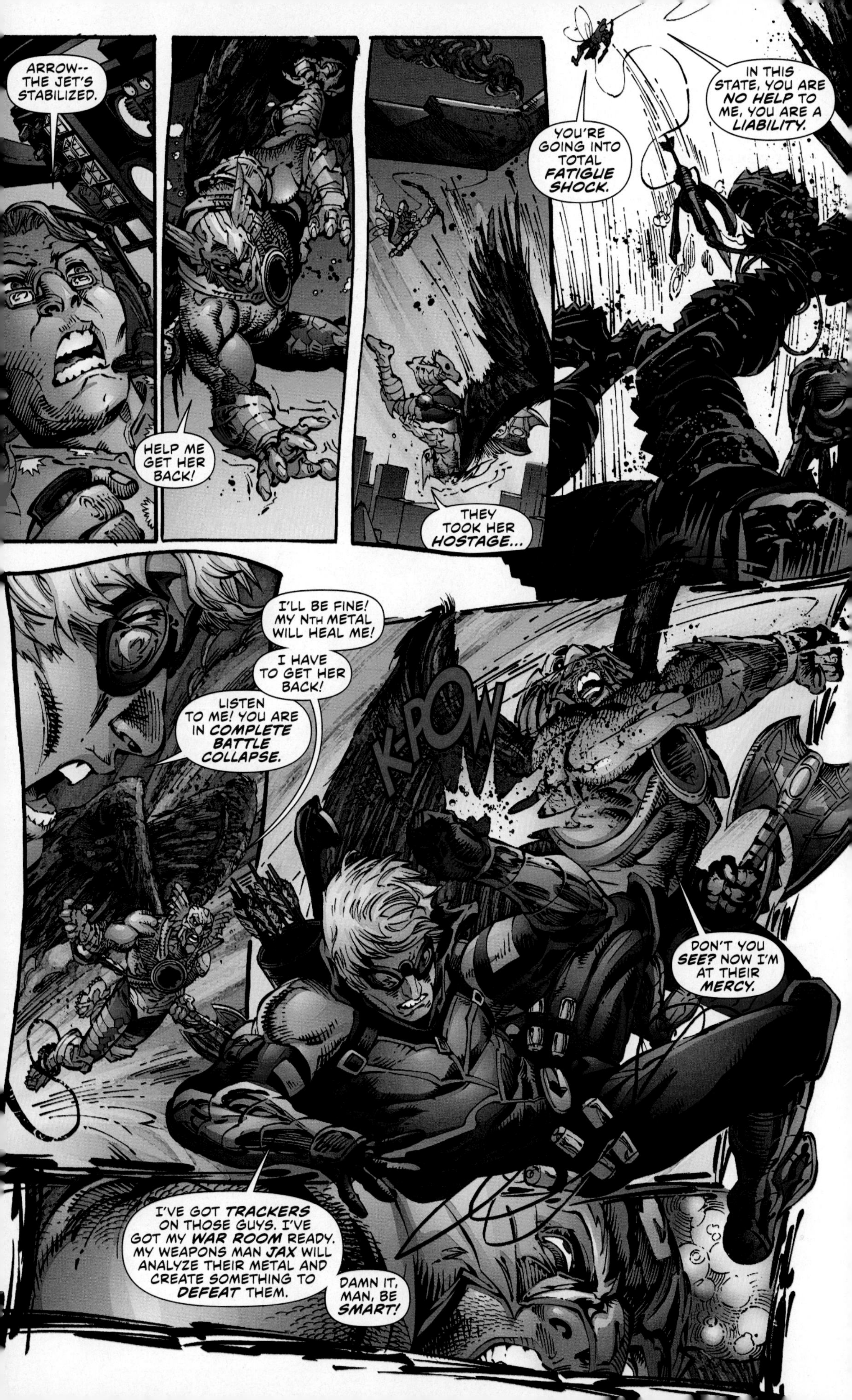

ARROW-- THE JET'S STABILIZED.
HELP ME GET HER BACK!
THEY TOOK HER HOSTAGE...
YOU'RE GOING INTO TOTAL FATIGUE SHOCK.
IN THIS STATE, YOU ARE NO HELP TO ME, YOU ARE A LIABILITY.
I'LL BE FINE! MY NTH METAL WILL HEAL ME!
I HAVE TO GET HER BACK!
LISTEN TO ME! YOU ARE IN COMPLETE BATTLE COLLAPSE.
K-POW
DON'T YOU SEE? NOW I'M AT THEIR MERCY.
I'VE GOT TRACKERS ON THOSE GUYS. I'VE GOT MY WAR ROOM READY. MY WEAPONS MAN JAX WILL ANALYZE THEIR METAL AND CREATE SOMETHING TO DEFEAT THEM.
DAMN IT, MAN, BE SMART!

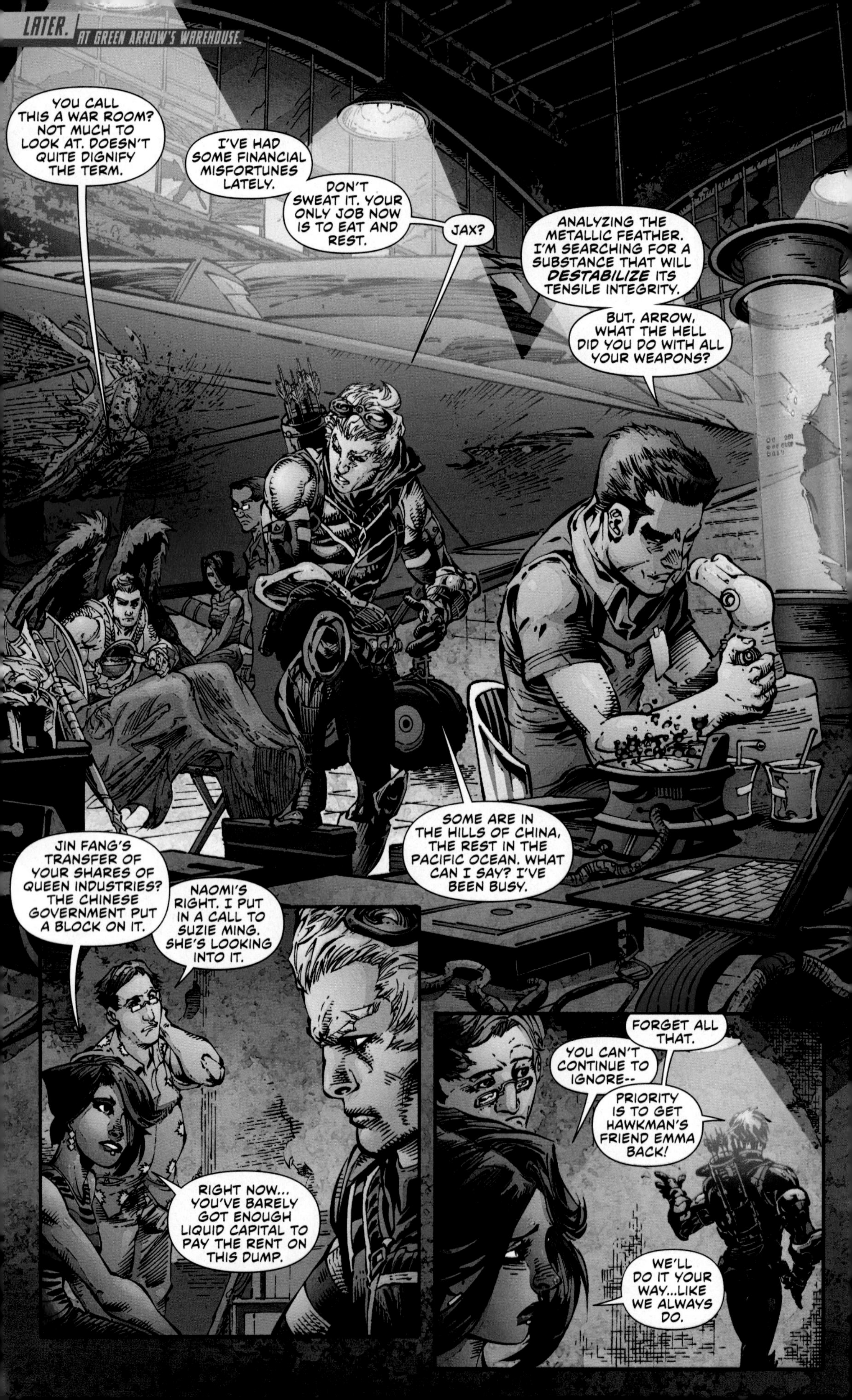
LATER.
AT GREEN ARROW'S WAREHOUSE.
YOU CALL THIS A WAR ROOM? NOT MUCH TO LOOK AT. DOESN'T QUITE DIGNIFY THE TERM.
I'VE HAD SOME FINANCIAL MISFORTUNES LATELY.
DON'T SWEAT IT. YOUR ONLY JOB NOW IS TO EAT AND REST.
JAX?
ANALYZING THE METALLIC FEATHER. I'M SEARCHING FOR A SUBSTANCE THAT WILL DESTABILIZE ITS TENSILE INTEGRITY.
BUT, ARROW, WHAT THE HELL DID YOU DO WITH ALL YOUR WEAPONS?
SOME ARE IN THE HILLS OF CHINA, THE REST IN THE PACIFIC OCEAN. WHAT CAN I SAY? I'VE BEEN BUSY.
JIN FANG'S TRANSFER OF YOUR SHARES OF QUEEN INDUSTRIES? THE CHINESE GOVERNMENT PUT A BLOCK ON IT.
NAOMI'S RIGHT. I PUT IN A CALL TO SUZIE MING. SHE'S LOOKING INTO IT.
RIGHT NOW... YOU'VE BARELY GOT ENOUGH LIQUID CAPITAL TO PAY THE RENT ON THIS DUMP.
FORGET ALL THAT.
YOU CAN'T CONTINUE TO IGNORE--
PRIORITY IS TO GET HAWKMAN'S FRIEND EMMA BACK!
WE'LL DO IT YOUR WAY...LIKE WE ALWAYS DO.

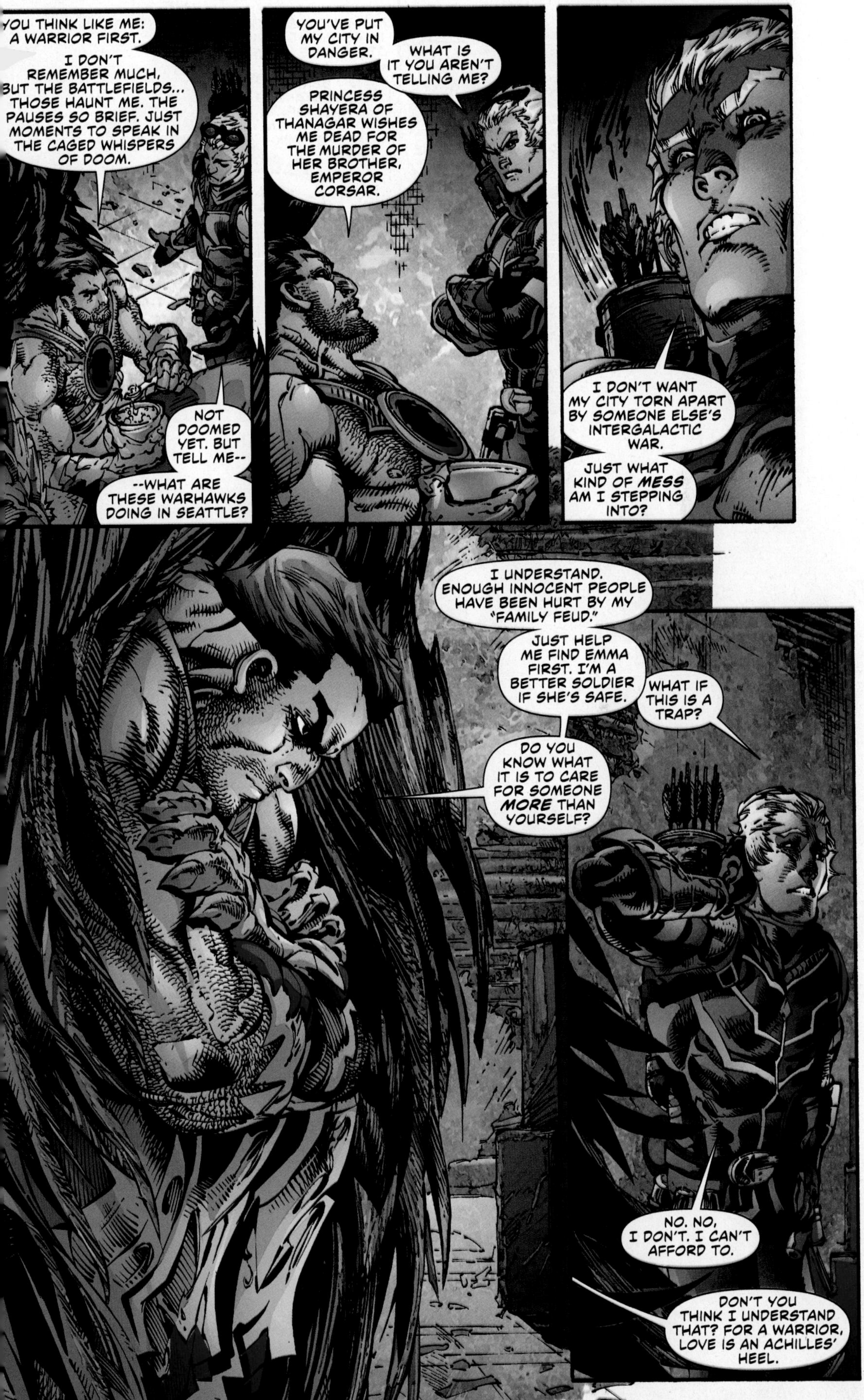
YOU THINK LIKE ME: A WARRIOR FIRST.
I DON'T REMEMBER MUCH, BUT THE BATTLEFIELDS... THOSE HAUNT ME. THE PAUSES SO BRIEF. JUST MOMENTS TO SPEAK IN THE CAGED WHISPERS OF DOOM.
NOT DOOMED YET. BUT TELL ME--
--WHAT ARE THESE WARHAWKS DOING IN SEATTLE?
YOU'VE PUT MY CITY IN DANGER.
WHAT IS IT YOU AREN'T TELLING ME?
PRINCESS SHAYERA OF THANAGAR WISHES ME DEAD FOR THE MURDER OF HER BROTHER, EMPEROR CORSAR.
I DON'T WANT MY CITY TORN APART BY SOMEONE ELSE'S INTERGALACTIC WAR.
JUST WHAT KIND OF *MESS* AM I STEPPING INTO?
I UNDERSTAND. ENOUGH INNOCENT PEOPLE HAVE BEEN HURT BY MY "FAMILY FEUD."
JUST HELP ME FIND EMMA FIRST. I'M A BETTER SOLDIER IF SHE'S SAFE.
WHAT IF THIS IS A TRAP?
DO YOU KNOW WHAT IT IS TO CARE FOR SOMEONE *MORE* THAN YOURSELF?
NO. NO, I DON'T. I CAN'T AFFORD TO.
DON'T YOU THINK I UNDERSTAND THAT? FOR A WARRIOR, LOVE IS AN ACHILLES' HEEL.

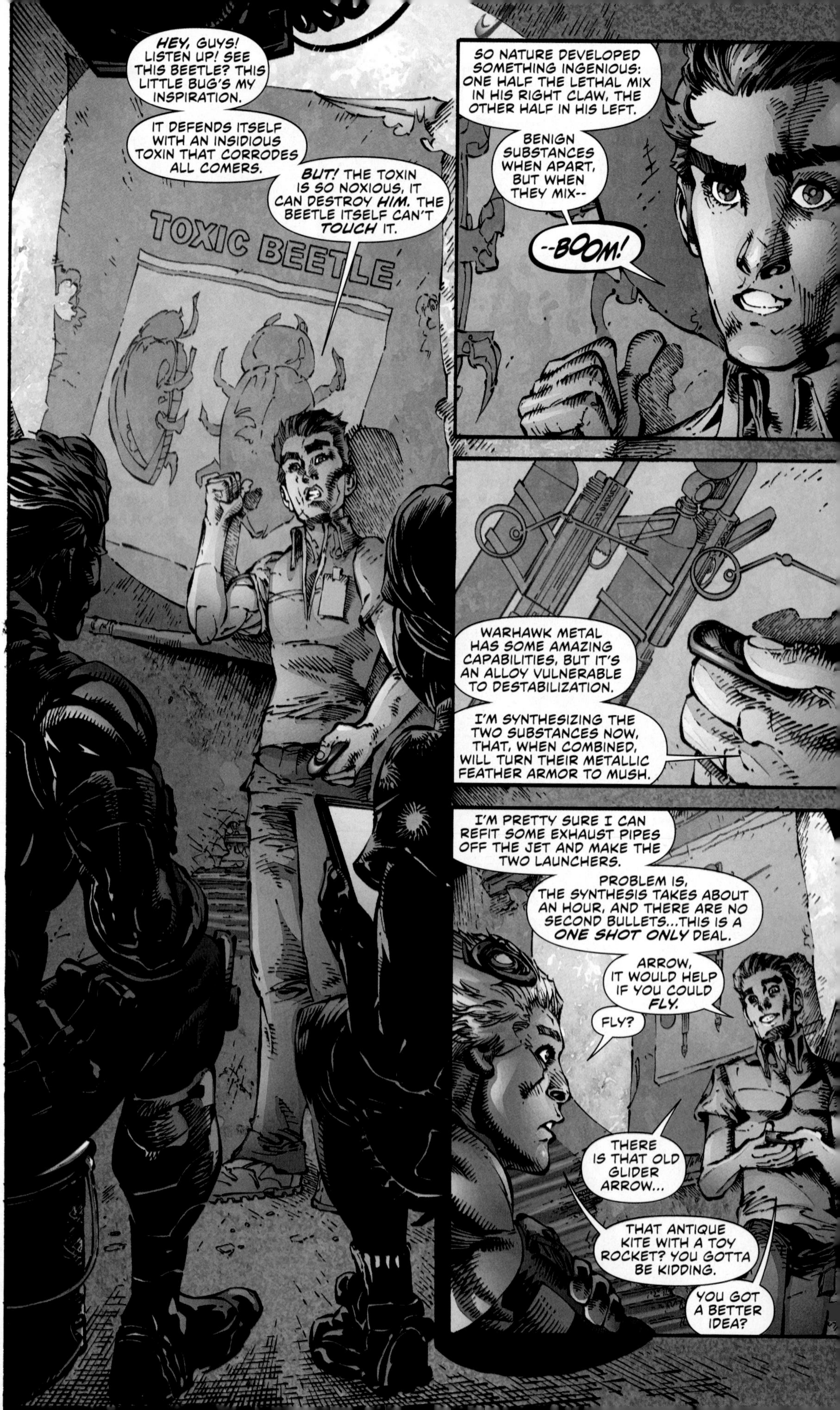
HEY, GUYS! LISTEN UP! SEE THIS BEETLE? THIS LITTLE BUG'S MY INSPIRATION.
IT DEFENDS ITSELF WITH AN INSIDIOUS TOXIN THAT CORRODES ALL COMERS.
BUT! THE TOXIN IS SO NOXIOUS, IT CAN DESTROY HIM. THE BEETLE ITSELF CAN'T TOUCH IT.
TOXIC BEETLE
SO NATURE DEVELOPED SOMETHING INGENIOUS: ONE HALF THE LETHAL MIX IN HIS RIGHT CLAW, THE OTHER HALF IN HIS LEFT.
BENIGN SUBSTANCES WHEN APART, BUT WHEN THEY MIX--
--BOOM!
WARHAWK METAL HAS SOME AMAZING CAPABILITIES, BUT IT'S AN ALLOY VULNERABLE TO DESTABILIZATION.
I'M SYNTHESIZING THE TWO SUBSTANCES NOW, THAT, WHEN COMBINED, WILL TURN THEIR METALLIC FEATHER ARMOR TO MUSH.
I'M PRETTY SURE I CAN REFIT SOME EXHAUST PIPES OFF THE JET AND MAKE THE TWO LAUNCHERS.
PROBLEM IS, THE SYNTHESIS TAKES ABOUT AN HOUR, AND THERE ARE NO SECOND BULLETS...THIS IS A ONE SHOT ONLY DEAL.
ARROW, IT WOULD HELP IF YOU COULD FLY.
FLY?
THERE IS THAT OLD GLIDER ARROW...
THAT ANTIQUE KITE WITH A TOY ROCKET? YOU GOTTA BE KIDDING.
YOU GOT A BETTER IDEA?

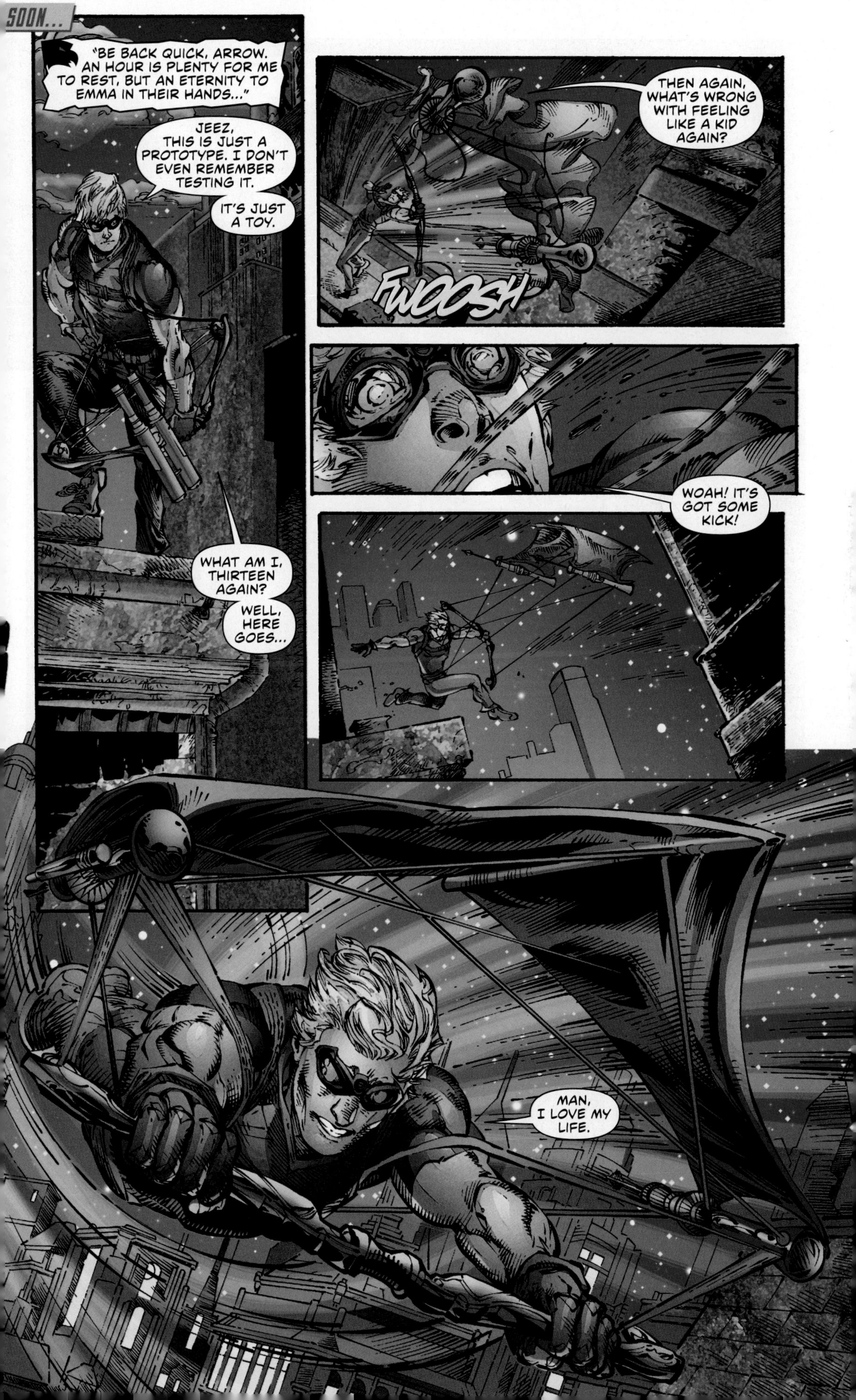
SOON...
"BE BACK QUICK, ARROW. AN HOUR IS PLENTY FOR ME TO REST, BUT AN ETERNITY TO EMMA IN THEIR HANDS..."
JEEZ, THIS IS JUST A PROTOTYPE. I DON'T EVEN REMEMBER TESTING IT.
IT'S JUST A TOY.
WHAT AM I, THIRTEEN AGAIN?
WELL, HERE GOES...
THEN AGAIN, WHAT'S WRONG WITH FEELING LIKE A KID AGAIN?
FWOOSH
WOAH! IT'S GOT SOME KICK!
MAN, I LOVE MY LIFE.

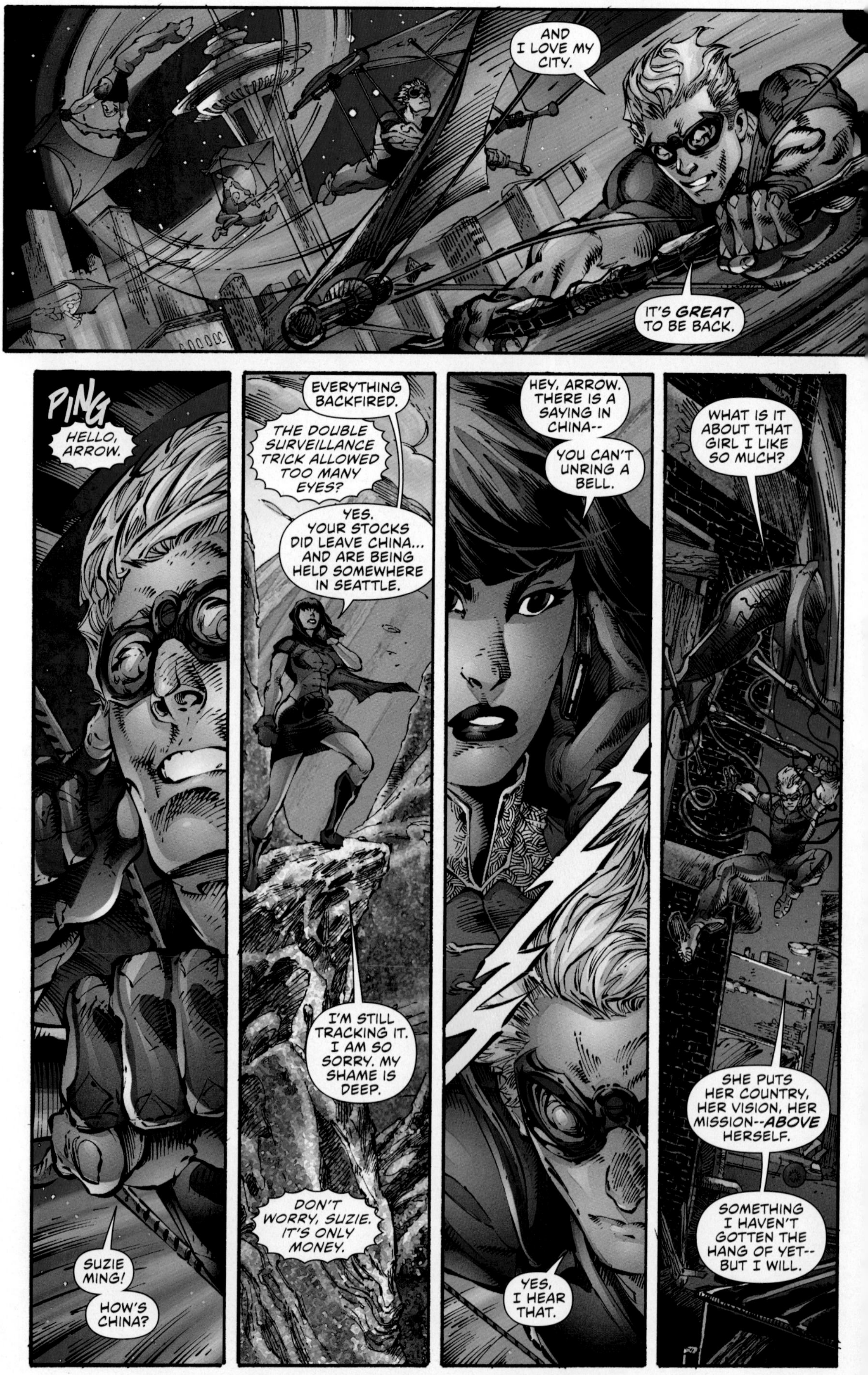
AND I LOVE MY CITY.
IT'S *GREAT* TO BE BACK.
PING
HELLO, ARROW.
SUZIE MING!
HOW'S CHINA?
EVERYTHING BACKFIRED.
THE DOUBLE SURVEILLANCE TRICK ALLOWED TOO MANY EYES?
YES. YOUR STOCKS DID LEAVE CHINA... AND ARE BEING HELD SOMEWHERE IN SEATTLE.
I'M STILL TRACKING IT. I AM SO SORRY. MY SHAME IS DEEP.
DON'T WORRY, SUZIE. IT'S ONLY MONEY.
HEY, ARROW. THERE IS A SAYING IN CHINA--
YOU CAN'T UNRING A BELL.
YES, I HEAR THAT.
WHAT IS IT ABOUT THAT GIRL I LIKE SO MUCH?
SHE PUTS HER COUNTRY, HER VISION, HER MISSION--*ABOVE* HERSELF.
SOMETHING I HAVEN'T GOTTEN THE HANG OF YET-- BUT I WILL.

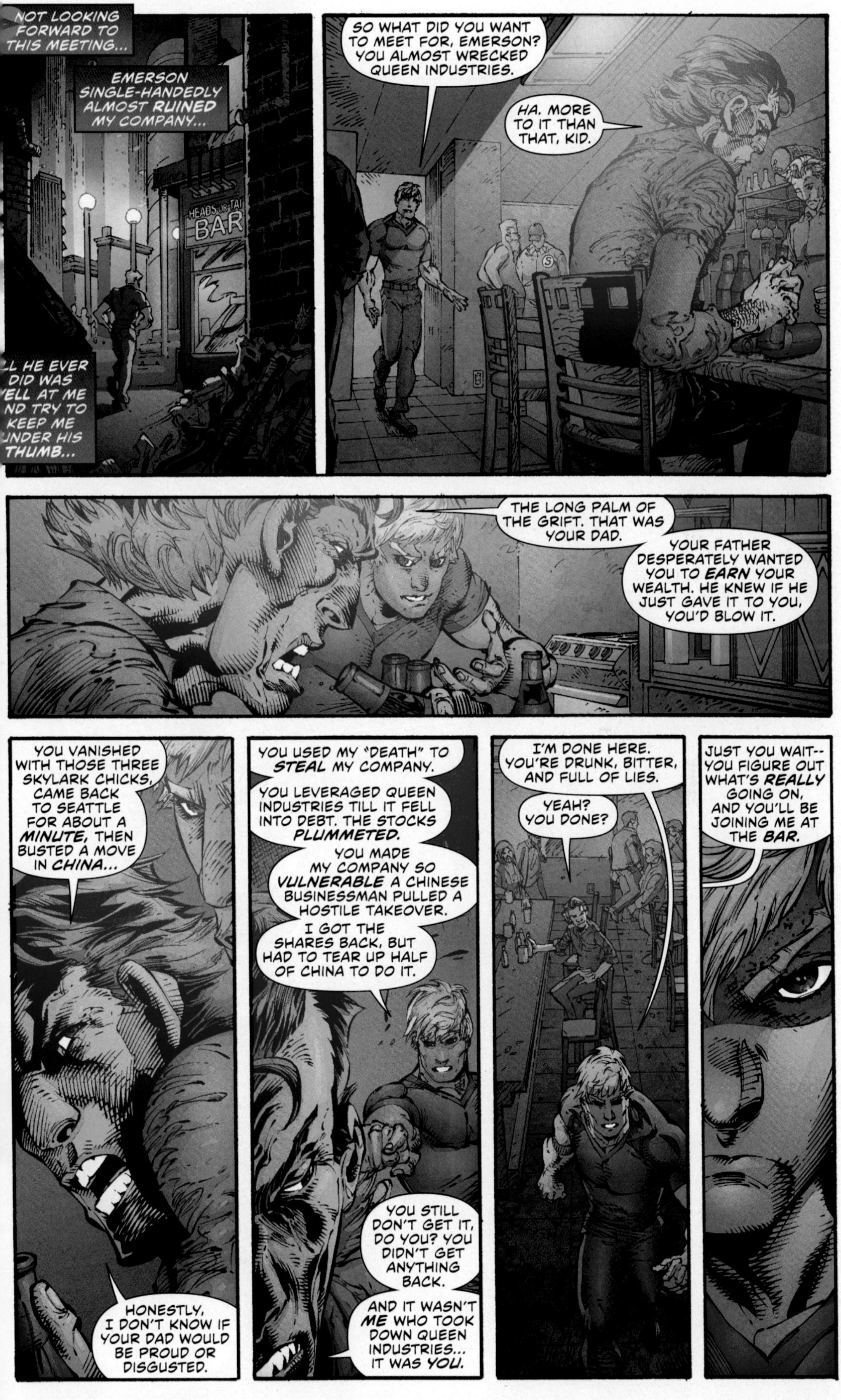
NOT LOOKING FORWARD TO THIS MEETING...
EMERSON SINGLE-HANDEDLY ALMOST RUINED MY COMPANY...
L HE EVER DID WAS YELL AT ME ND TRY TO KEEP ME NDER HIS THUMB...
HEADS OR TAI
BAR
SO WHAT DID YOU WANT TO MEET FOR, EMERSON? YOU ALMOST WRECKED QUEEN INDUSTRIES.
HA. MORE TO IT THAN THAT, KID.
THE LONG PALM OF THE GRIFT. THAT WAS YOUR DAD.
YOUR FATHER DESPERATELY WANTED YOU TO EARN YOUR WEALTH. HE KNEW IF HE JUST GAVE IT TO YOU, YOU'D BLOW IT.
YOU VANISHED WITH THOSE THREE SKYLARK CHICKS, CAME BACK TO SEATTLE FOR ABOUT A MINUTE, THEN BUSTED A MOVE IN CHINA...
HONESTLY, I DON'T KNOW IF YOUR DAD WOULD BE PROUD OR DISGUSTED.
YOU USED MY "DEATH" TO STEAL MY COMPANY.
YOU LEVERAGED QUEEN INDUSTRIES TILL IT FELL INTO DEBT. THE STOCKS PLUMMETED.
YOU MADE MY COMPANY SO VULNERABLE A CHINESE BUSINESSMAN PULLED A HOSTILE TAKEOVER.
I GOT THE SHARES BACK, BUT HAD TO TEAR UP HALF OF CHINA TO DO IT.
YOU STILL DON'T GET IT, DO YOU? YOU DIDN'T GET ANYTHING BACK.
AND IT WASN'T ME WHO TOOK DOWN QUEEN INDUSTRIES... IT WAS YOU.
I'M DONE HERE. YOU'RE DRUNK, BITTER, AND FULL OF LIES.
YEAH? YOU DONE?
JUST YOU WAIT-- YOU FIGURE OUT WHAT'S REALLY GOING ON, AND YOU'LL BE JOINING ME AT THE BAR.

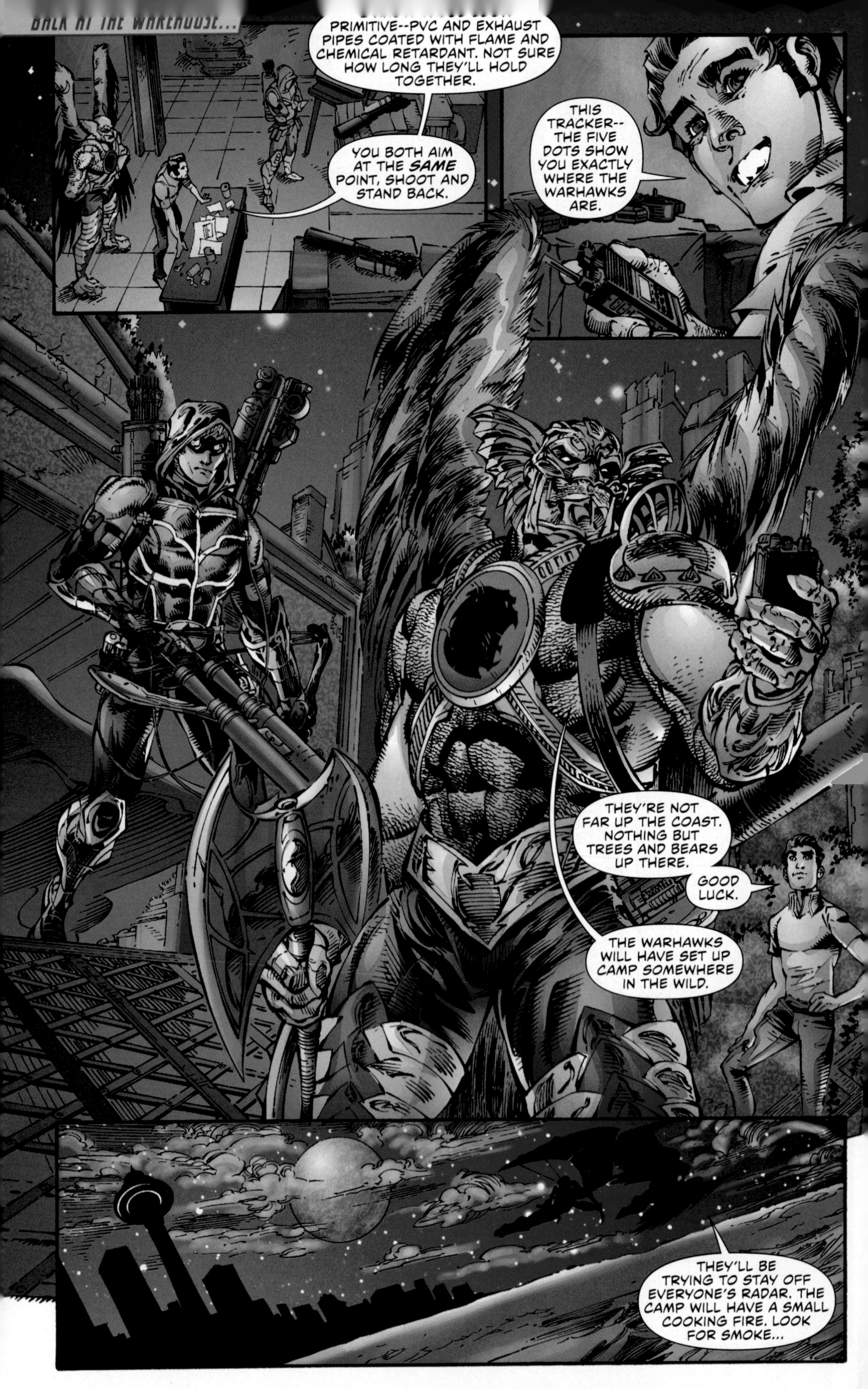

BACK AT THE WAREHOUSE...
PRIMITIVE--PVC AND EXHAUST PIPES COATED WITH FLAME AND CHEMICAL RETARDANT. NOT SURE HOW LONG THEY'LL HOLD TOGETHER.
YOU BOTH AIM AT THE *SAME* POINT, SHOOT AND STAND BACK.
THIS TRACKER-- THE FIVE DOTS SHOW YOU EXACTLY WHERE THE WARHAWKS ARE.
THEY'RE NOT FAR UP THE COAST. NOTHING BUT TREES AND BEARS UP THERE.
GOOD LUCK.
THE WARHAWKS WILL HAVE SET UP CAMP SOMEWHERE IN THE WILD.
THEY'LL BE TRYING TO STAY OFF EVERYONE'S RADAR. THE CAMP WILL HAVE A SMALL COOKING FIRE. LOOK FOR SMOKE...

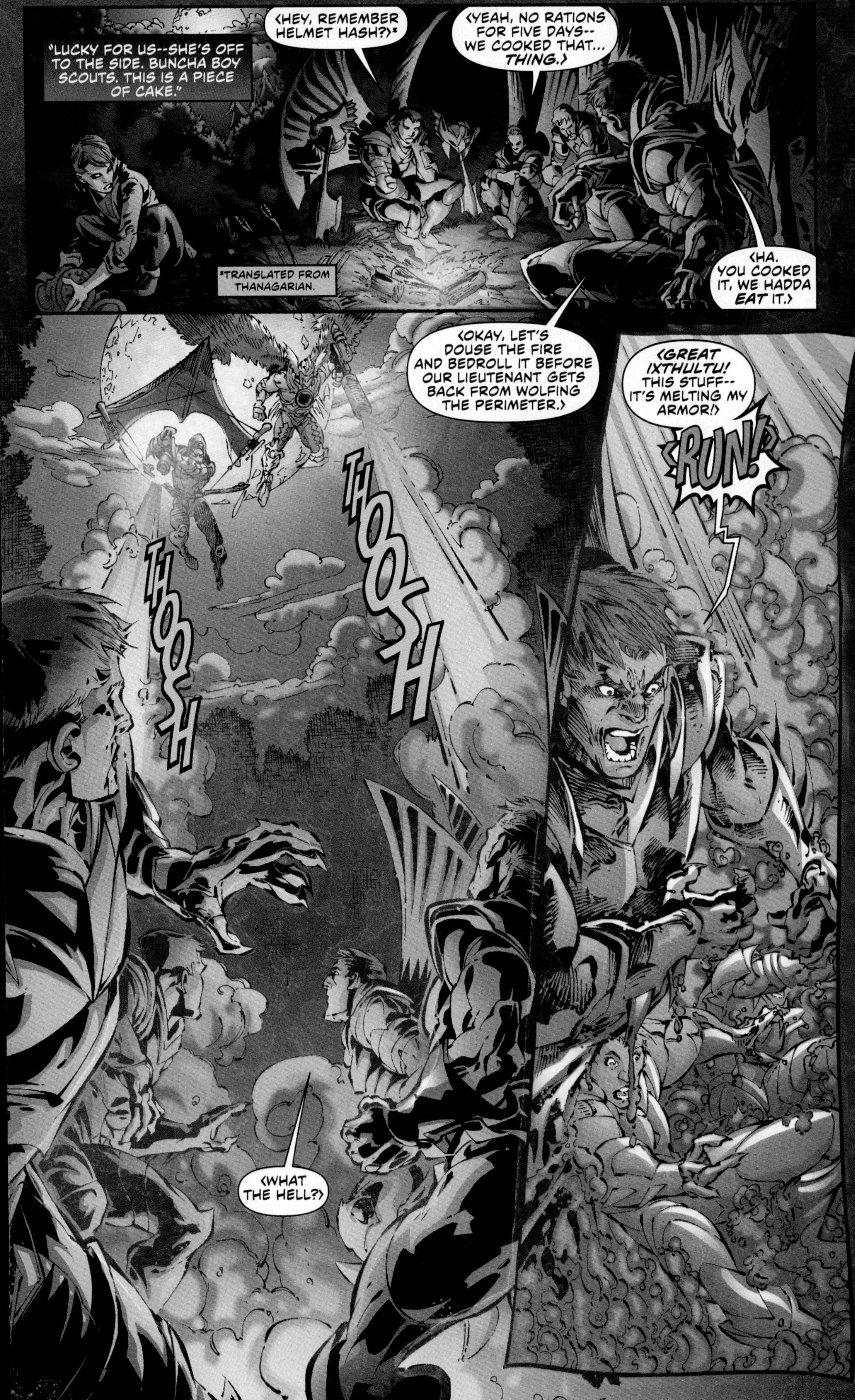
"LUCKY FOR US--SHE'S OFF TO THE SIDE. BUNCHA BOY SCOUTS. THIS IS A PIECE OF CAKE."
‹HEY, REMEMBER HELMET HASH?›*
‹YEAH, NO RATIONS FOR FIVE DAYS-- WE COOKED THAT... THING.›
*TRANSLATED FROM THANAGARIAN.
‹HA. YOU COOKED IT, WE HADDA EAT IT.›
‹OKAY, LET'S DOUSE THE FIRE AND BEDROLL IT BEFORE OUR LIEUTENANT GETS BACK FROM WOLFING THE PERIMETER.›
THOOSH
THOOSH
‹WHAT THE HELL?›
‹GREAT IXTHULTU! THIS STUFF-- IT'S MELTING MY ARMOR!›
‹RUN!›

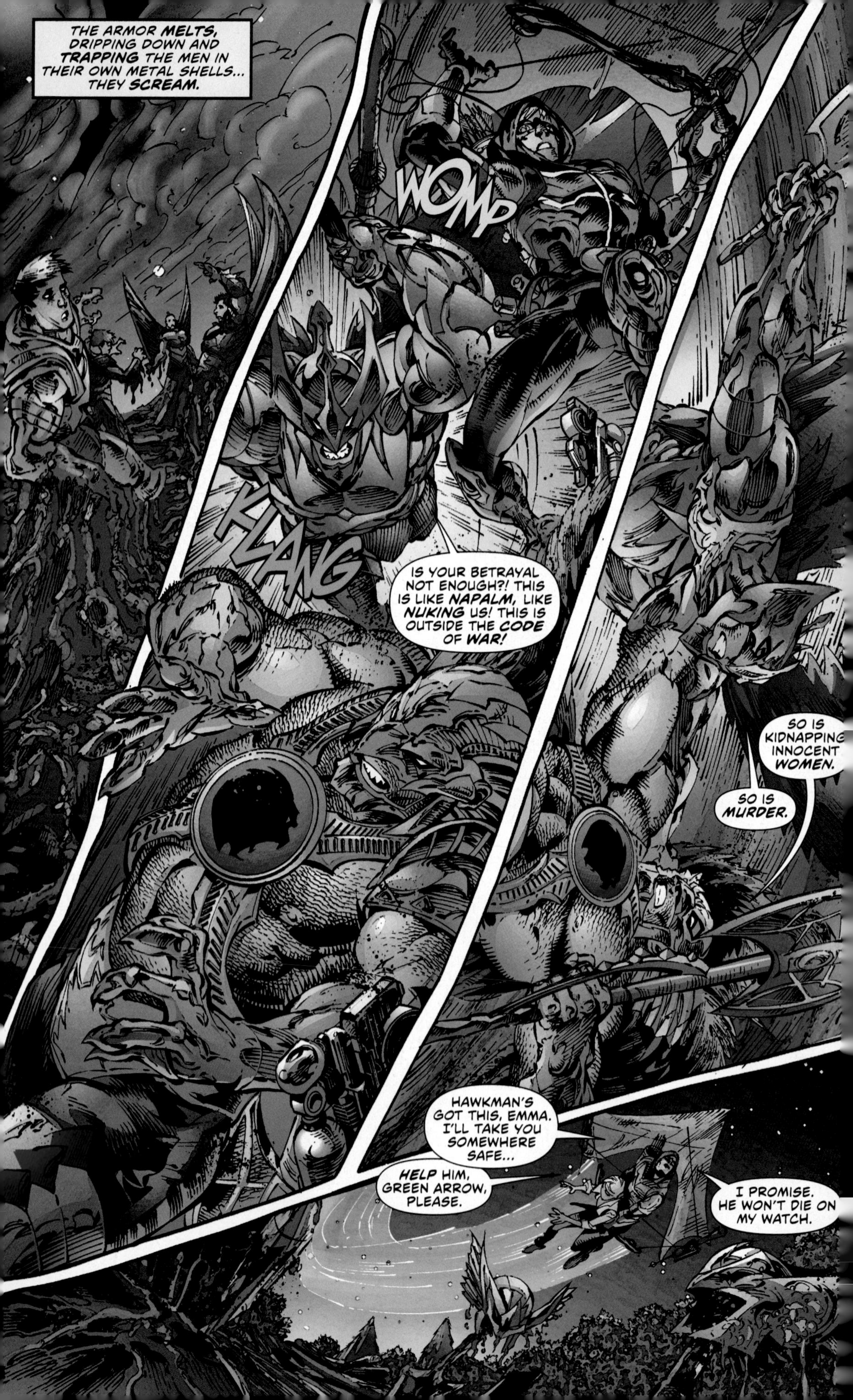
THE ARMOR MELTS, DRIPPING DOWN AND TRAPPING THE MEN IN THEIR OWN METAL SHELLS... THEY SCREAM.
WOMP
KLANG
IS YOUR BETRAYAL NOT ENOUGH?! THIS IS LIKE NAPALM, LIKE NUKING US! THIS IS OUTSIDE THE CODE OF WAR!
SO IS KIDNAPPING INNOCENT WOMEN.
SO IS MURDER.
HAWKMAN'S GOT THIS, EMMA. I'LL TAKE YOU SOMEWHERE SAFE...
HELP HIM, GREEN ARROW, PLEASE.
I PROMISE. HE WON'T DIE ON MY WATCH.

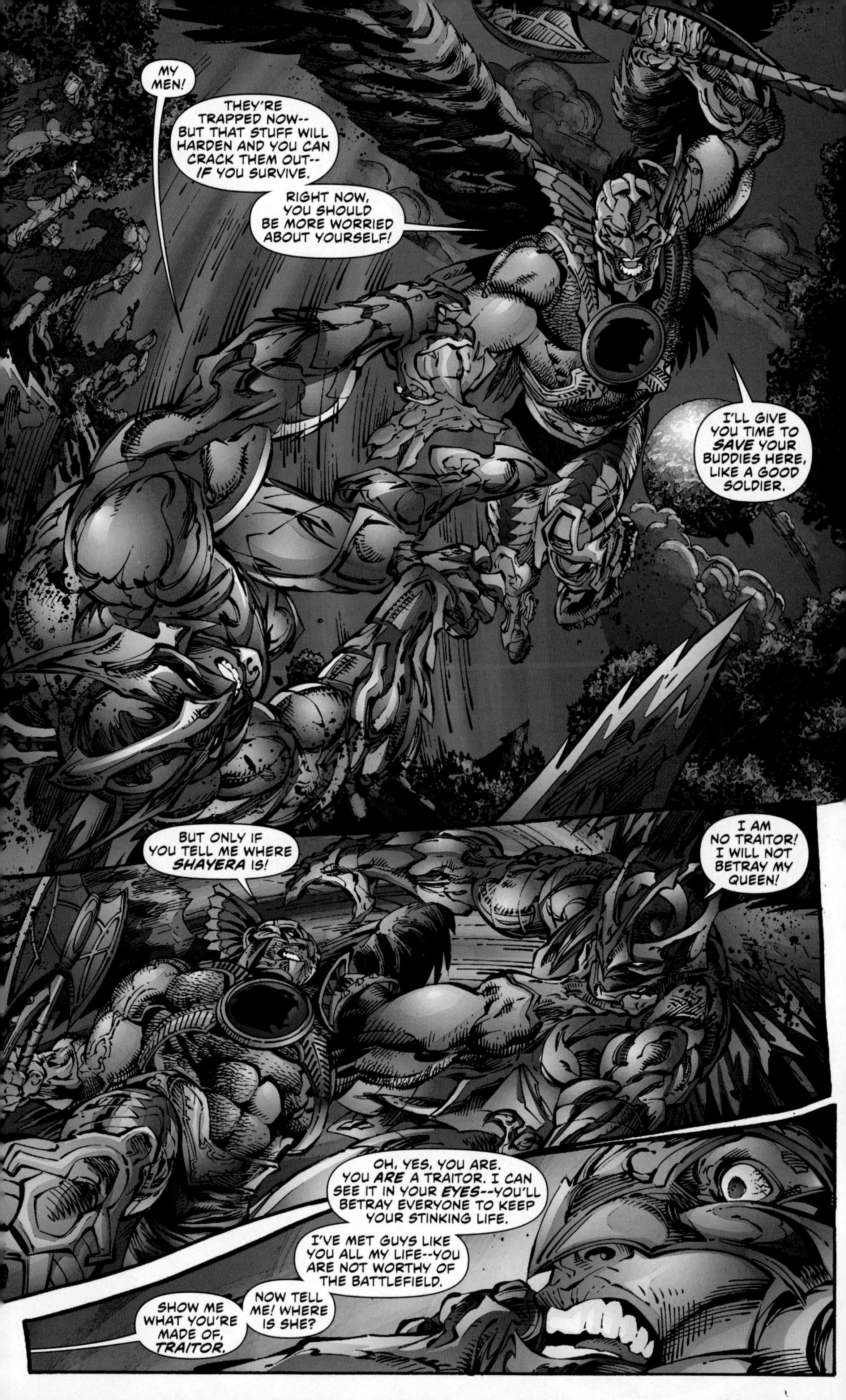
MY MEN!
THEY'RE TRAPPED NOW-- BUT THAT STUFF WILL HARDEN AND YOU CAN CRACK THEM OUT-- IF YOU SURVIVE.
RIGHT NOW, YOU SHOULD BE MORE WORRIED ABOUT YOURSELF!
I'LL GIVE YOU TIME TO SAVE YOUR BUDDIES HERE, LIKE A GOOD SOLDIER.
BUT ONLY IF YOU TELL ME WHERE SHAYERA IS!
I AM NO TRAITOR! I WILL NOT BETRAY MY QUEEN!
OH, YES, YOU ARE. YOU ARE A TRAITOR. I CAN SEE IT IN YOUR EYES--YOU'LL BETRAY EVERYONE TO KEEP YOUR STINKING LIFE.
I'VE MET GUYS LIKE YOU ALL MY LIFE--YOU ARE NOT WORTHY OF THE BATTLEFIELD.
NOW TELL ME! WHERE IS SHE?
SHOW ME WHAT YOU'RE MADE OF, TRAITOR.

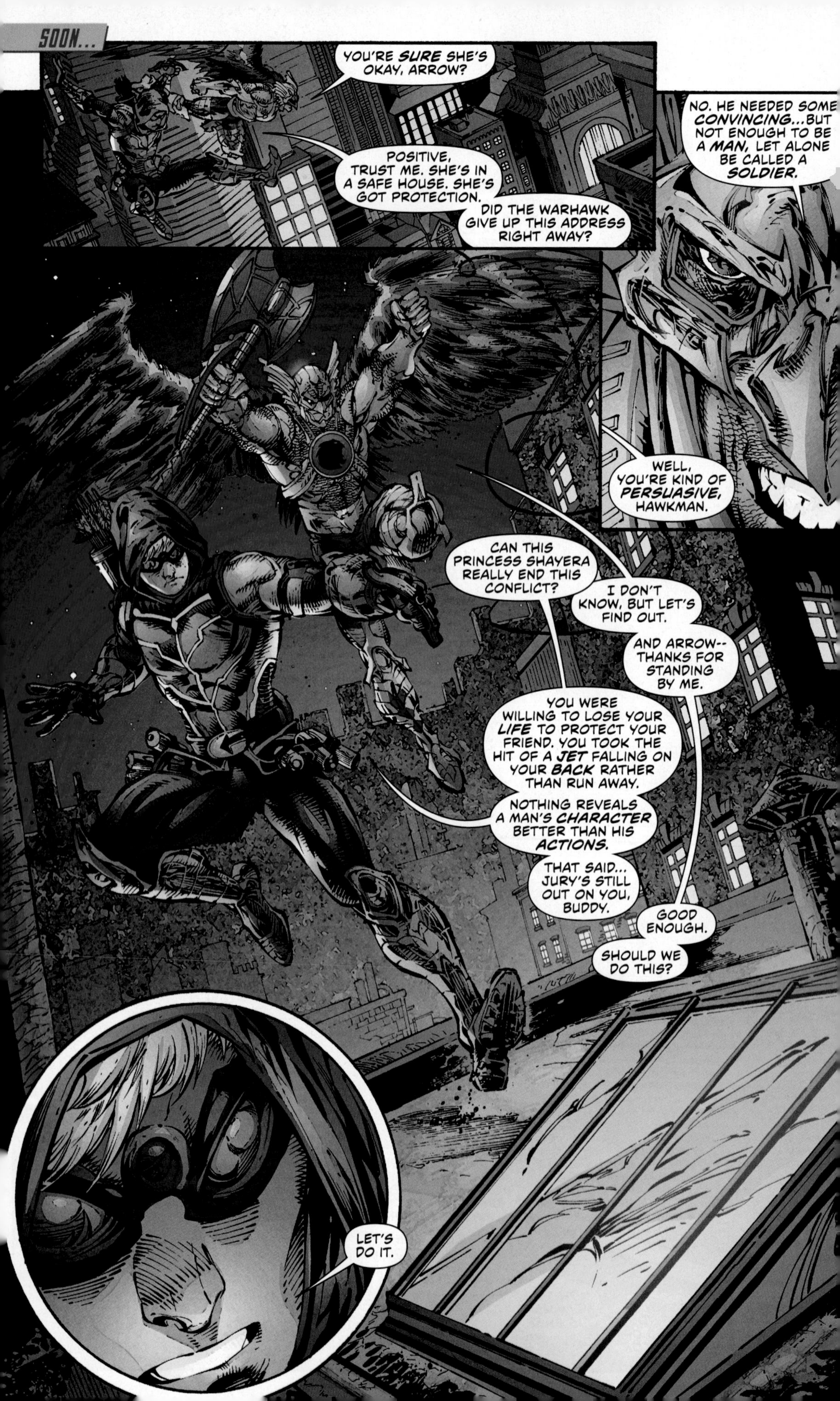
SOON...
YOU'RE SURE SHE'S OKAY, ARROW?
POSITIVE, TRUST ME. SHE'S IN A SAFE HOUSE. SHE'S GOT PROTECTION.
DID THE WARHAWK GIVE UP THIS ADDRESS RIGHT AWAY?
NO. HE NEEDED SOME CONVINCING...BUT NOT ENOUGH TO BE A MAN, LET ALONE BE CALLED A SOLDIER.
WELL, YOU'RE KIND OF PERSUASIVE, HAWKMAN.
CAN THIS PRINCESS SHAYERA REALLY END THIS CONFLICT?
I DON'T KNOW, BUT LET'S FIND OUT.
AND ARROW-- THANKS FOR STANDING BY ME.
YOU WERE WILLING TO LOSE YOUR LIFE TO PROTECT YOUR FRIEND. YOU TOOK THE HIT OF A JET FALLING ON YOUR BACK RATHER THAN RUN AWAY.
NOTHING REVEALS A MAN'S CHARACTER BETTER THAN HIS ACTIONS.
THAT SAID... JURY'S STILL OUT ON YOU, BUDDY.
GOOD ENOUGH.
SHOULD WE DO THIS?
LET'S DO IT.

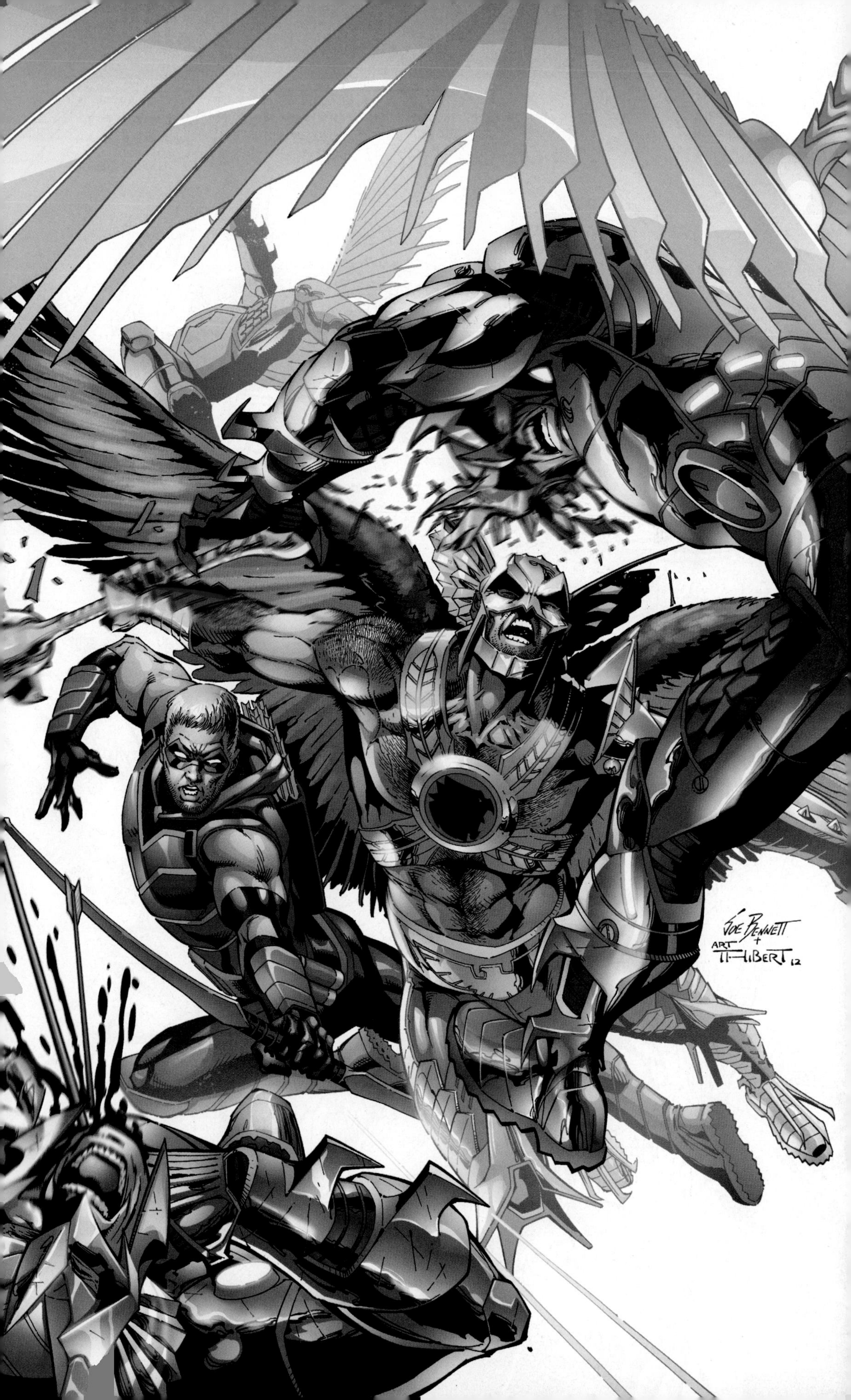
JOE BENNETT
+
ART THIBERT 12

BIRDS OF A FEATHER

ROB LIEFELD & FRANK TIERI writers **JOE BENNETT & JACK JADSON** pencillers **ART THIBERT & WAYNE FAUCHER** inkers
cover by **JOE BENNETT** and **ART THIBERT** with **GUY MAJOR**

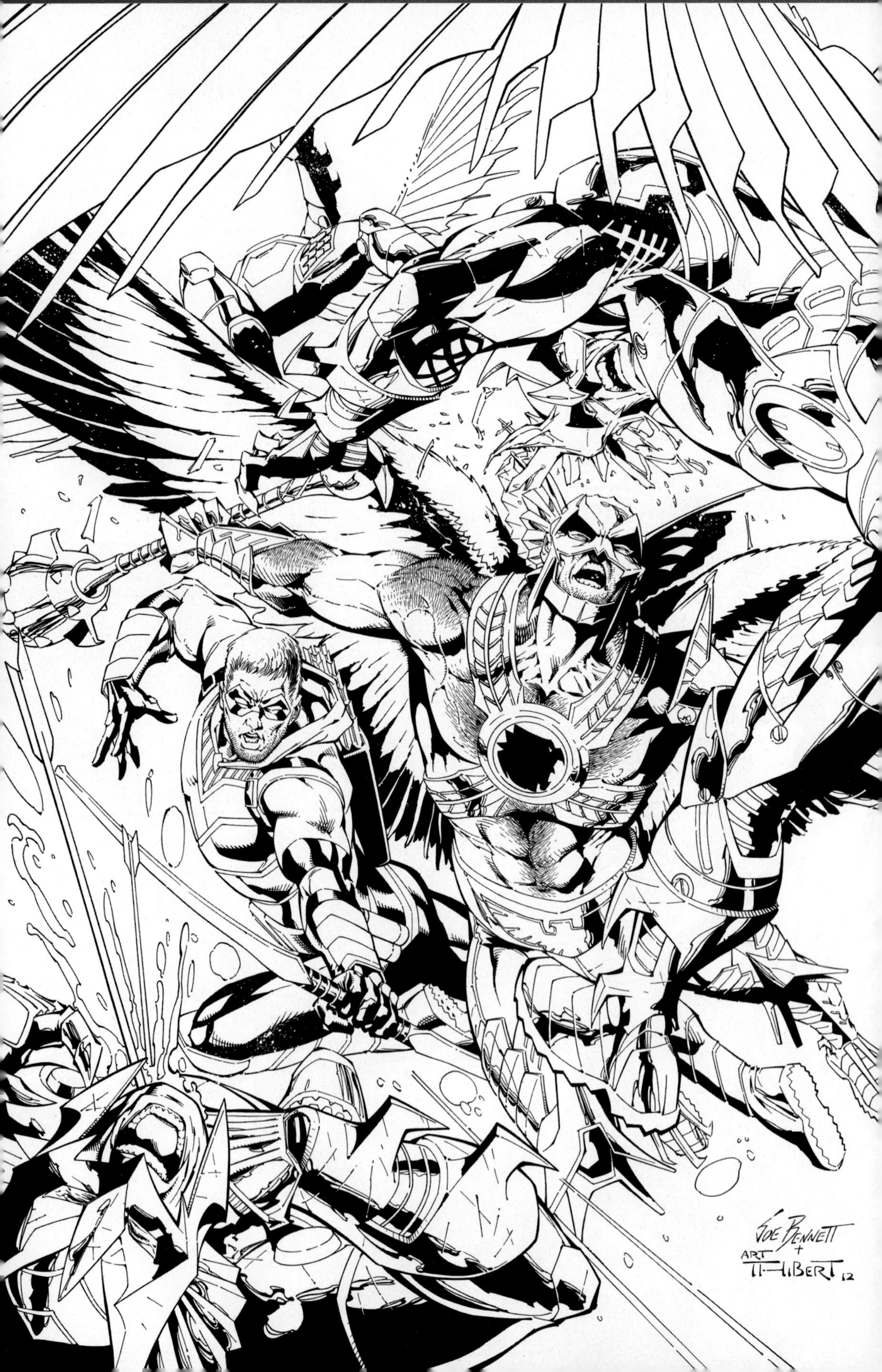
JOE BENNETT + ART THIBERT 12

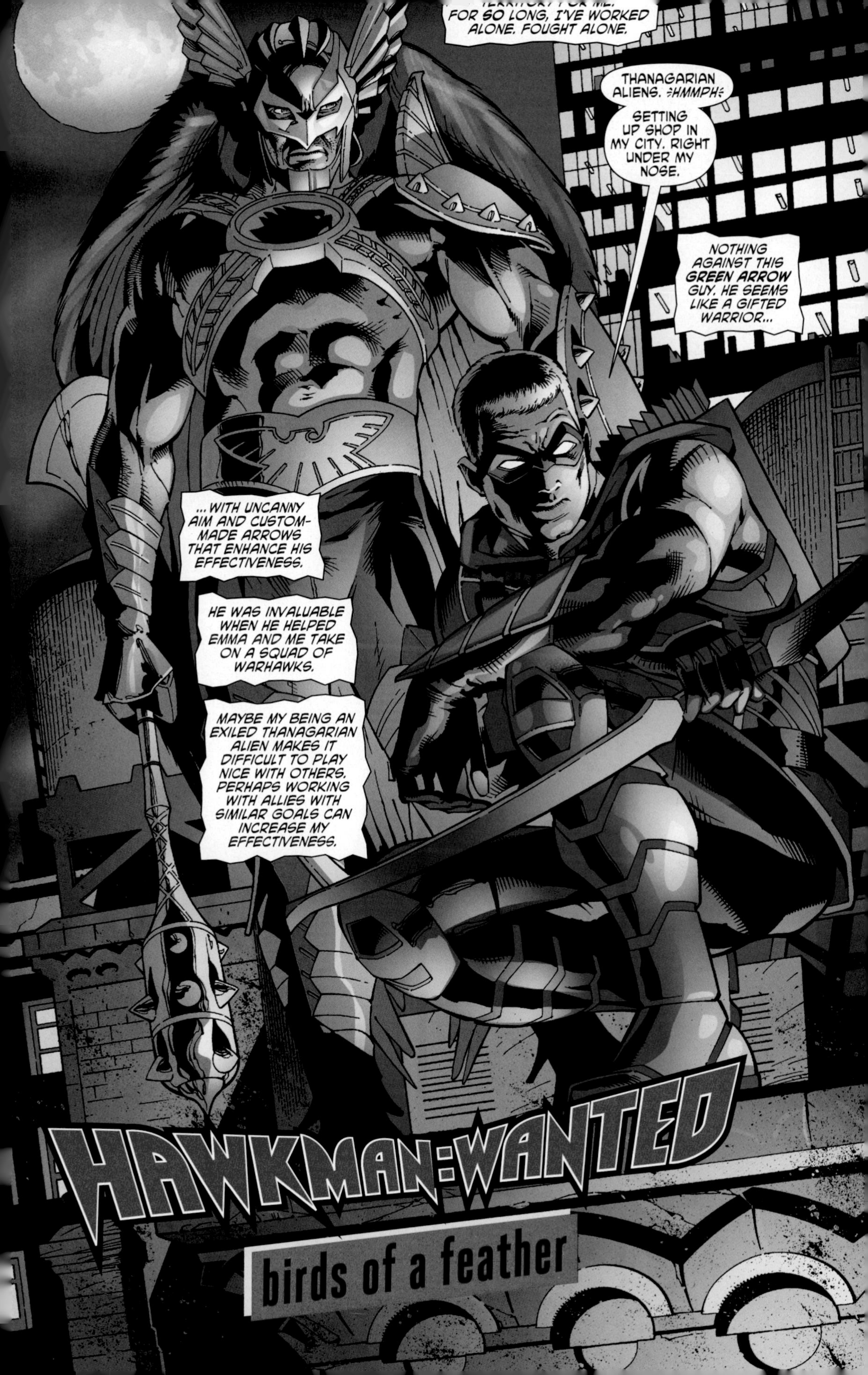
FOR SO LONG, I'VE WORKED ALONE. FOUGHT ALONE.
THANAGARIAN ALIENS. ≈HMMPH≈
SETTING UP SHOP IN MY CITY. RIGHT UNDER MY NOSE.
NOTHING AGAINST THIS GREEN ARROW GUY. HE SEEMS LIKE A GIFTED WARRIOR...
...WITH UNCANNY AIM AND CUSTOM-MADE ARROWS THAT ENHANCE HIS EFFECTIVENESS.
HE WAS INVALUABLE WHEN HE HELPED EMMA AND ME TAKE ON A SQUAD OF WARHAWKS.
MAYBE MY BEING AN EXILED THANAGARIAN ALIEN MAKES IT DIFFICULT TO PLAY NICE WITH OTHERS. PERHAPS WORKING WITH ALLIES WITH SIMILAR GOALS CAN INCREASE MY EFFECTIVENESS.
HAWKMAN: WANTED
birds of a feather

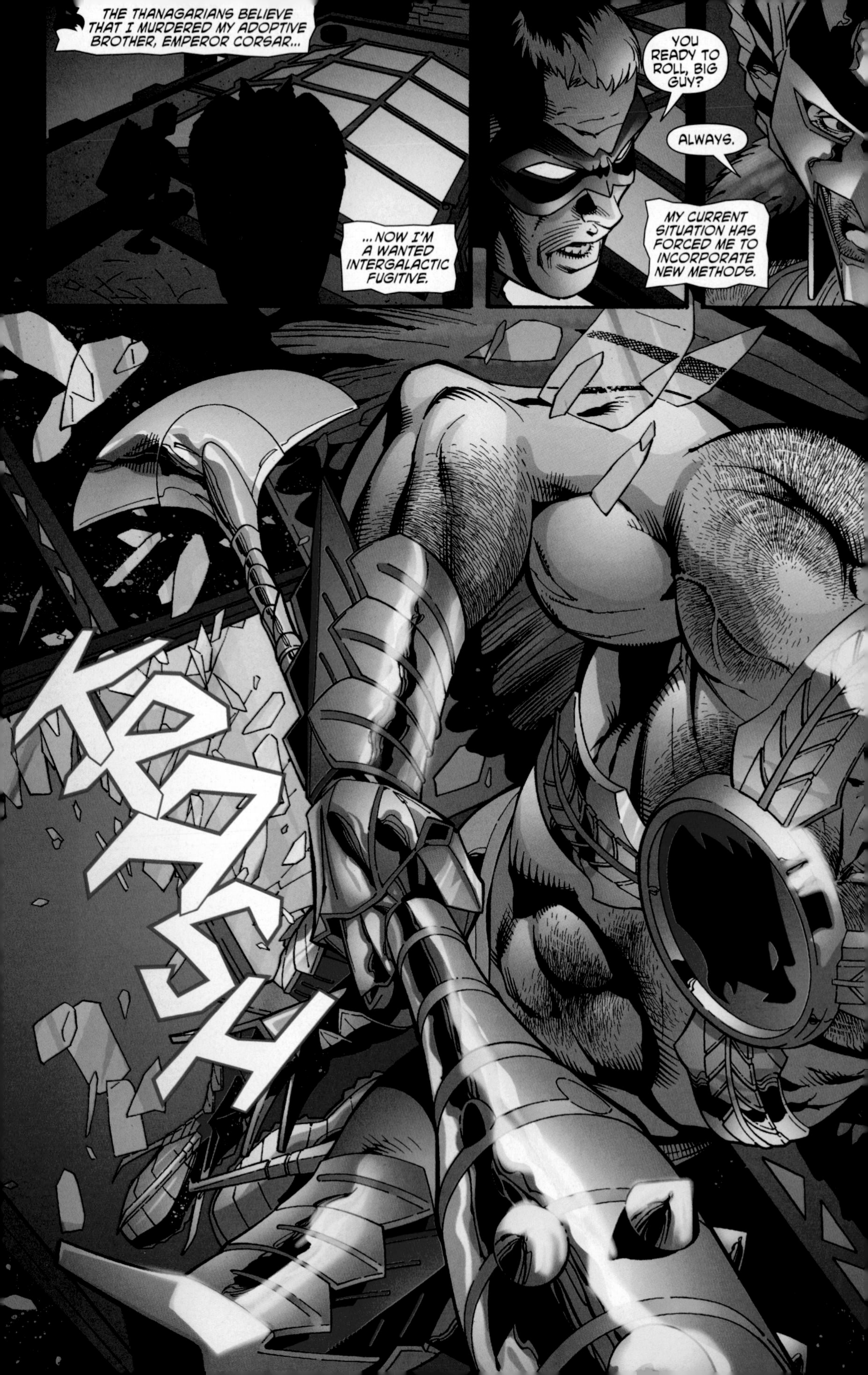
THE THANAGARIANS BELIEVE THAT I MURDERED MY ADOPTIVE BROTHER, EMPEROR CORSAR...
...NOW I'M A WANTED INTERGALACTIC FUGITIVE.
YOU READY TO ROLL, BIG GUY?
ALWAYS.
MY CURRENT SITUATION HAS FORCED ME TO INCORPORATE NEW METHODS.
KRASH

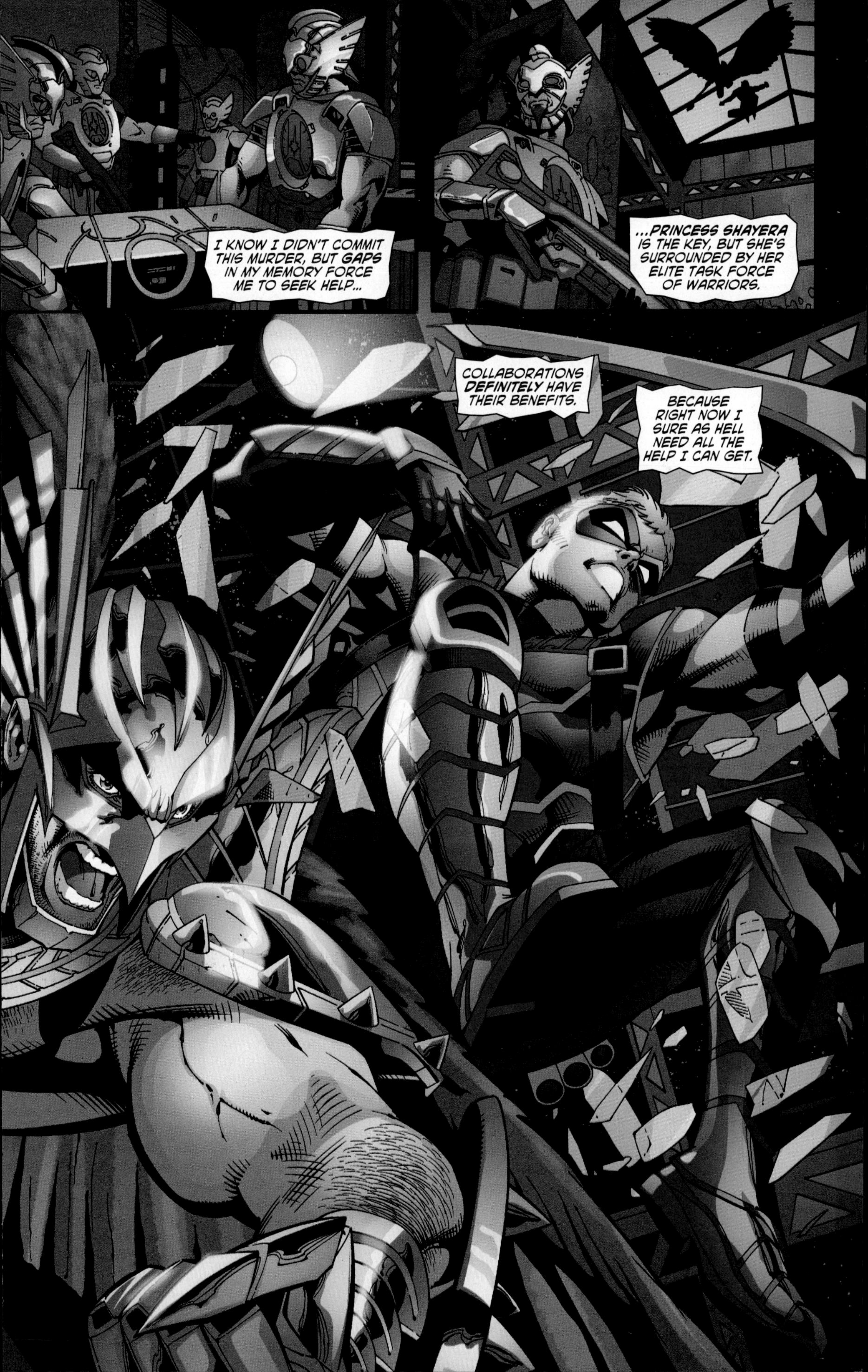
I KNOW I DIDN'T COMMIT THIS MURDER, BUT GAPS IN MY MEMORY FORCE ME TO SEEK HELP...
...PRINCESS SHAYERA IS THE KEY, BUT SHE'S SURROUNDED BY HER ELITE TASK FORCE OF WARRIORS.
COLLABORATIONS DEFINITELY HAVE THEIR BENEFITS.
BECAUSE RIGHT NOW I SURE AS HELL NEED ALL THE HELP I CAN GET.

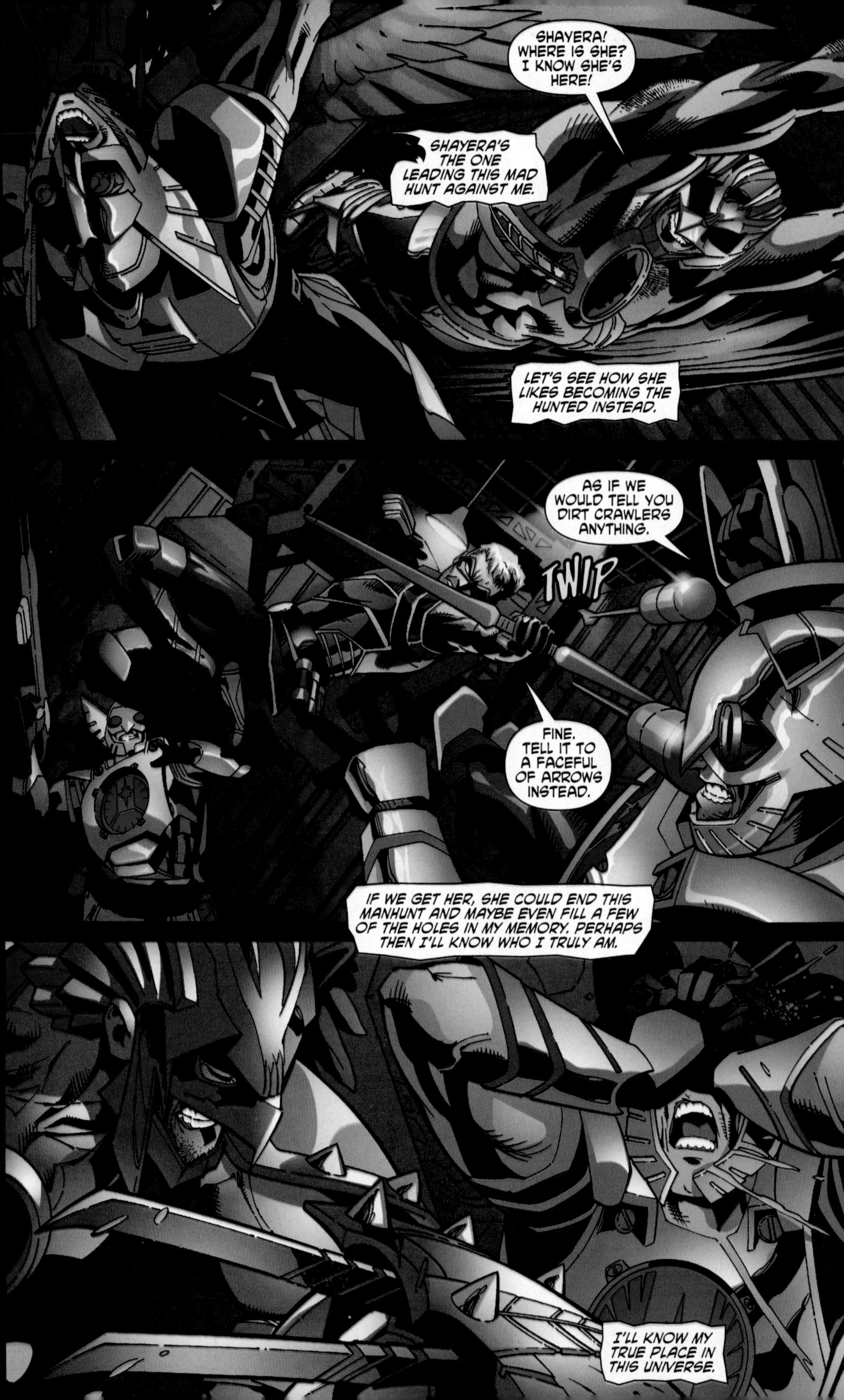

SHAYERA! WHERE IS SHE? I KNOW SHE'S HERE!
SHAYERA'S THE ONE LEADING THIS MAD HUNT AGAINST ME.
LET'S SEE HOW SHE LIKES BECOMING THE HUNTED INSTEAD.
AS IF WE WOULD TELL YOU DIRT CRAWLERS ANYTHING.
TWIP
FINE. TELL IT TO A FACEFUL OF ARROWS INSTEAD.
IF WE GET HER, SHE COULD END THIS MANHUNT AND MAYBE EVEN FILL A FEW OF THE HOLES IN MY MEMORY. PERHAPS THEN I'LL KNOW WHO I TRULY AM.
I'LL KNOW MY TRUE PLACE IN THIS UNIVERSE.

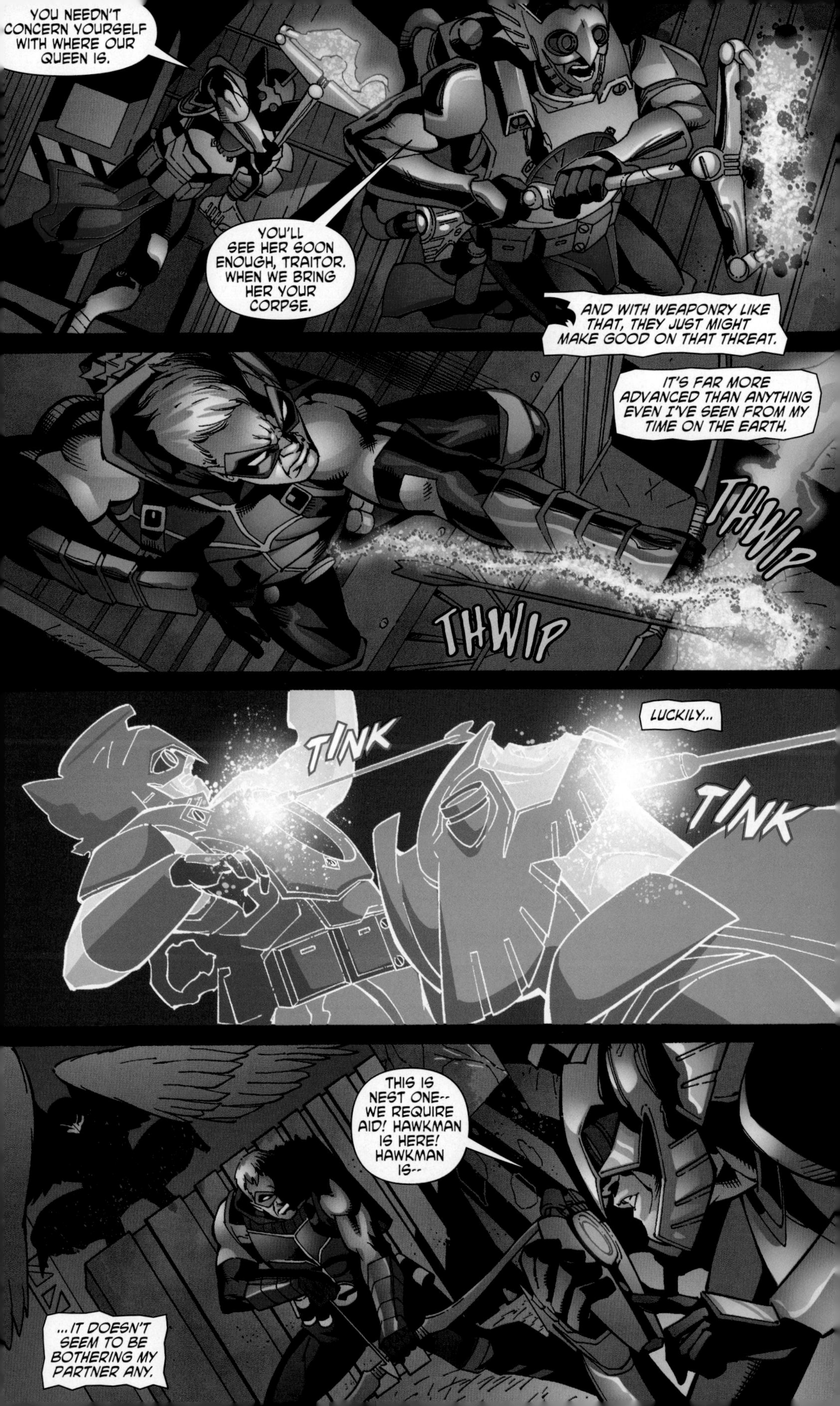
YOU NEEDN'T CONCERN YOURSELF WITH WHERE OUR QUEEN IS.
YOU'LL SEE HER SOON ENOUGH, TRAITOR. WHEN WE BRING HER YOUR CORPSE.
AND WITH WEAPONRY LIKE THAT, THEY JUST MIGHT MAKE GOOD ON THAT THREAT.
IT'S FAR MORE ADVANCED THAN ANYTHING EVEN I'VE SEEN FROM MY TIME ON THE EARTH.
THWIP
THWIP
LUCKILY...
TINK
TINK
THIS IS NEST ONE-- WE REQUIRE AID! HAWKMAN IS HERE! HAWKMAN IS--
...IT DOESN'T SEEM TO BE BOTHERING MY PARTNER ANY.

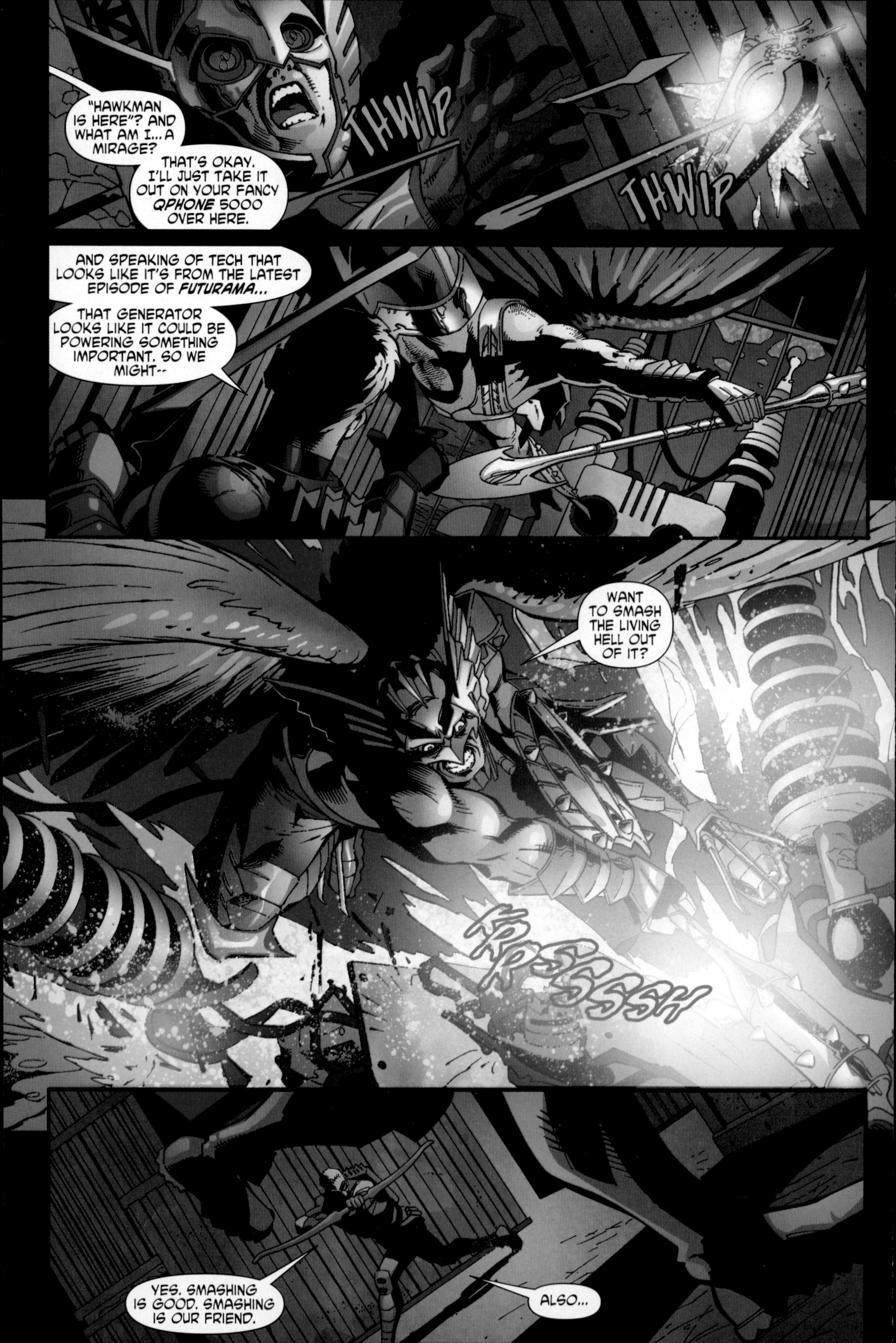
"HAWKMAN IS HERE"? AND WHAT AM I... A MIRAGE?
THAT'S OKAY. I'LL JUST TAKE IT OUT ON YOUR FANCY *QPHONE* 5000 OVER HERE.
THWIP
THWIP
AND SPEAKING OF TECH THAT LOOKS LIKE IT'S FROM THE LATEST EPISODE OF *FUTURAMA*...
THAT GENERATOR LOOKS LIKE IT COULD BE POWERING SOMETHING IMPORTANT. SO WE MIGHT--
WANT TO SMASH THE LIVING HELL OUT OF IT?
KRSSSSH
YES. SMASHING IS GOOD. SMASHING IS OUR FRIEND.
ALSO...

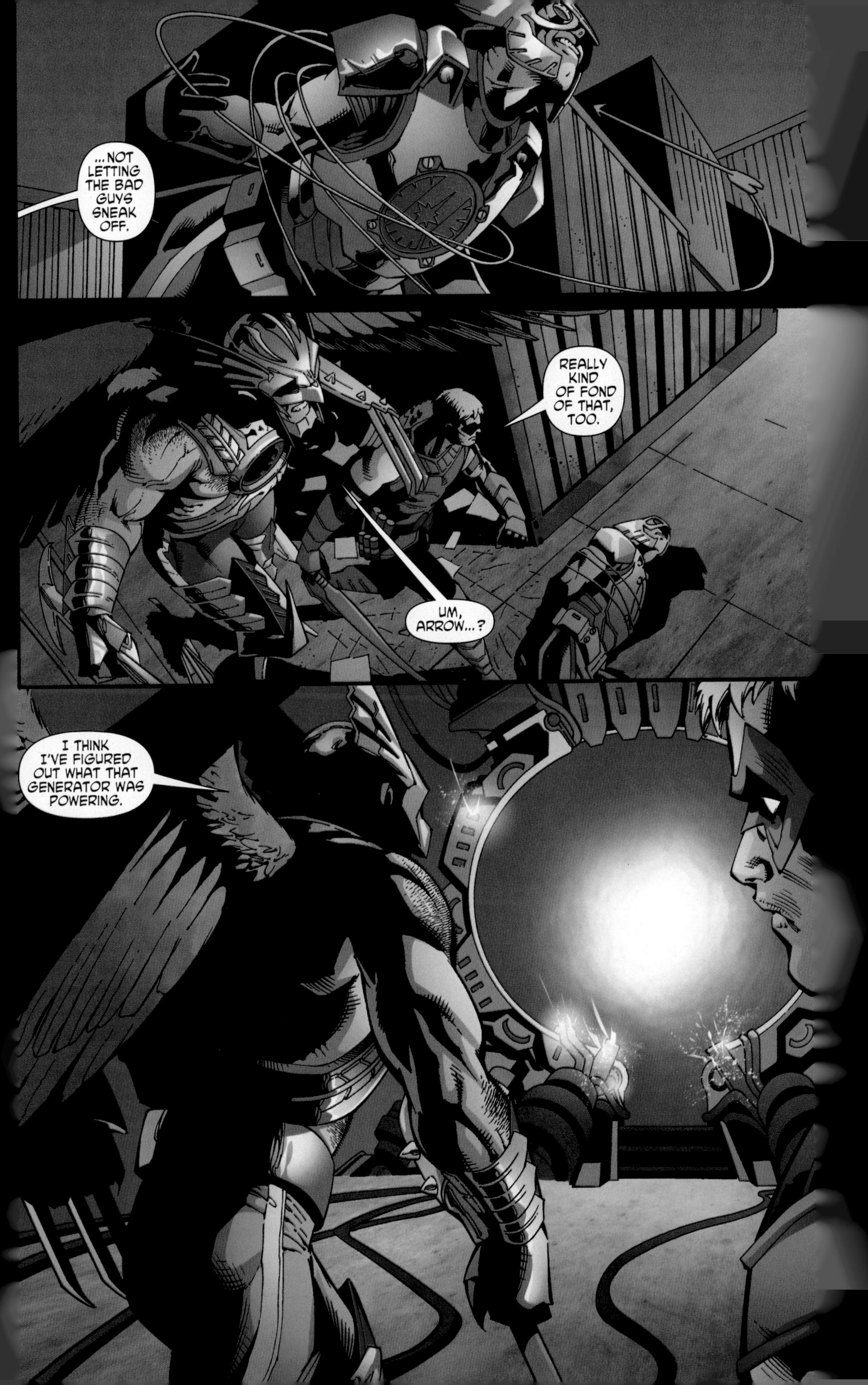
...NOT LETTING THE BAD GUYS SNEAK OFF.
REALLY KIND OF FOND OF THAT, TOO.
UM, ARROW...?
I THINK I'VE FIGURED OUT WHAT THAT GENERATOR WAS POWERING.

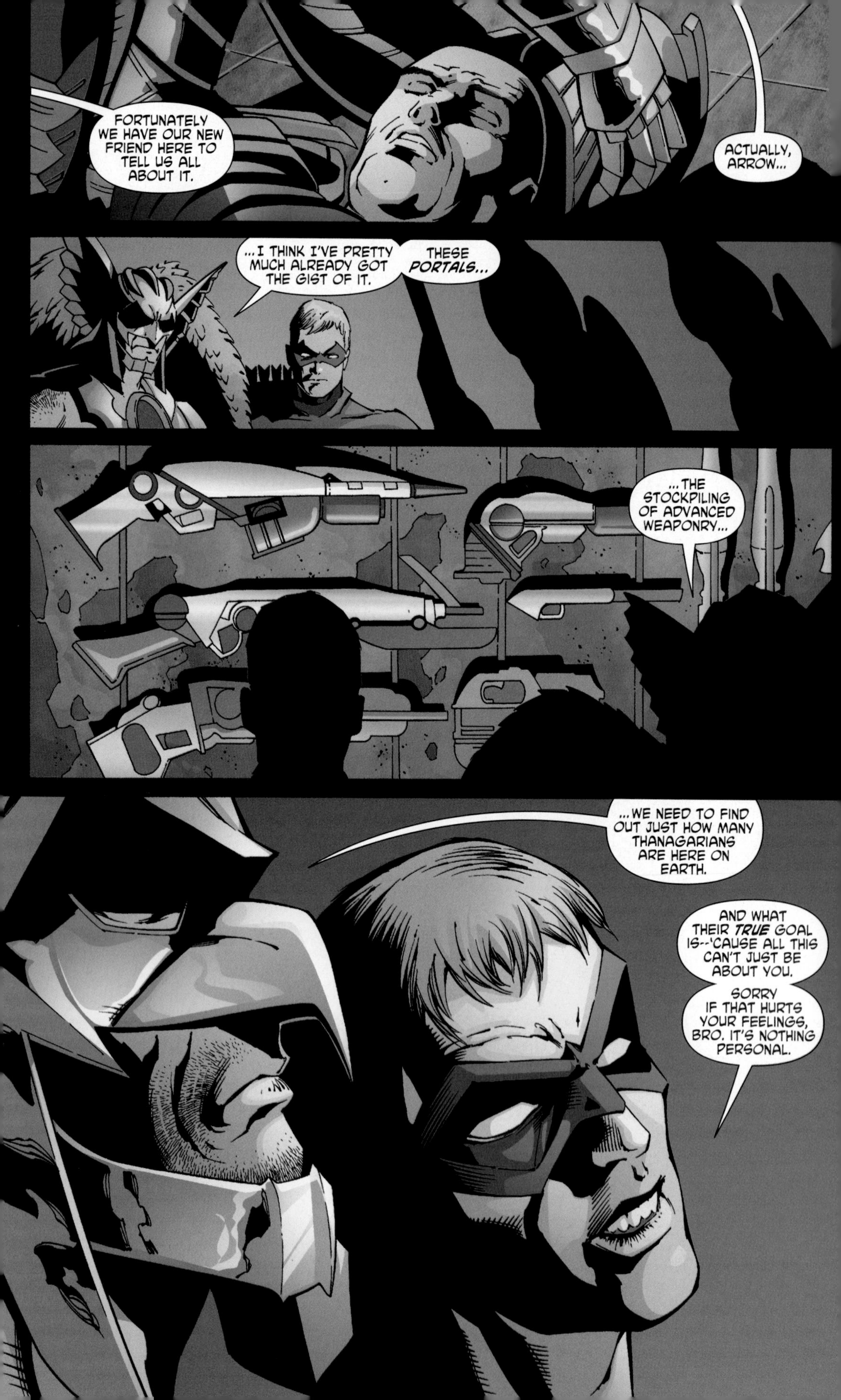
FORTUNATELY WE HAVE OUR NEW FRIEND HERE TO TELL US ALL ABOUT IT.
ACTUALLY, ARROW...
...I THINK I'VE PRETTY MUCH ALREADY GOT THE GIST OF IT.
THESE *PORTALS*...
...THE STOCKPILING OF ADVANCED WEAPONRY...
...WE NEED TO FIND OUT JUST HOW MANY THANAGARIANS ARE HERE ON EARTH.
AND WHAT THEIR *TRUE* GOAL IS--'CAUSE ALL THIS CAN'T JUST BE ABOUT YOU.
SORRY IF THAT HURTS YOUR FEELINGS, BRO. IT'S NOTHING PERSONAL.

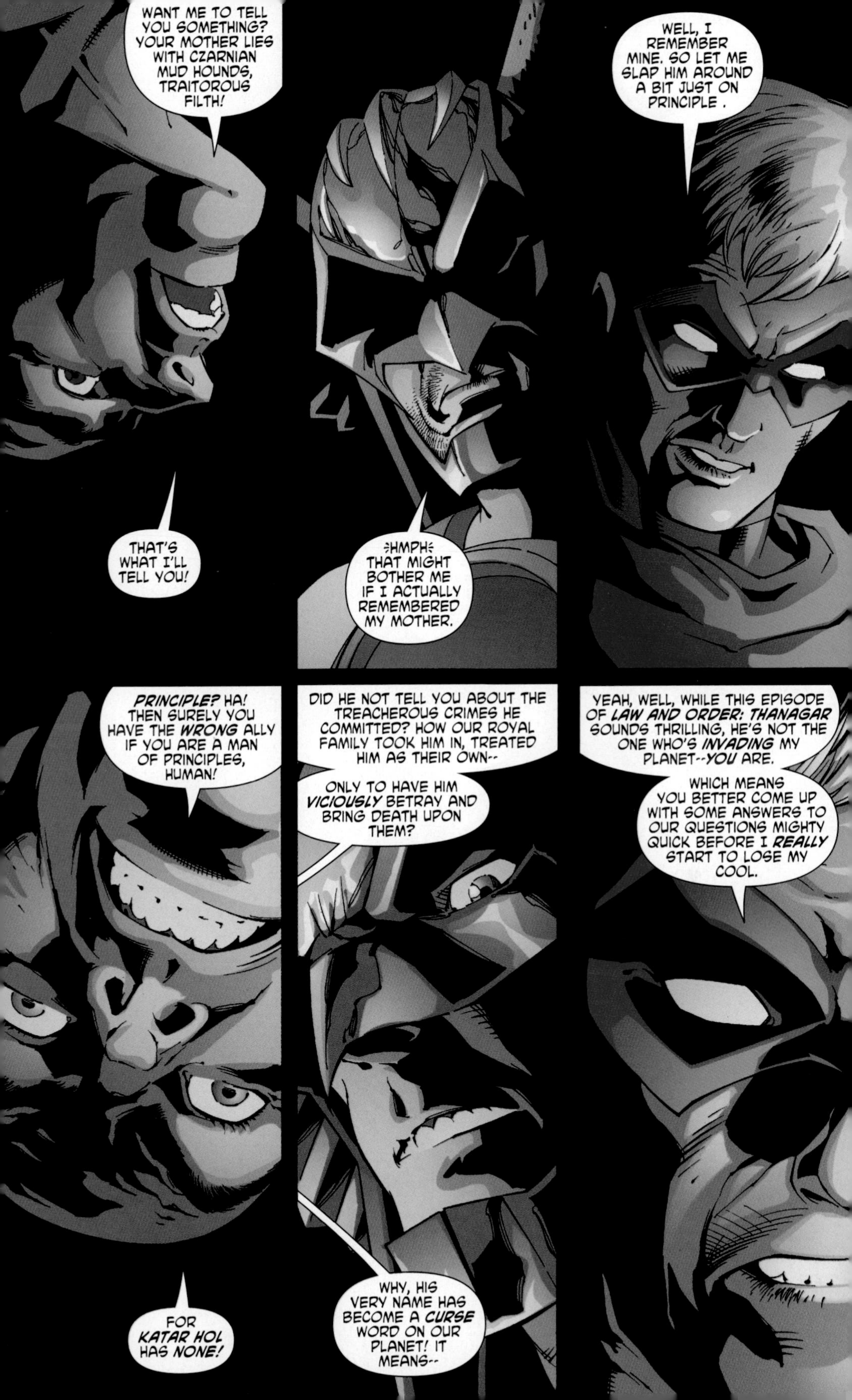
WANT ME TO TELL YOU SOMETHING? YOUR MOTHER LIES WITH CZARNIAN MUD HOUNDS, TRAITOROUS FILTH!
THAT'S WHAT I'LL TELL YOU!
HMPH THAT MIGHT BOTHER ME IF I ACTUALLY REMEMBERED MY MOTHER.
WELL, I REMEMBER MINE. SO LET ME SLAP HIM AROUND A BIT JUST ON PRINCIPLE .
PRINCIPLE? HA! THEN SURELY YOU HAVE THE WRONG ALLY IF YOU ARE A MAN OF PRINCIPLES, HUMAN!
FOR KATAR HOL HAS NONE!
DID HE NOT TELL YOU ABOUT THE TREACHEROUS CRIMES HE COMMITTED? HOW OUR ROYAL FAMILY TOOK HIM IN, TREATED HIM AS THEIR OWN--
ONLY TO HAVE HIM VICIOUSLY BETRAY AND BRING DEATH UPON THEM?
WHY, HIS VERY NAME HAS BECOME A CURSE WORD ON OUR PLANET! IT MEANS--
YEAH, WELL, WHILE THIS EPISODE OF LAW AND ORDER: THANAGAR SOUNDS THRILLING, HE'S NOT THE ONE WHO'S INVADING MY PLANET--YOU ARE.
WHICH MEANS YOU BETTER COME UP WITH SOME ANSWERS TO OUR QUESTIONS MIGHTY QUICK BEFORE I REALLY START TO LOSE MY COOL.

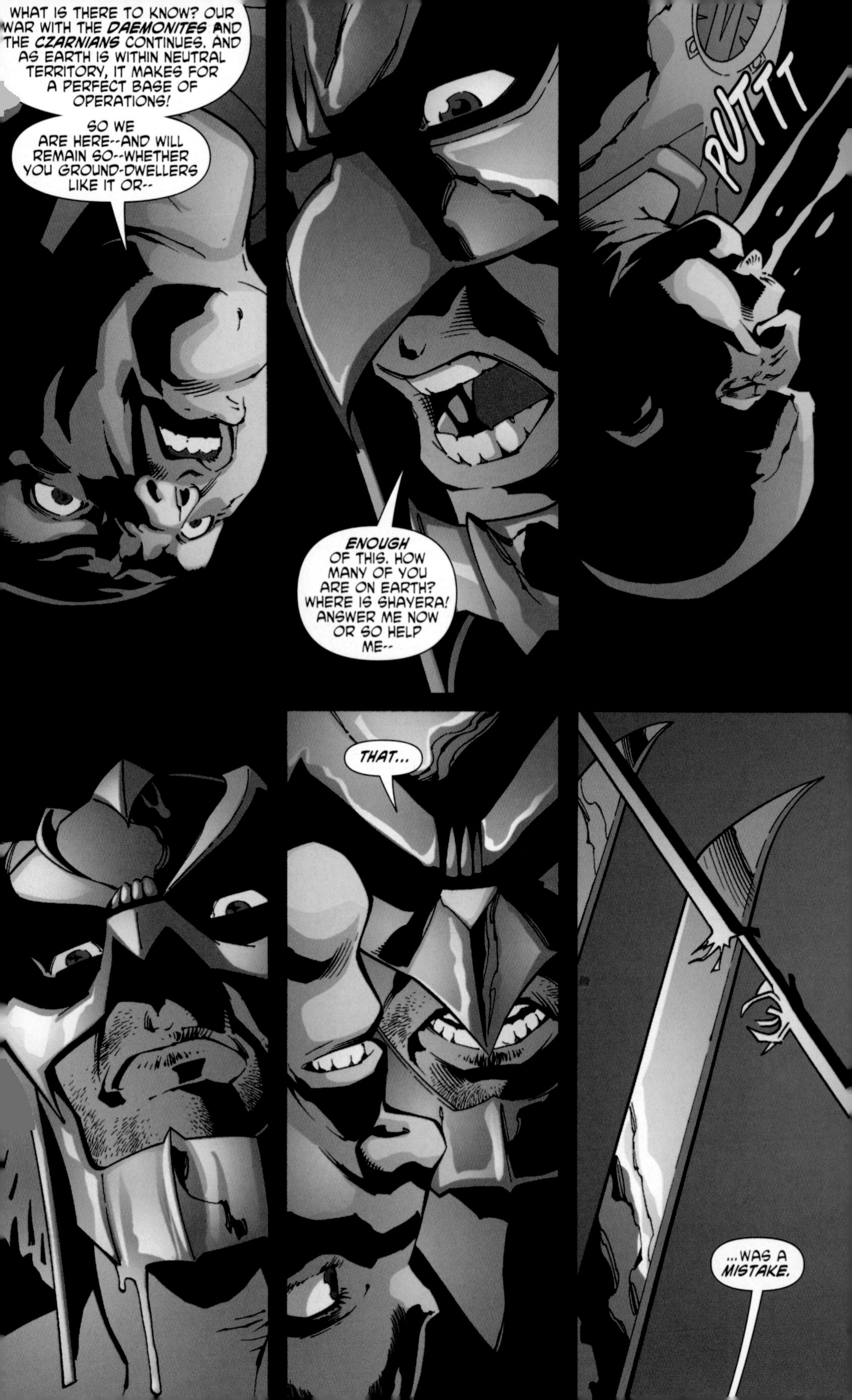

WHAT IS THERE TO KNOW? OUR WAR WITH THE *DAEMONITES* AND THE *CZARNIANS* CONTINUES. AND AS EARTH IS WITHIN NEUTRAL TERRITORY, IT MAKES FOR A PERFECT BASE OF OPERATIONS!
SO WE ARE HERE--AND WILL REMAIN SO--WHETHER YOU GROUND-DWELLERS LIKE IT OR--
ENOUGH OF THIS. HOW MANY OF YOU ARE ON EARTH? WHERE IS SHAYERA! ANSWER ME NOW OR SO HELP ME--
PUTTT
THAT...
...WAS A *MISTAKE.*

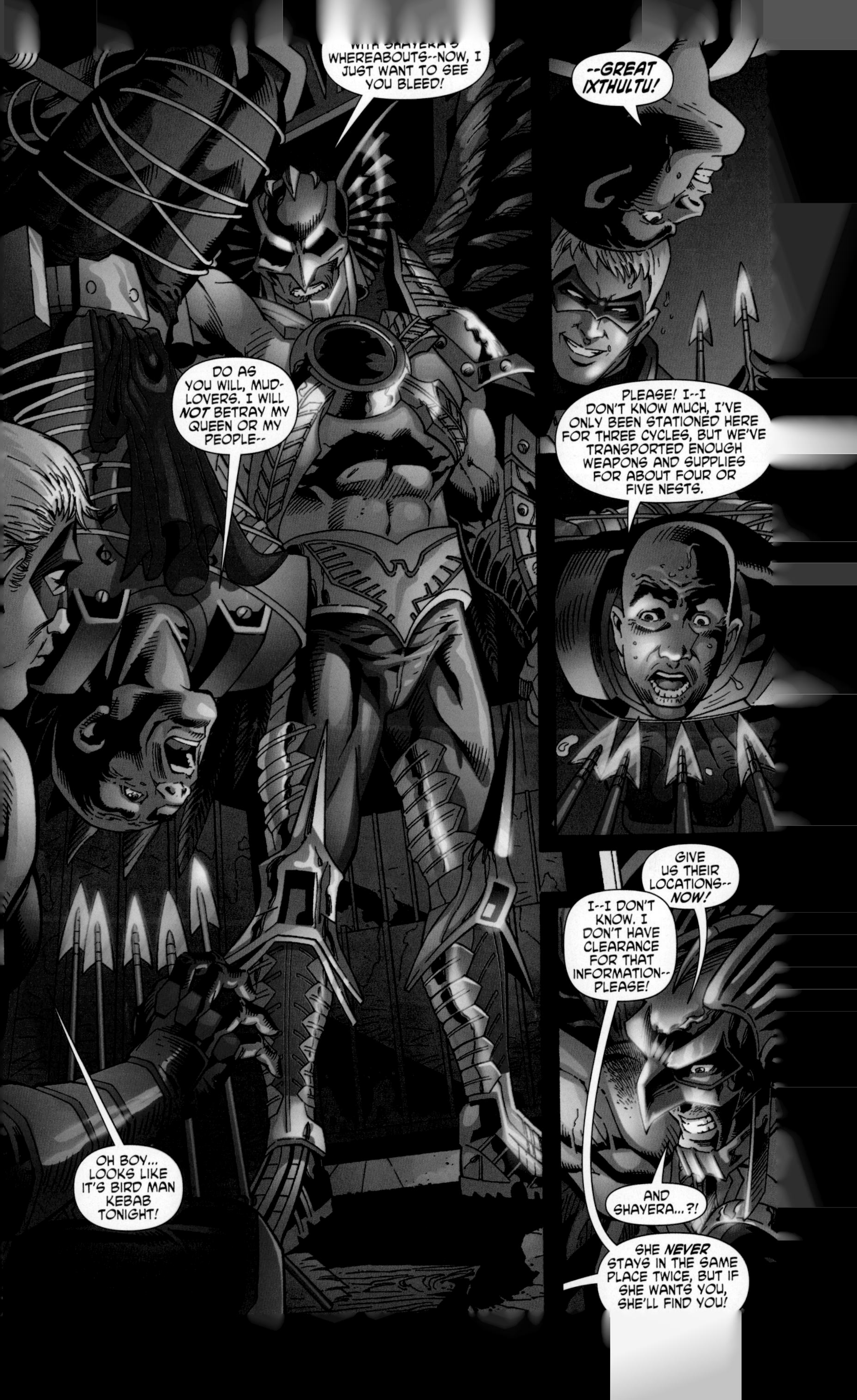
WHEREABOUTS--NOW, I JUST WANT TO SEE YOU BLEED!
DO AS YOU WILL, MUD-LOVERS. I WILL NOT BETRAY MY QUEEN OR MY PEOPLE--
OH BOY... LOOKS LIKE IT'S BIRD MAN KEBAB TONIGHT!
--GREAT IXTHULTU!
PLEASE! I--I DON'T KNOW MUCH, I'VE ONLY BEEN STATIONED HERE FOR THREE CYCLES, BUT WE'VE TRANSPORTED ENOUGH WEAPONS AND SUPPLIES FOR ABOUT FOUR OR FIVE NESTS.
GIVE US THEIR LOCATIONS--NOW!
I--I DON'T KNOW. I DON'T HAVE CLEARANCE FOR THAT INFORMATION--PLEASE!
AND SHAYERA...?!
SHE NEVER STAYS IN THE SAME PLACE TWICE, BUT IF SHE WANTS YOU, SHE'LL FIND YOU!

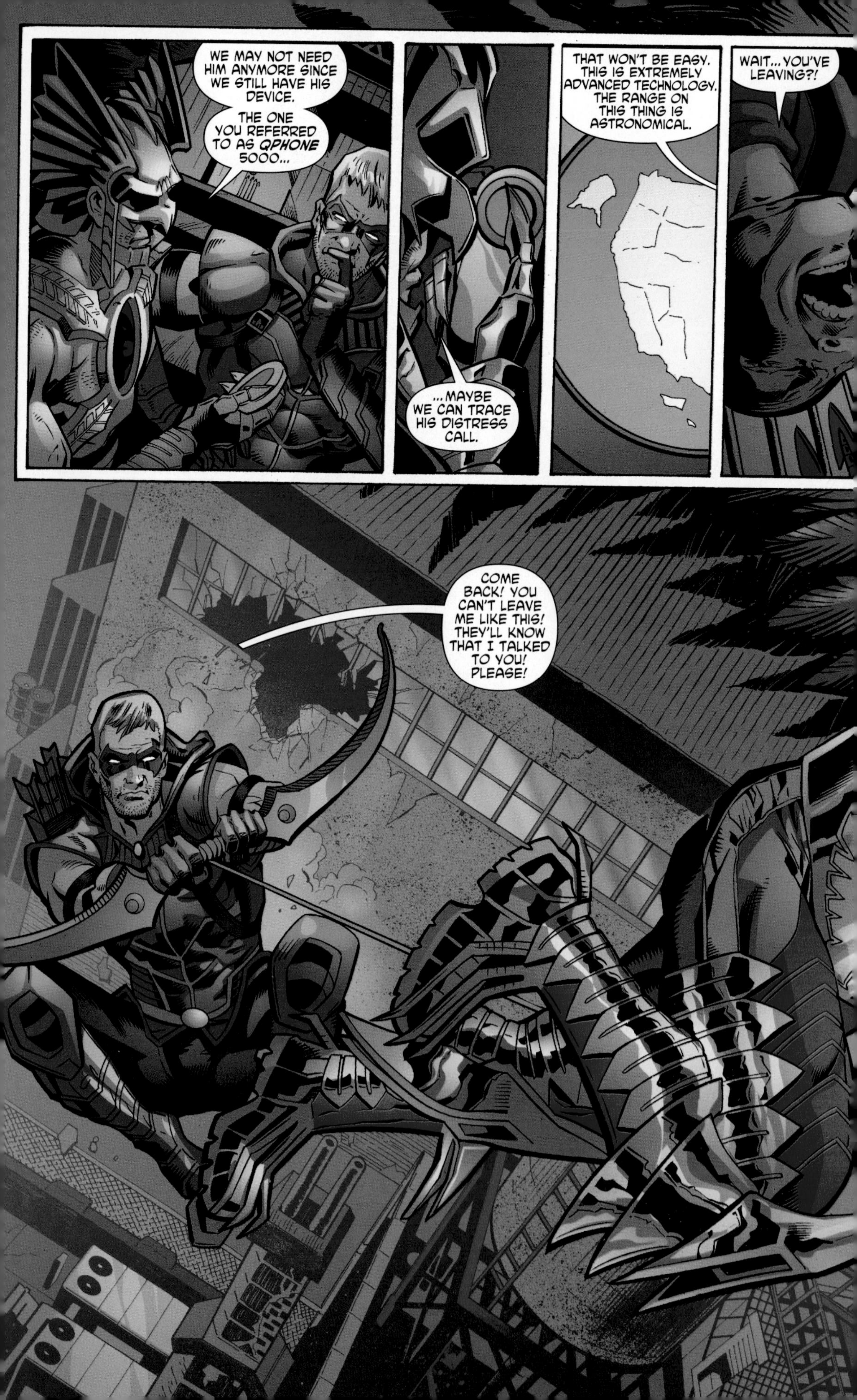

WE MAY NOT NEED HIM ANYMORE SINCE WE STILL HAVE HIS DEVICE.
THE ONE YOU REFERRED TO AS *QPHONE* 5000...
...MAYBE WE CAN TRACE HIS DISTRESS CALL.
THAT WON'T BE EASY. THIS IS EXTREMELY ADVANCED TECHNOLOGY. THE RANGE ON THIS THING IS ASTRONOMICAL.
WAIT... YOU'VE LEAVING?!
COME BACK! YOU CAN'T LEAVE ME LIKE THIS! THEY'LL KNOW THAT I TALKED TO YOU! PLEASE!

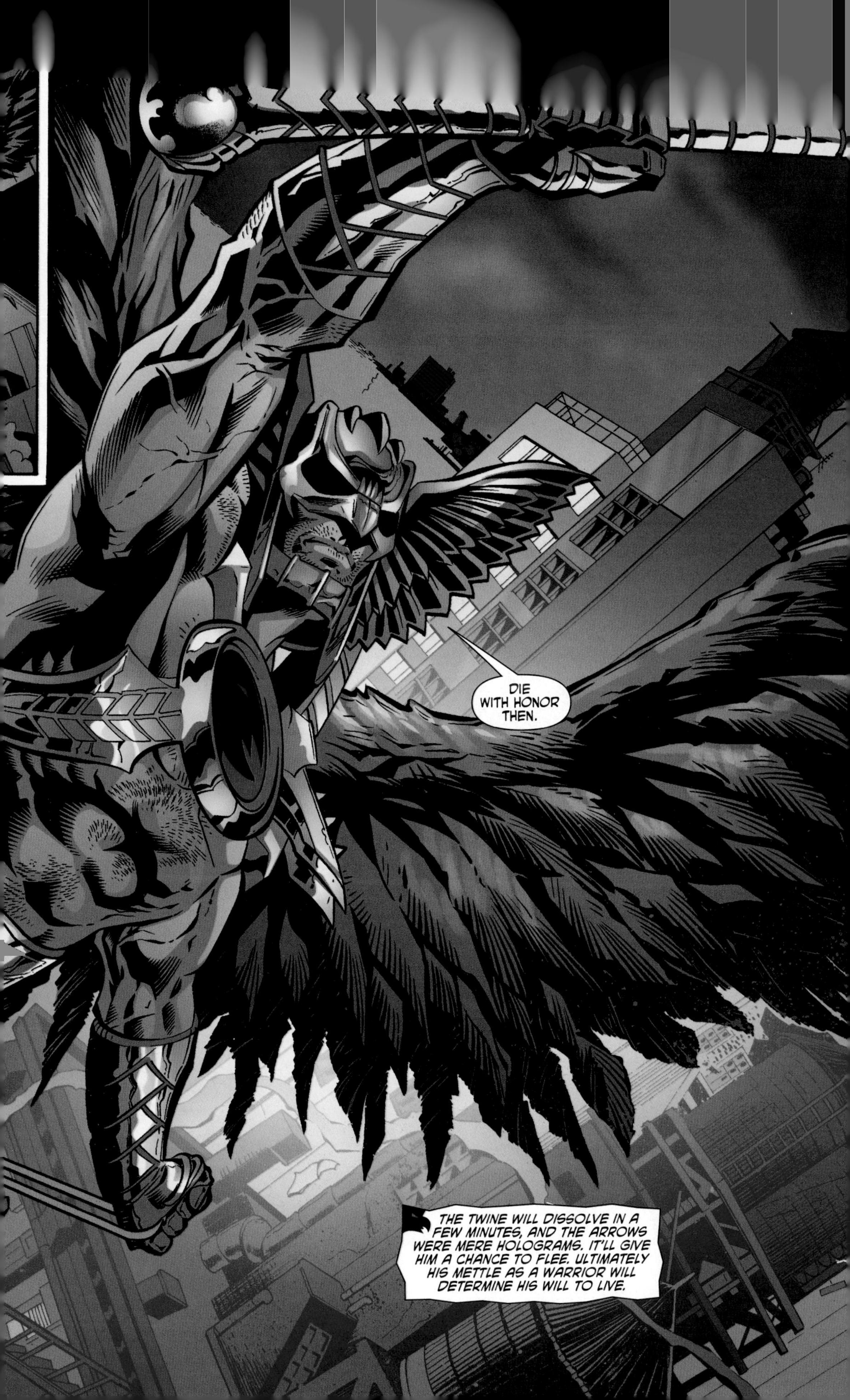
DIE WITH HONOR THEN.
THE TWINE WILL DISSOLVE IN A FEW MINUTES, AND THE ARROWS WERE MERE HOLOGRAMS. IT'LL GIVE HIM A CHANCE TO FLEE. ULTIMATELY HIS METTLE AS A WARRIOR WILL DETERMINE HIS WILL TO LIVE.

HARROW

ANN NOCENTI writer FREDDIE WILLIAMS II penciller
FREDDIE WILLIAMS II - pgs. 7, 8, 11, 20 ROB HUNTER - pgs. 1-6, 9, 10, 12, 13 ROBIN RIGGS - pgs. 14-19 inkers cover by AARON LOPRESTI with HI-FI

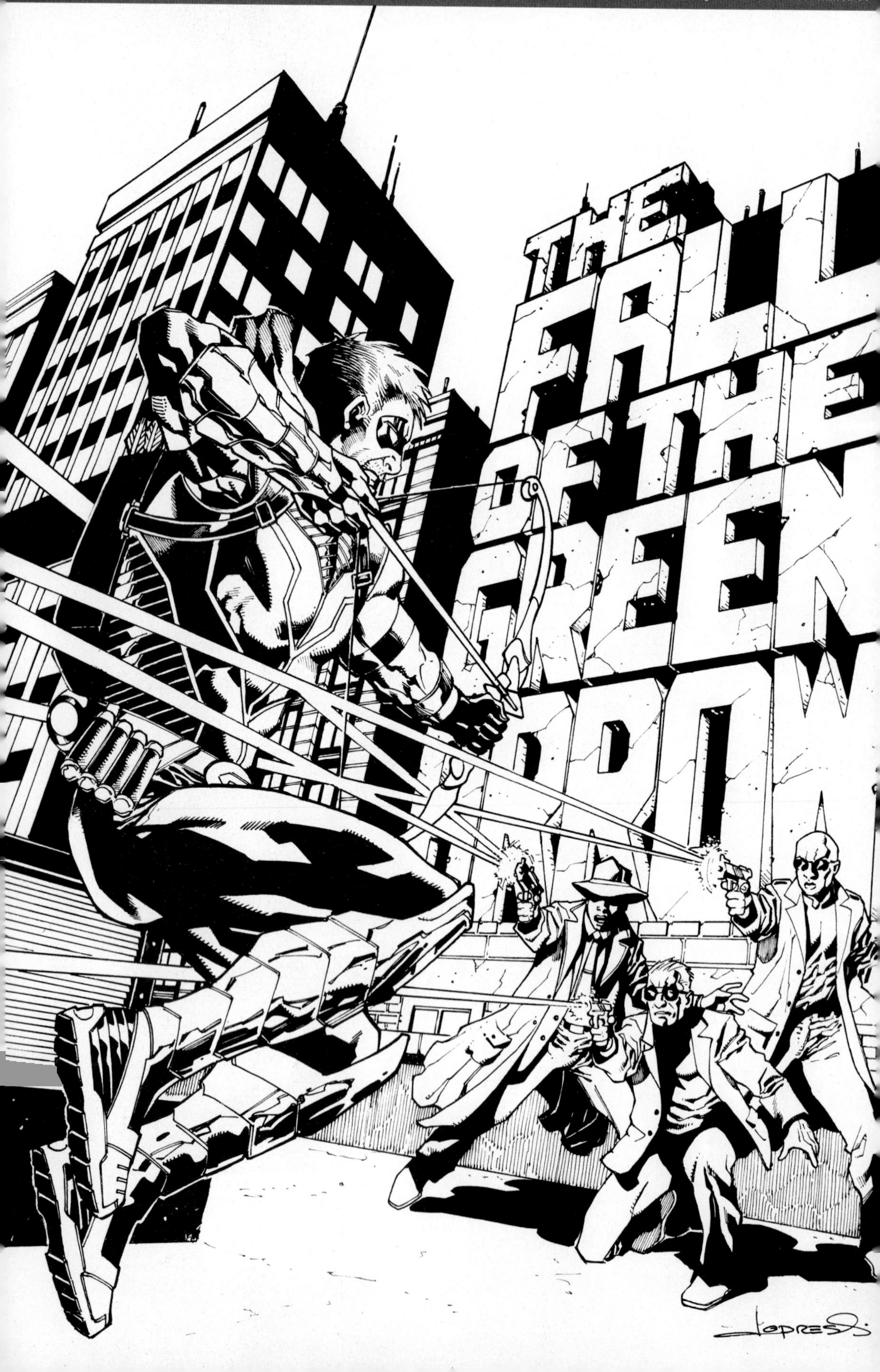

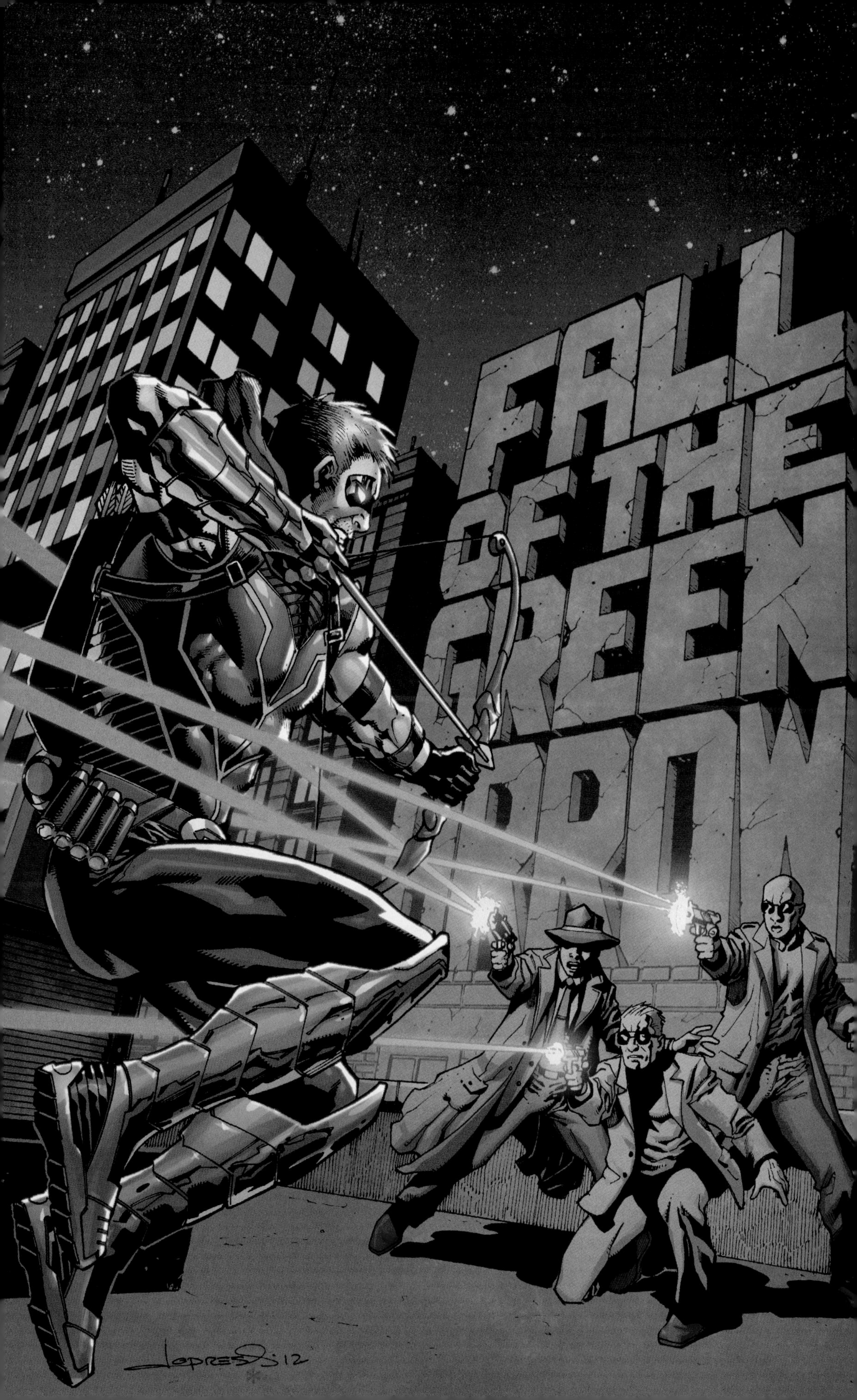
FALL OF THE GREEN ARROW

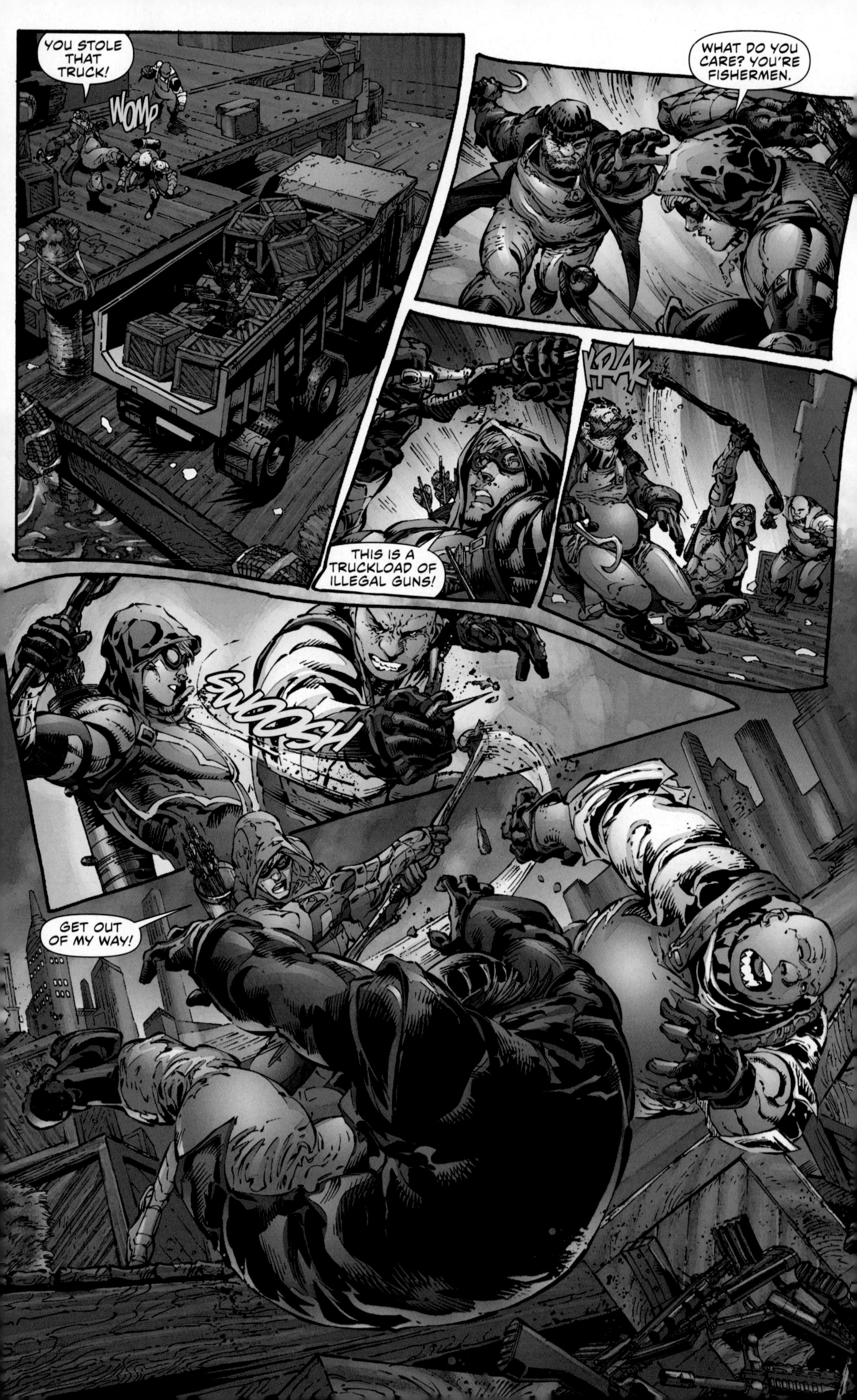

YOU STOLE THAT TRUCK!
WOMP
WHAT DO YOU CARE? YOU'RE FISHERMEN.
THIS IS A TRUCKLOAD OF ILLEGAL GUNS!
KRAK
SWOOSH
GET OUT OF MY WAY!

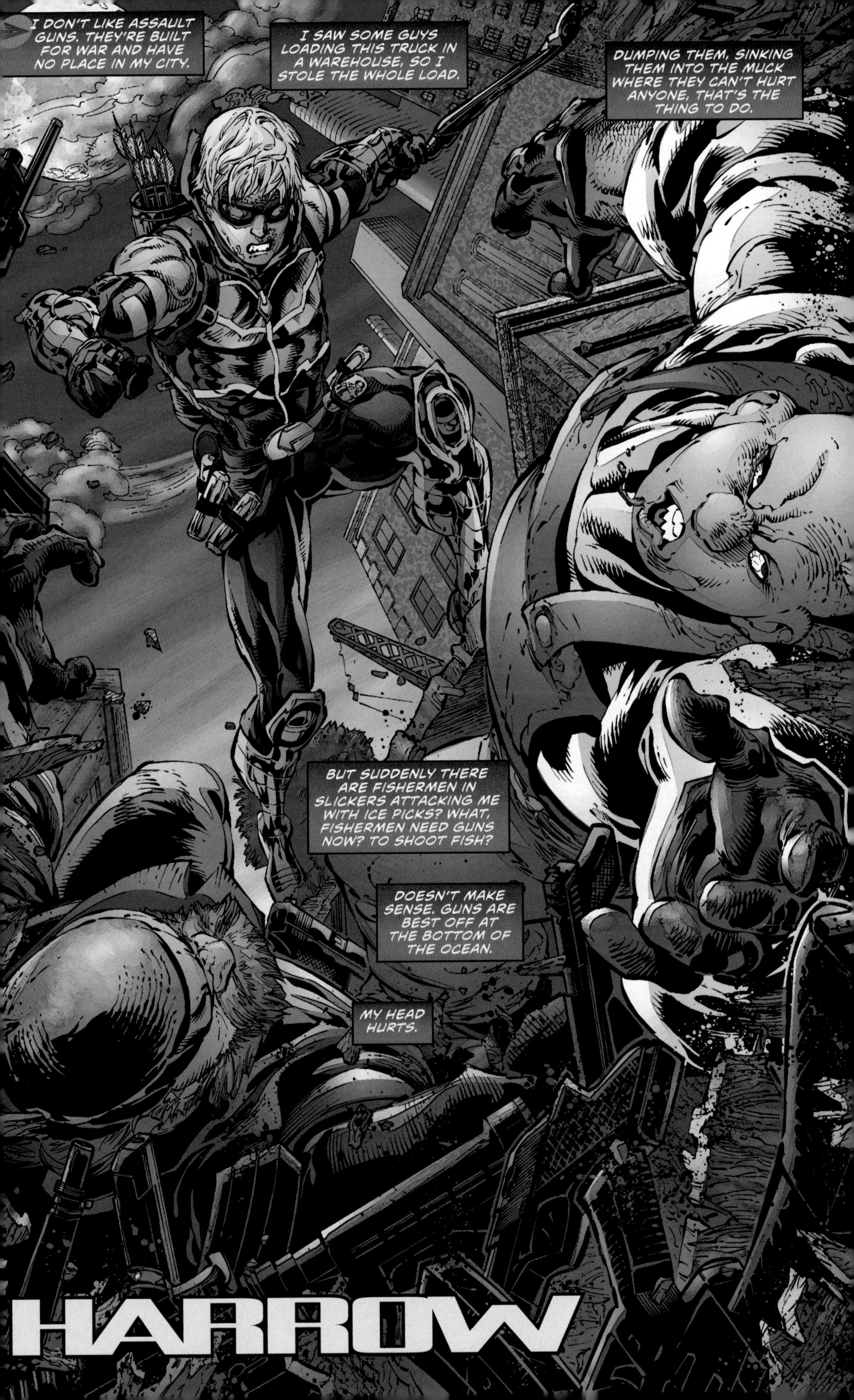
I DON'T LIKE ASSAULT GUNS. THEY'RE BUILT FOR WAR AND HAVE NO PLACE IN MY CITY.
I SAW SOME GUYS LOADING THIS TRUCK IN A WAREHOUSE, SO I STOLE THE WHOLE LOAD.
DUMPING THEM, SINKING THEM INTO THE MUCK WHERE THEY CAN'T HURT ANYONE, THAT'S THE THING TO DO.
BUT SUDDENLY THERE ARE FISHERMEN IN SLICKERS ATTACKING ME WITH ICE PICKS? WHAT, FISHERMEN NEED GUNS NOW? TO SHOOT FISH?
DOESN'T MAKE SENSE. GUNS ARE BEST OFF AT THE BOTTOM OF THE OCEAN.
MY HEAD HURTS.
HARROW

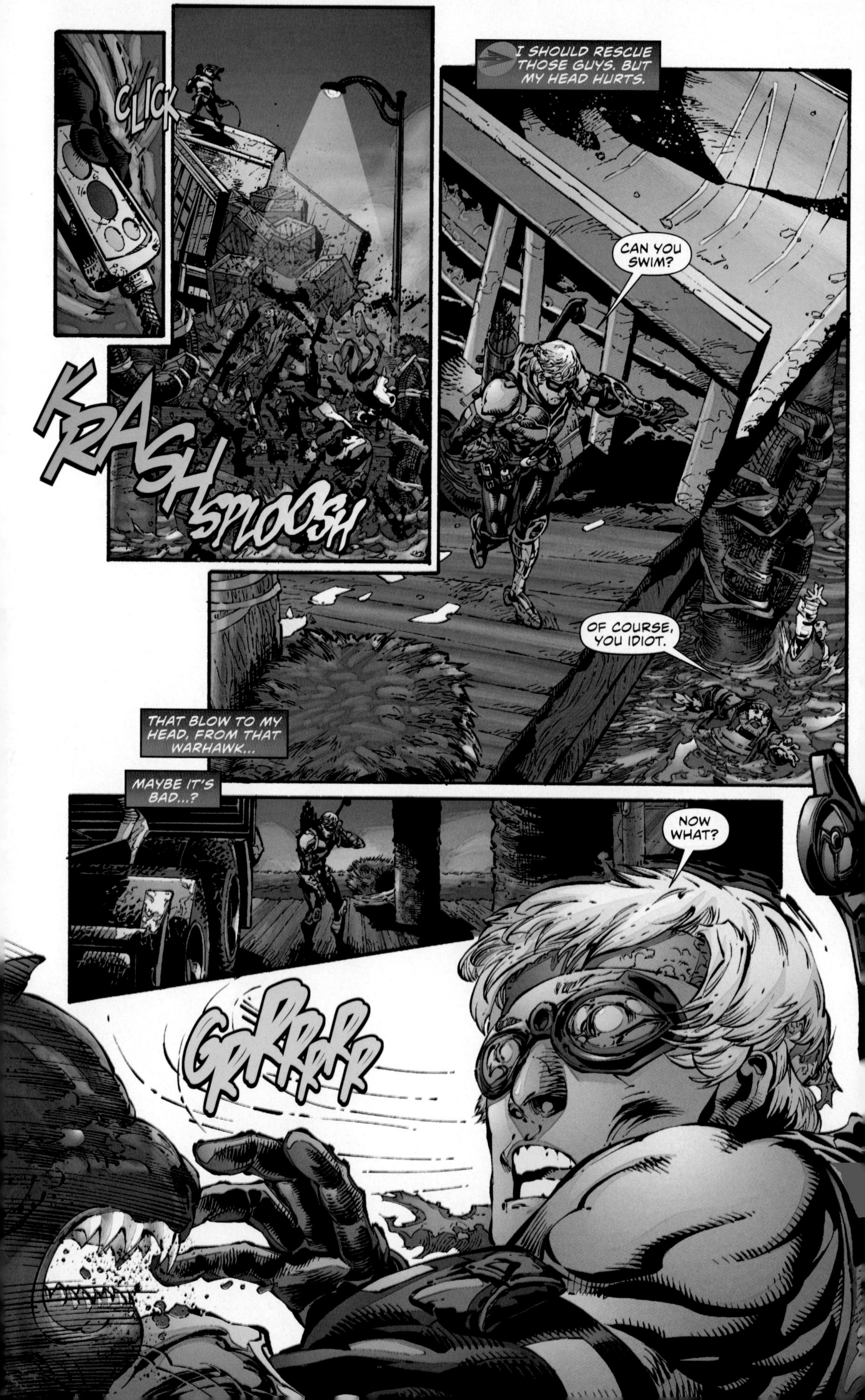
CLICK
KRASH
SPLOOSH
I SHOULD RESCUE THOSE GUYS. BUT MY HEAD HURTS.
CAN YOU SWIM?
OF COURSE, YOU IDIOT.
THAT BLOW TO MY HEAD, FROM THAT WARHAWK...
MAYBE IT'S BAD...?
NOW WHAT?
GRRRRR

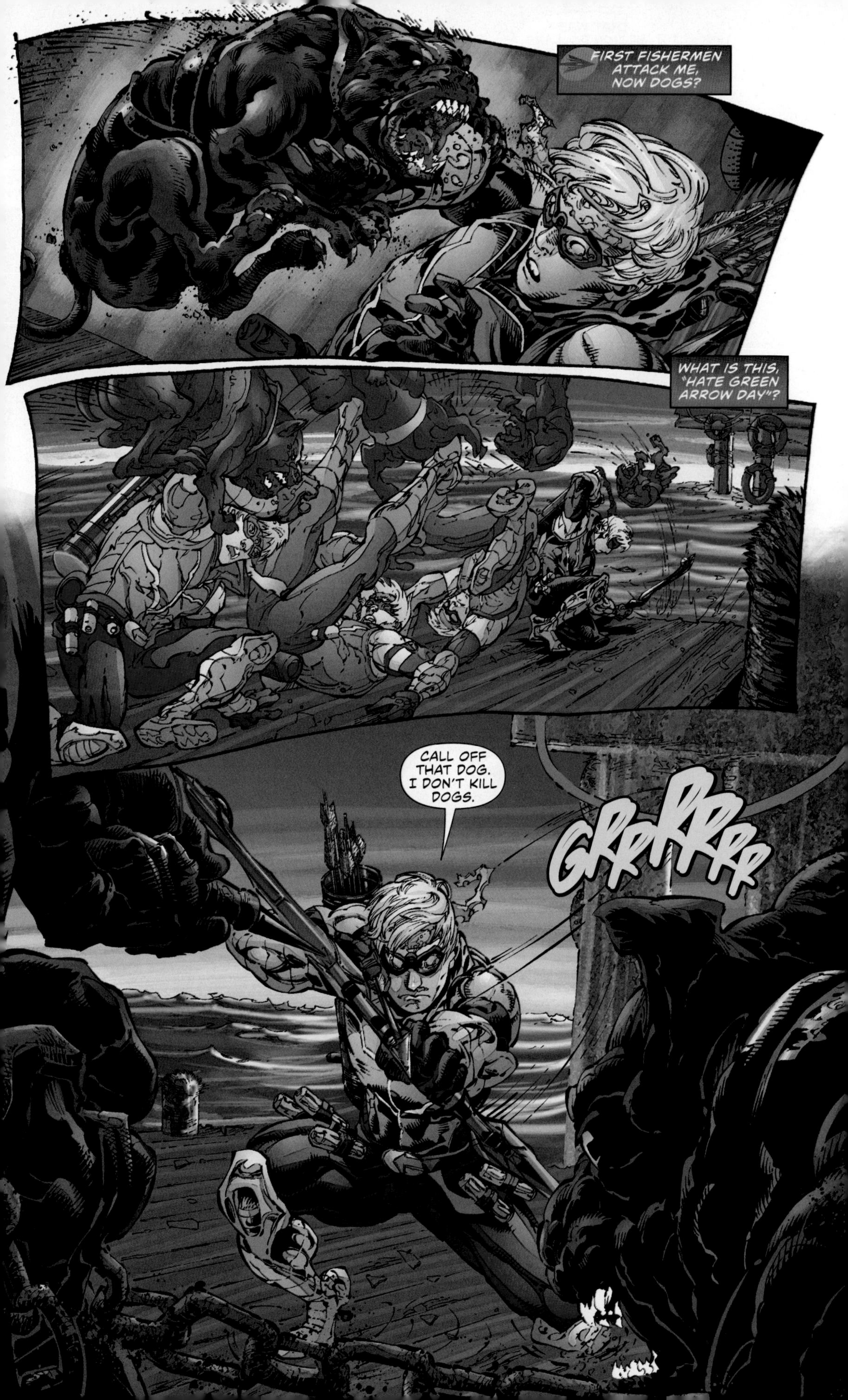
FIRST FISHERMEN ATTACK ME, NOW DOGS?
WHAT IS THIS, "HATE GREEN ARROW DAY"?
CALL OFF THAT DOG. I DON'T KILL DOGS.
GRRRRRR

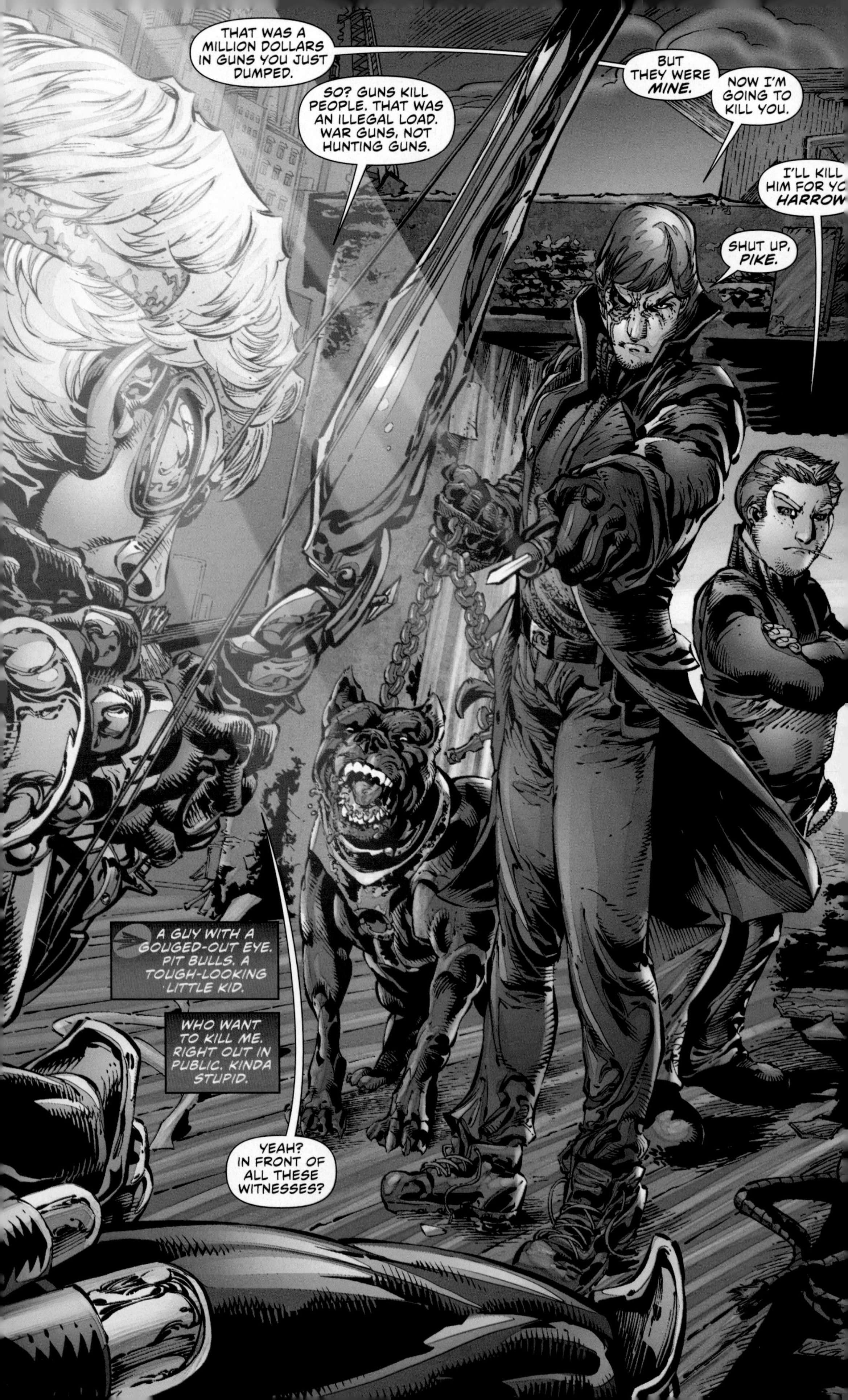
THAT WAS A MILLION DOLLARS IN GUNS YOU JUST DUMPED.
SO? GUNS KILL PEOPLE. THAT WAS AN ILLEGAL LOAD. WAR GUNS, NOT HUNTING GUNS.
BUT THEY WERE MINE.
NOW I'M GOING TO KILL YOU.
I'LL KILL HIM FOR YO HARROW
SHUT UP, PIKE.
A GUY WITH A GOUGED-OUT EYE. PIT BULLS. A TOUGH-LOOKING LITTLE KID.
WHO WANT TO KILL ME. RIGHT OUT IN PUBLIC. KINDA STUPID.
YEAH? IN FRONT OF ALL THESE WITNESSES?

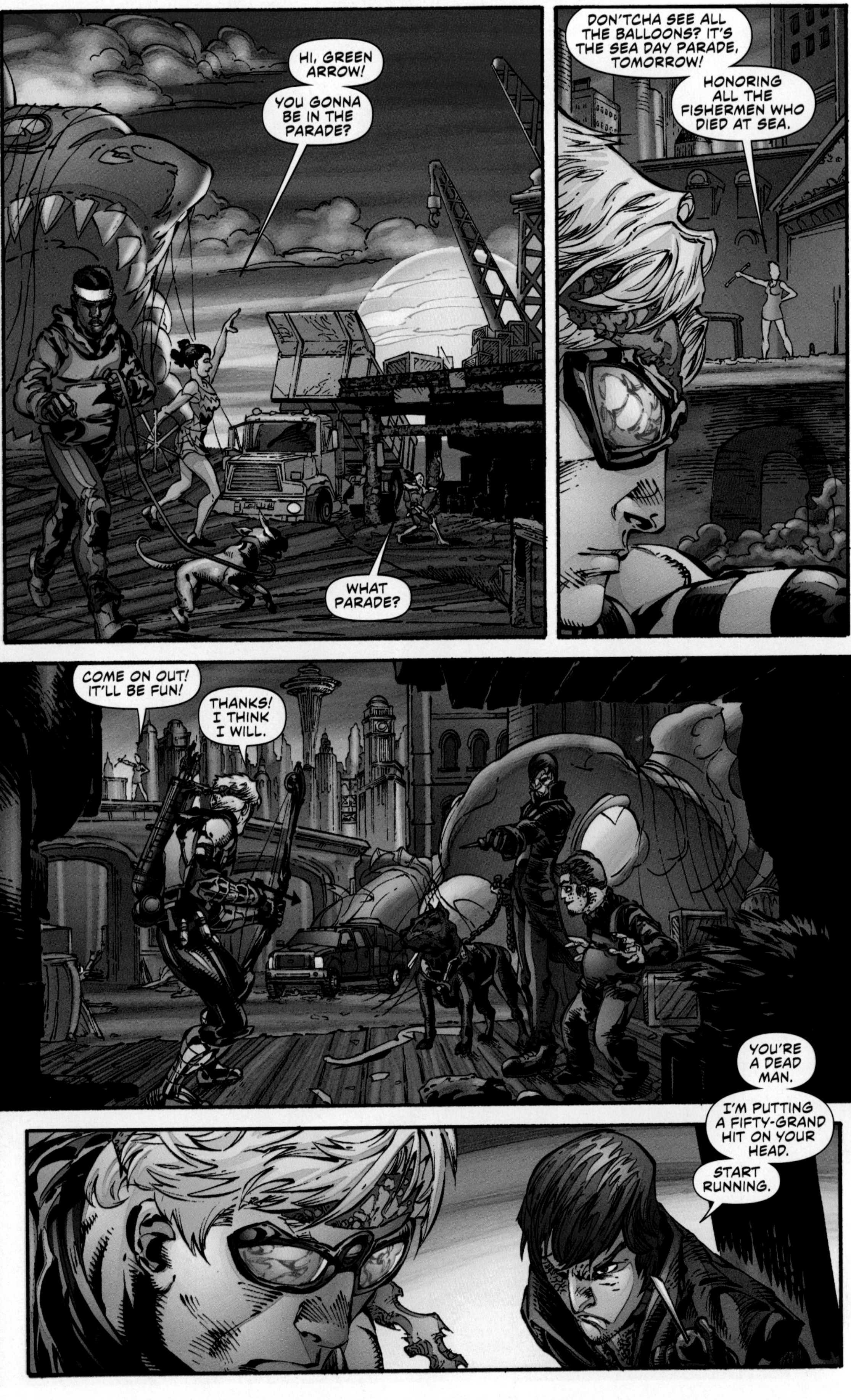
HI, GREEN ARROW!
YOU GONNA BE IN THE PARADE?
WHAT PARADE?
DON'TCHA SEE ALL THE BALLOONS? IT'S THE SEA DAY PARADE, TOMORROW!
HONORING ALL THE FISHERMEN WHO DIED AT SEA.
COME ON OUT! IT'LL BE FUN!
THANKS! I THINK I WILL.
YOU'RE A DEAD MAN.
I'M PUTTING A FIFTY-GRAND HIT ON YOUR HEAD.
START RUNNING.

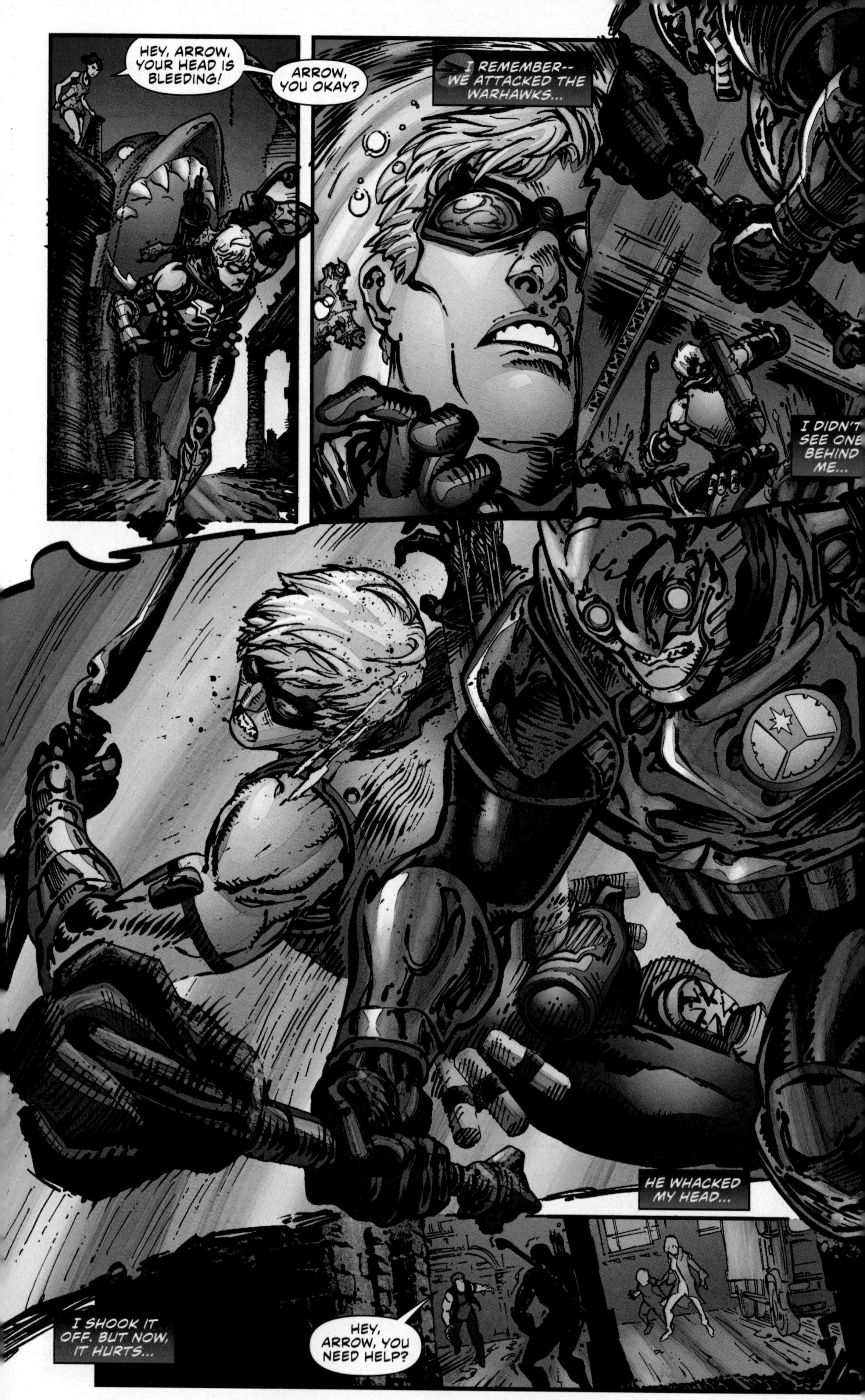
HEY, ARROW, YOUR HEAD IS BLEEDING!
ARROW, YOU OKAY?
I REMEMBER-- WE ATTACKED THE WARHAWKS...
I DIDN'T SEE ONE BEHIND ME...
HE WHACKED MY HEAD...
I SHOOK IT OFF. BUT NOW, IT HURTS...
HEY, ARROW, YOU NEED HELP?

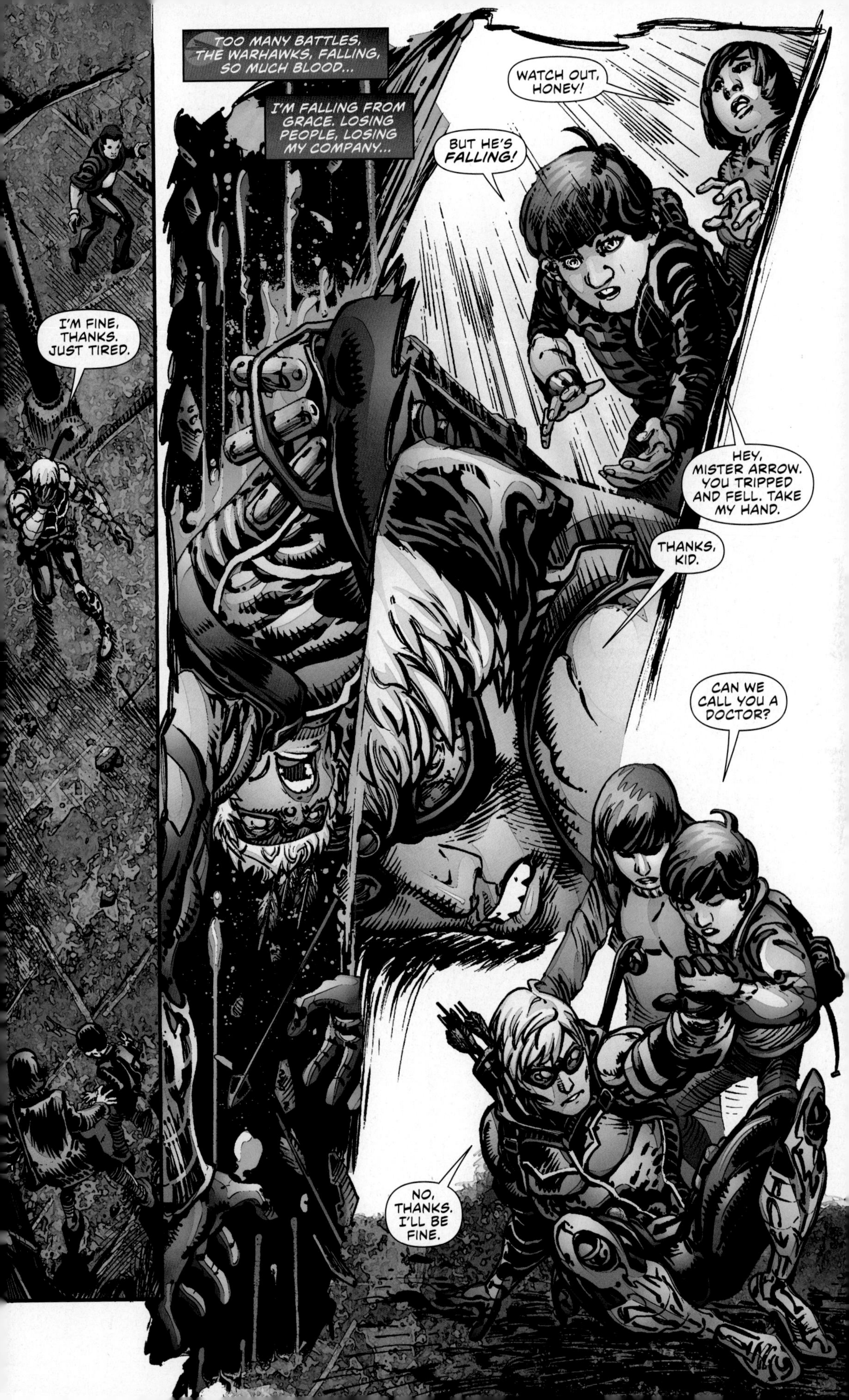
I'M FINE, THANKS. JUST TIRED.
TOO MANY BATTLES, THE WARHAWKS, FALLING, SO MUCH BLOOD...
I'M FALLING FROM GRACE. LOSING PEOPLE, LOSING MY COMPANY...
WATCH OUT, HONEY!
BUT HE'S FALLING!
HEY, MISTER ARROW. YOU TRIPPED AND FELL. TAKE MY HAND.
THANKS, KID.
CAN WE CALL YOU A DOCTOR?
NO, THANKS. I'LL BE FINE.

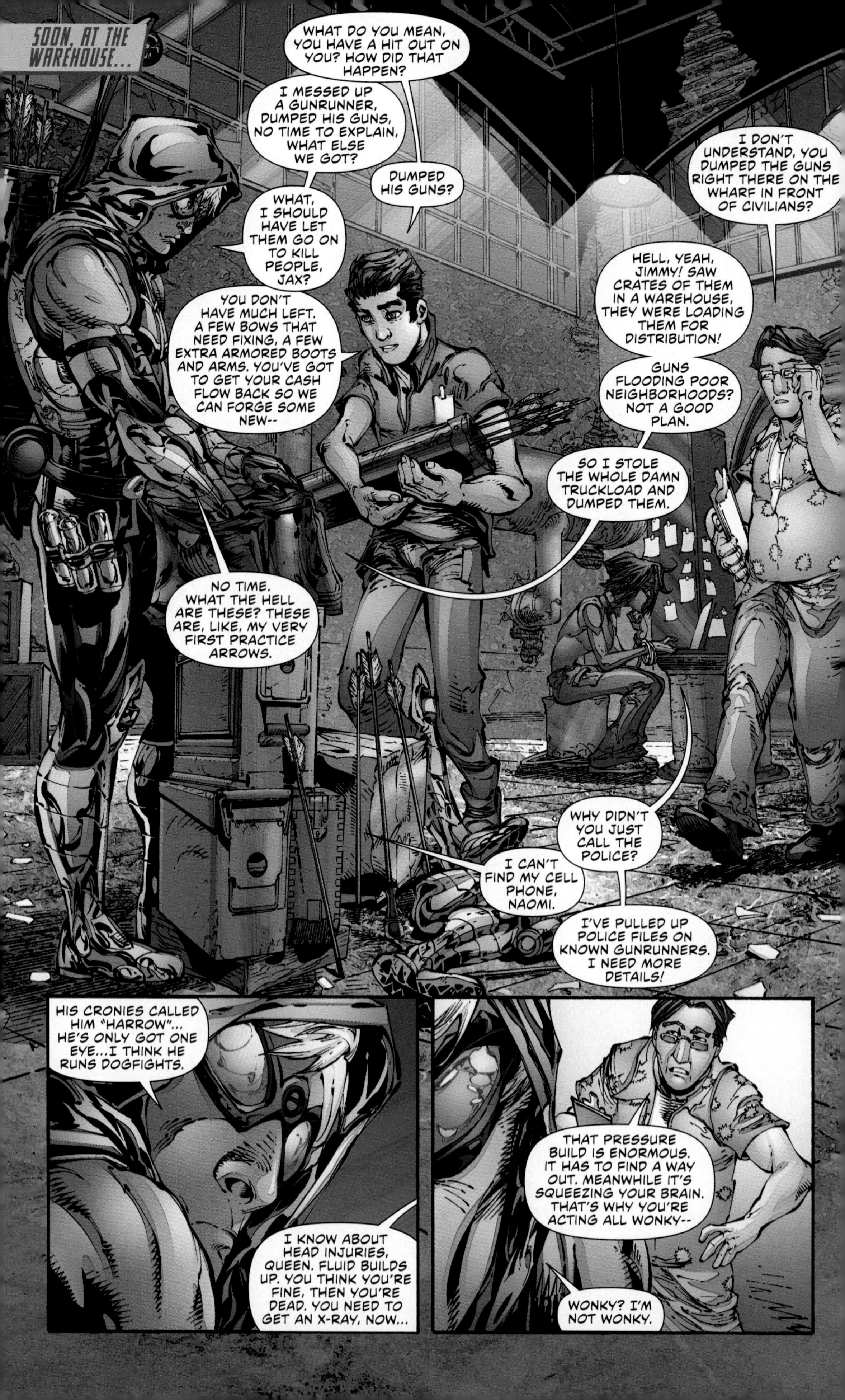
SOON, AT THE WAREHOUSE...
WHAT DO YOU MEAN, YOU HAVE A HIT OUT ON YOU? HOW DID THAT HAPPEN?
I MESSED UP A GUNRUNNER, DUMPED HIS GUNS, NO TIME TO EXPLAIN, WHAT ELSE WE GOT?
DUMPED HIS GUNS?
WHAT, I SHOULD HAVE LET THEM GO ON TO KILL PEOPLE, JAX?
I DON'T UNDERSTAND, YOU DUMPED THE GUNS RIGHT THERE ON THE WHARF IN FRONT OF CIVILIANS?
HELL, YEAH, JIMMY! SAW CRATES OF THEM IN A WAREHOUSE, THEY WERE LOADING THEM FOR DISTRIBUTION!
GUNS FLOODING POOR NEIGHBORHOODS? NOT A GOOD PLAN.
SO I STOLE THE WHOLE DAMN TRUCKLOAD AND DUMPED THEM.
YOU DON'T HAVE MUCH LEFT. A FEW BOWS THAT NEED FIXING, A FEW EXTRA ARMORED BOOTS AND ARMS. YOU'VE GOT TO GET YOUR CASH FLOW BACK SO WE CAN FORGE SOME NEW--
NO TIME. WHAT THE HELL ARE THESE? THESE ARE, LIKE, MY VERY FIRST PRACTICE ARROWS.
WHY DIDN'T YOU JUST CALL THE POLICE?
I CAN'T FIND MY CELL PHONE, NAOMI.
I'VE PULLED UP POLICE FILES ON KNOWN GUNRUNNERS. I NEED MORE DETAILS!
HIS CRONIES CALLED HIM "HARROW"... HE'S ONLY GOT ONE EYE...I THINK HE RUNS DOGFIGHTS.
I KNOW ABOUT HEAD INJURIES, QUEEN. FLUID BUILDS UP. YOU THINK YOU'RE FINE, THEN YOU'RE DEAD. YOU NEED TO GET AN X-RAY, NOW...
THAT PRESSURE BUILD IS ENORMOUS. IT HAS TO FIND A WAY OUT. MEANWHILE IT'S SQUEEZING YOUR BRAIN. THAT'S WHY YOU'RE ACTING ALL WONKY--
WONKY? I'M NOT WONKY.

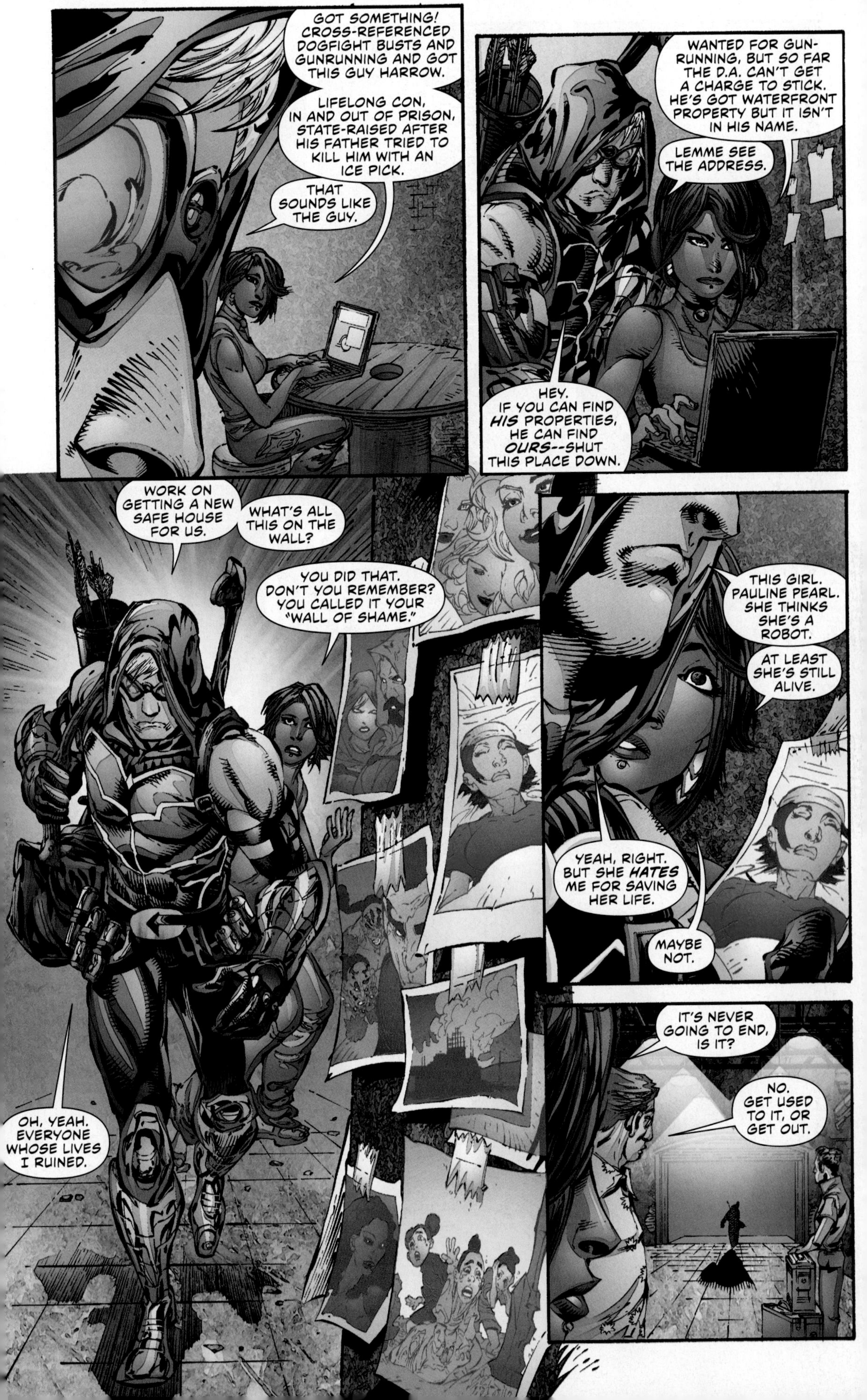
GOT SOMETHING! CROSS-REFERENCED DOGFIGHT BUSTS AND GUNRUNNING AND GOT THIS GUY HARROW.
LIFELONG CON, IN AND OUT OF PRISON, STATE-RAISED AFTER HIS FATHER TRIED TO KILL HIM WITH AN ICE PICK.
THAT SOUNDS LIKE THE GUY.
WANTED FOR GUN-RUNNING, BUT SO FAR THE D.A. CAN'T GET A CHARGE TO STICK. HE'S GOT WATERFRONT PROPERTY BUT IT ISN'T IN HIS NAME.
LEMME SEE THE ADDRESS.
HEY. IF YOU CAN FIND *HIS* PROPERTIES, HE CAN FIND *OURS*--SHUT THIS PLACE DOWN.
WORK ON GETTING A NEW SAFE HOUSE FOR US.
WHAT'S ALL THIS ON THE WALL?
YOU DID THAT. DON'T YOU REMEMBER? YOU CALLED IT YOUR "WALL OF SHAME."
OH, YEAH. EVERYONE WHOSE LIVES I RUINED.
THIS GIRL. PAULINE PEARL. SHE THINKS SHE'S A ROBOT.
AT LEAST SHE'S STILL ALIVE.
YEAH, RIGHT. BUT SHE *HATES* ME FOR SAVING HER LIFE.
MAYBE NOT.
IT'S NEVER GOING TO END, IS IT?
NO. GET USED TO IT, OR GET OUT.

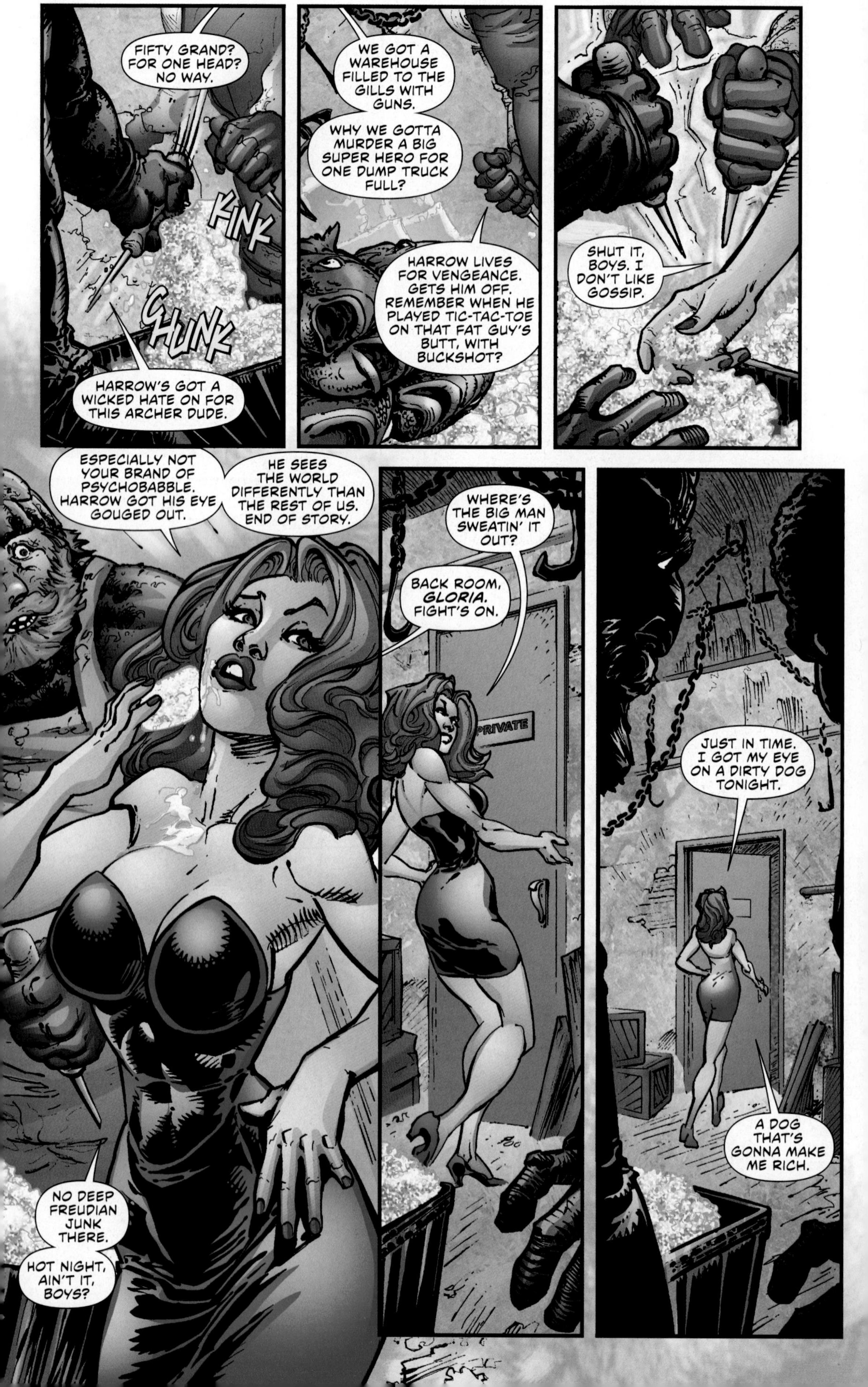
FIFTY GRAND? FOR ONE HEAD? NO WAY.
KINK
CHUNK
HARROW'S GOT A WICKED HATE ON FOR THIS ARCHER DUDE.
WE GOT A WAREHOUSE FILLED TO THE GILLS WITH GUNS.
WHY WE GOTTA MURDER A BIG SUPER HERO FOR ONE DUMP TRUCK FULL?
HARROW LIVES FOR VENGEANCE. GETS HIM OFF. REMEMBER WHEN HE PLAYED TIC-TAC-TOE ON THAT FAT GUY'S BUTT, WITH BUCKSHOT?
SHUT IT, BOYS. I DON'T LIKE GOSSIP.
ESPECIALLY NOT YOUR BRAND OF PSYCHOBABBLE. HARROW GOT HIS EYE GOUGED OUT.
HE SEES THE WORLD DIFFERENTLY THAN THE REST OF US. END OF STORY.
NO DEEP FREUDIAN JUNK THERE.
HOT NIGHT, AIN'T IT, BOYS?
WHERE'S THE BIG MAN SWEATIN' IT OUT?
BACK ROOM, GLORIA. FIGHT'S ON.
PRIVATE
JUST IN TIME. I GOT MY EYE ON A DIRTY DOG TONIGHT.
A DOG THAT'S GONNA MAKE ME RICH.

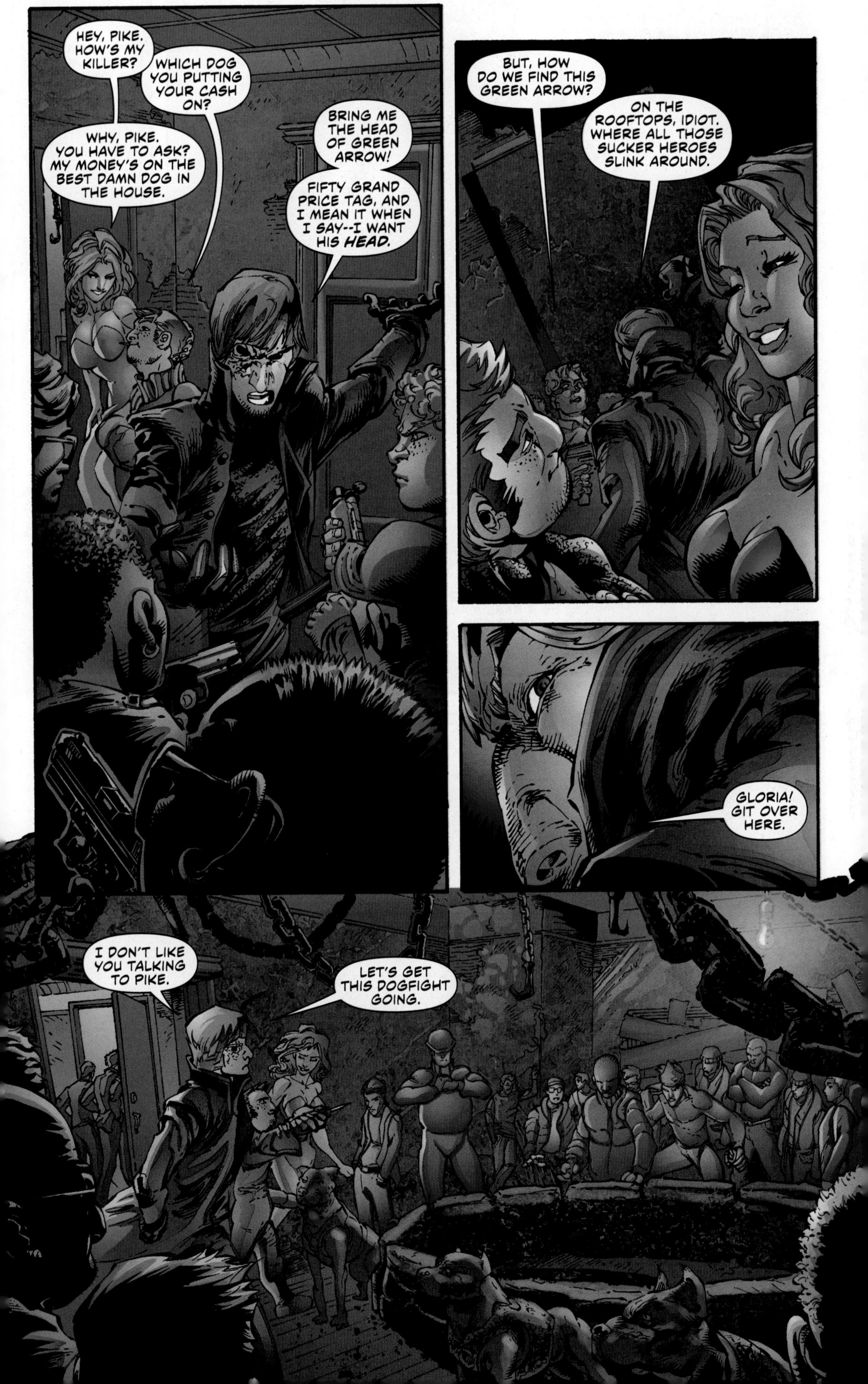
HEY, PIKE. HOW'S MY KILLER?
WHICH DOG YOU PUTTING YOUR CASH ON?
WHY, PIKE. YOU HAVE TO ASK? MY MONEY'S ON THE BEST DAMN DOG IN THE HOUSE.
BRING ME THE HEAD OF GREEN ARROW!
FIFTY GRAND PRICE TAG, AND I MEAN IT WHEN I SAY--I WANT HIS HEAD.
BUT, HOW DO WE FIND THIS GREEN ARROW?
ON THE ROOFTOPS, IDIOT. WHERE ALL THOSE SUCKER HEROES SLINK AROUND.
GLORIA! GIT OVER HERE.
I DON'T LIKE YOU TALKING TO PIKE.
LET'S GET THIS DOGFIGHT GOING.

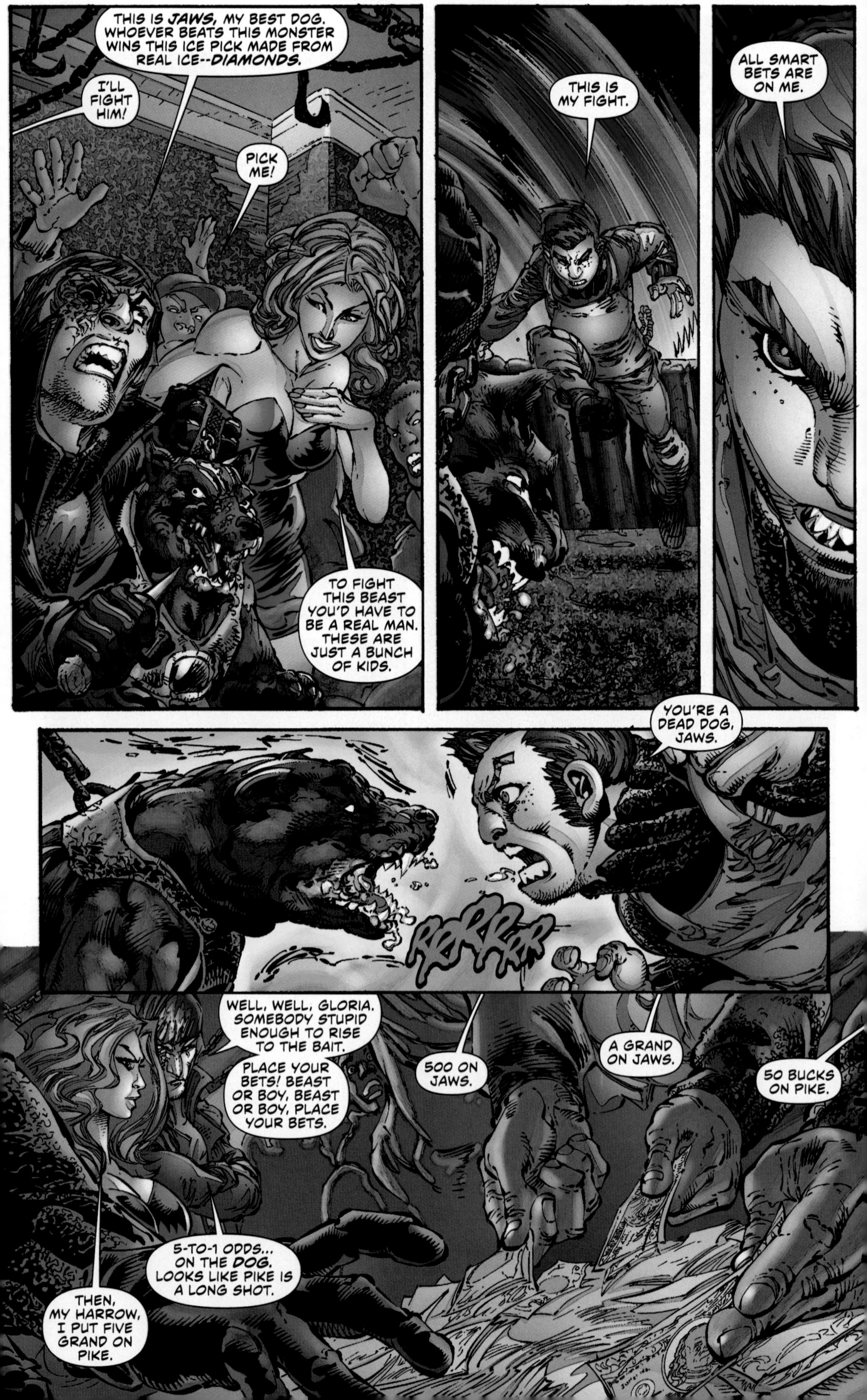
THIS IS JAWS, MY BEST DOG. WHOEVER BEATS THIS MONSTER WINS THIS ICE PICK MADE FROM REAL ICE--DIAMONDS.
I'LL FIGHT HIM!
PICK ME!
TO FIGHT THIS BEAST YOU'D HAVE TO BE A REAL MAN. THESE ARE JUST A BUNCH OF KIDS.
THIS IS MY FIGHT.
ALL SMART BETS ARE ON ME.
YOU'RE A DEAD DOG, JAWS.
RRRRRR
WELL, WELL, GLORIA. SOMEBODY STUPID ENOUGH TO RISE TO THE BAIT.
PLACE YOUR BETS! BEAST OR BOY, BEAST OR BOY, PLACE YOUR BETS.
500 ON JAWS.
A GRAND ON JAWS.
50 BUCKS ON PIKE.
5-TO-1 ODDS... ON THE DOG. LOOKS LIKE PIKE IS A LONG SHOT.
THEN, MY HARROW, I PUT FIVE GRAND ON PIKE.

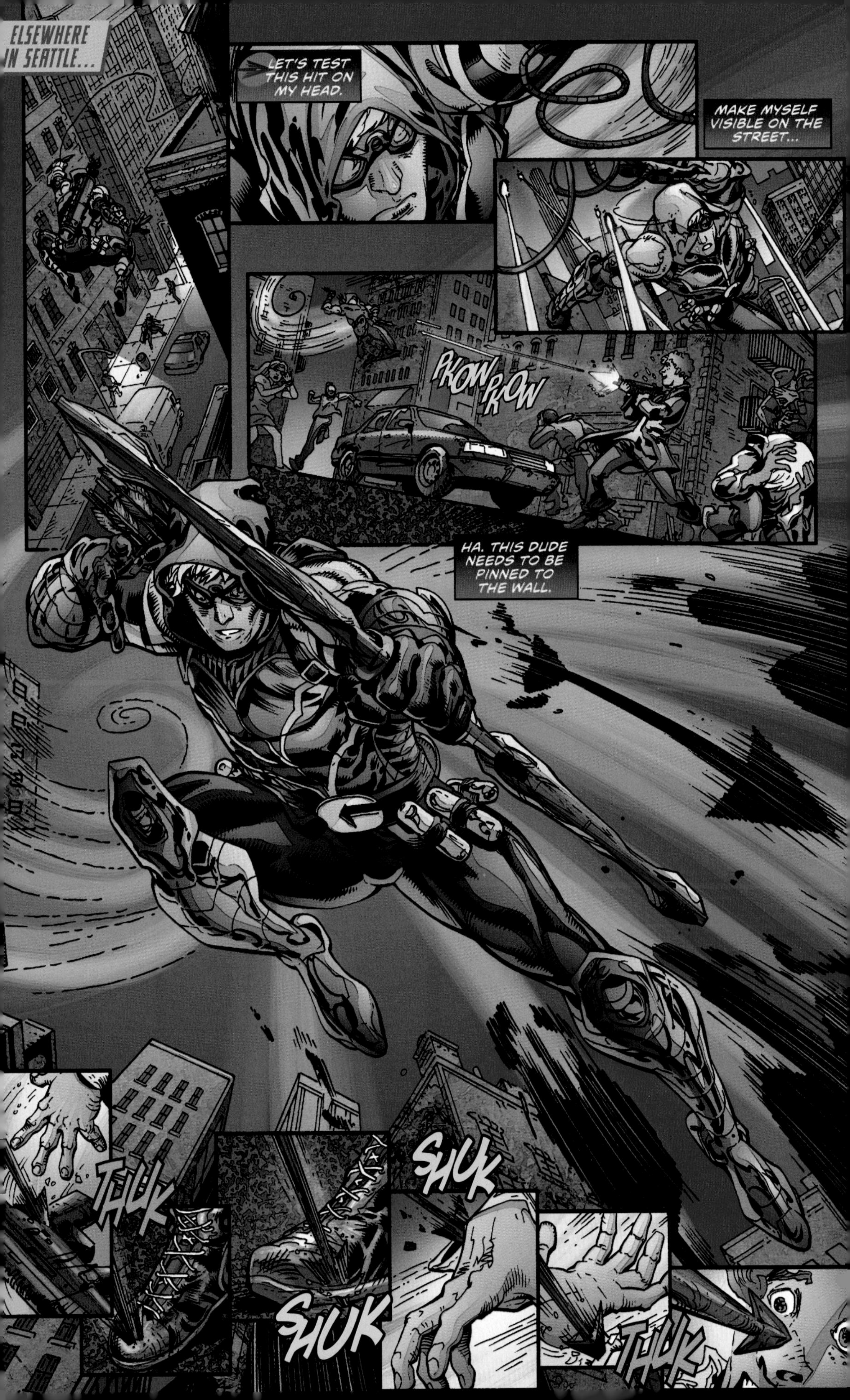

ELSEWHERE IN SEATTLE...
LET'S TEST THIS HIT ON MY HEAD.
MAKE MYSELF VISIBLE ON THE STREET...
PKOW PKOW
HA. THIS DUDE NEEDS TO BE PINNED TO THE WALL.
THUK
SHUK
SHUK
THUK

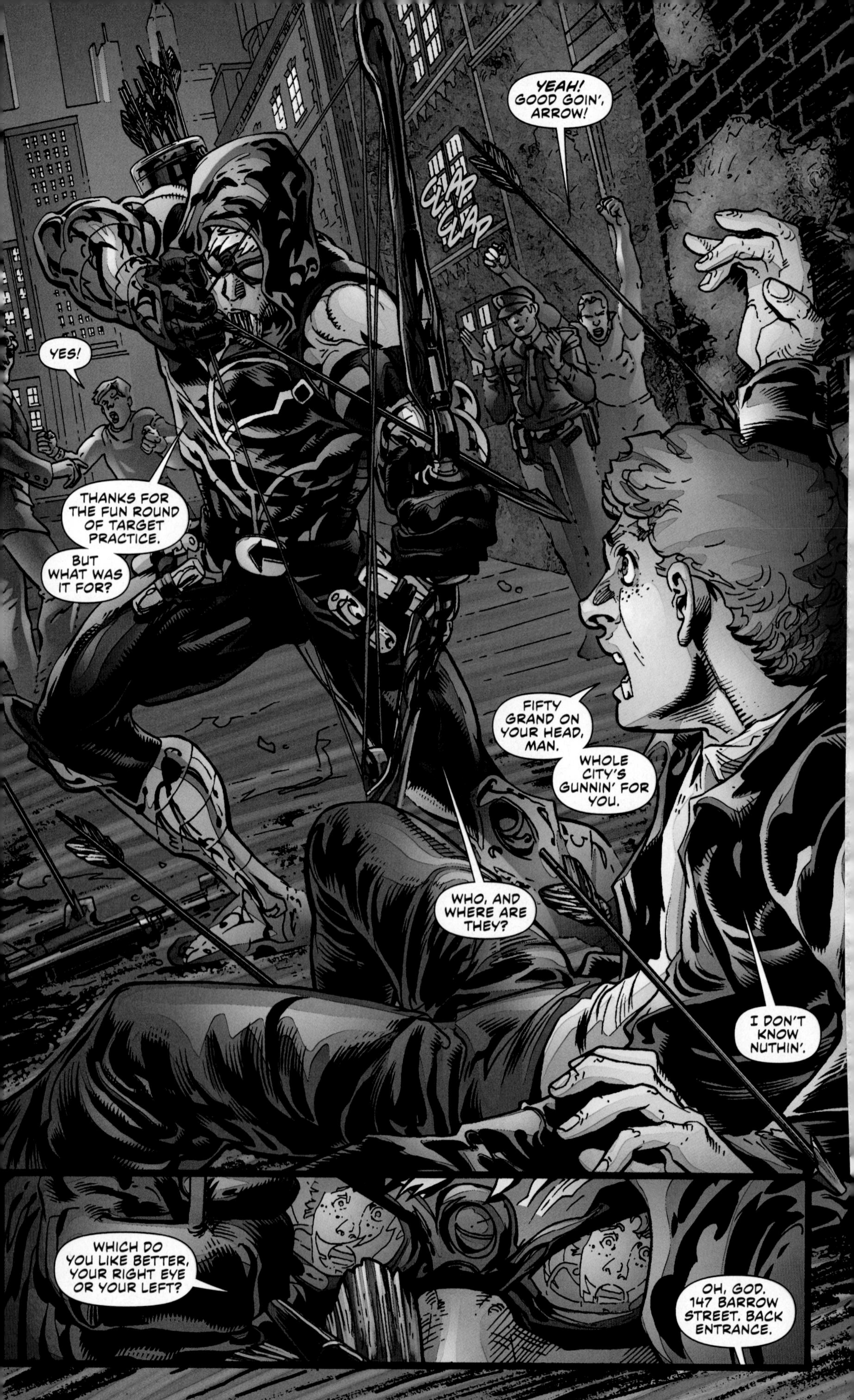
CLAP CLAP CLAP
YEAH! GOOD GOIN', ARROW!
YES!
THANKS FOR THE FUN ROUND OF TARGET PRACTICE.
BUT WHAT WAS IT FOR?
FIFTY GRAND ON YOUR HEAD, MAN.
WHOLE CITY'S GUNNIN' FOR YOU.
WHO, AND WHERE ARE THEY?
I DON'T KNOW NUTHIN'.
WHICH DO YOU LIKE BETTER, YOUR RIGHT EYE OR YOUR LEFT?
OH, GOD. 147 BARROW STREET. BACK ENTRANCE.

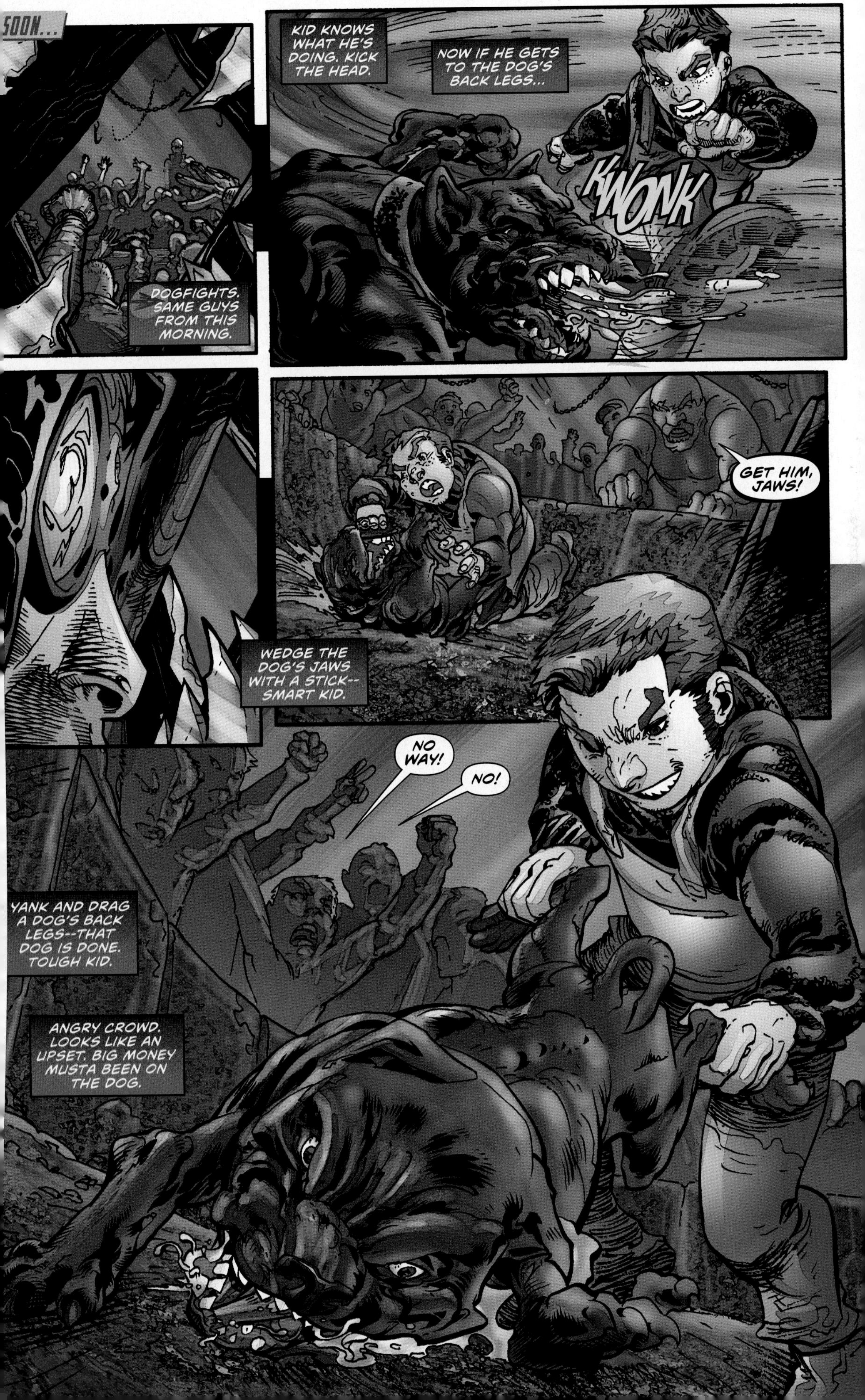
SOON...
DOGFIGHTS. SAME GUYS FROM THIS MORNING.
KID KNOWS WHAT HE'S DOING. KICK THE HEAD.
NOW IF HE GETS TO THE DOG'S BACK LEGS...
KWONK
GET HIM, JAWS!
WEDGE THE DOG'S JAWS WITH A STICK-- SMART KID.
NO WAY!
NO!
YANK AND DRAG A DOG'S BACK LEGS--THAT DOG IS DONE. TOUGH KID.
ANGRY CROWD. LOOKS LIKE AN UPSET. BIG MONEY MUSTA BEEN ON THE DOG.

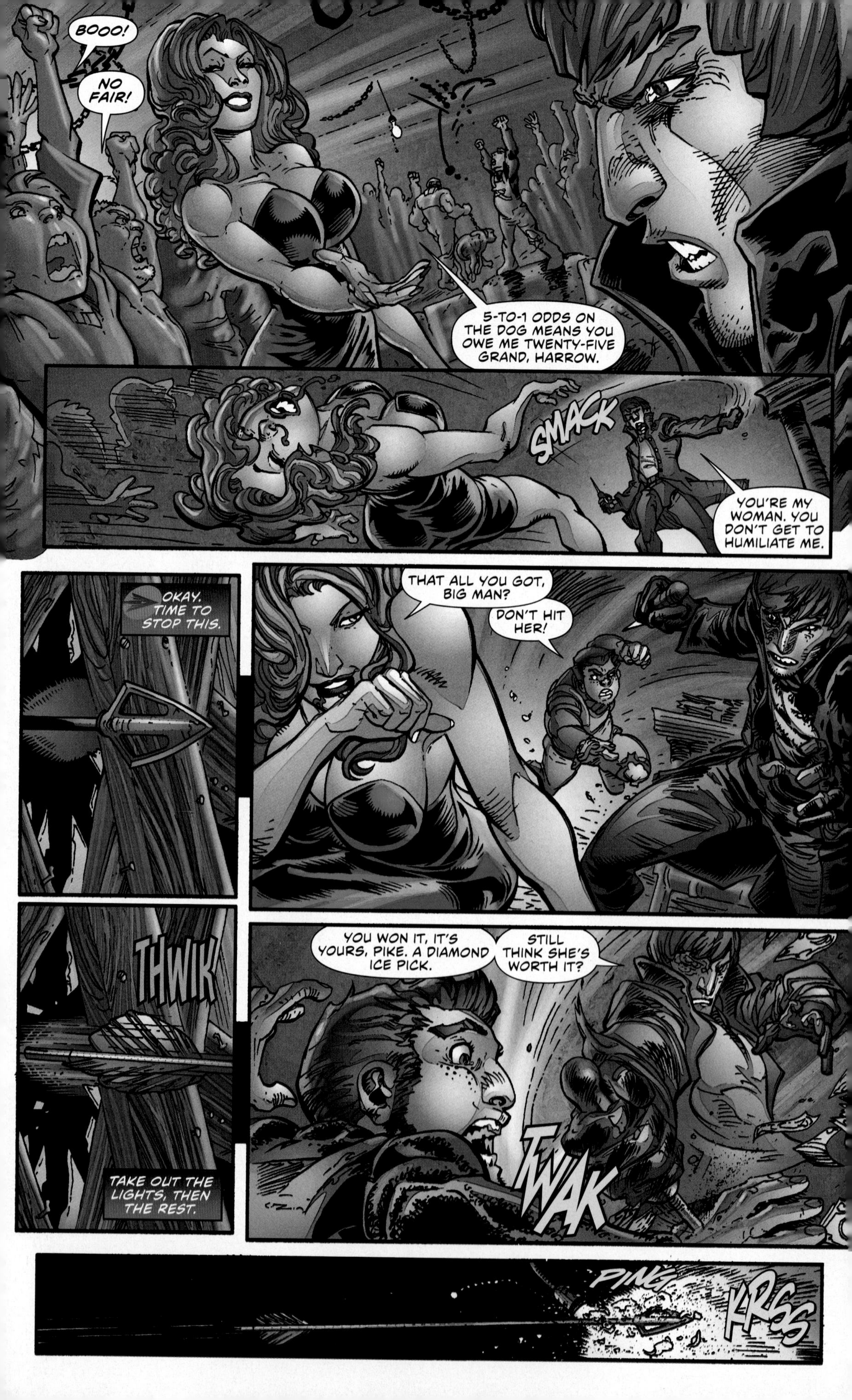
BOOO!
NO FAIR!
5-TO-1 ODDS ON THE DOG MEANS YOU OWE ME TWENTY-FIVE GRAND, HARROW.
SMACK
YOU'RE MY WOMAN. YOU DON'T GET TO HUMILIATE ME.
OKAY. TIME TO STOP THIS.
THAT ALL YOU GOT, BIG MAN?
DON'T HIT HER!
THWIK
TAKE OUT THE LIGHTS, THEN THE REST.
YOU WON IT, IT'S YOURS, PIKE. A DIAMOND ICE PICK.
STILL THINK SHE'S WORTH IT?
TWAK
PING!
KRSS

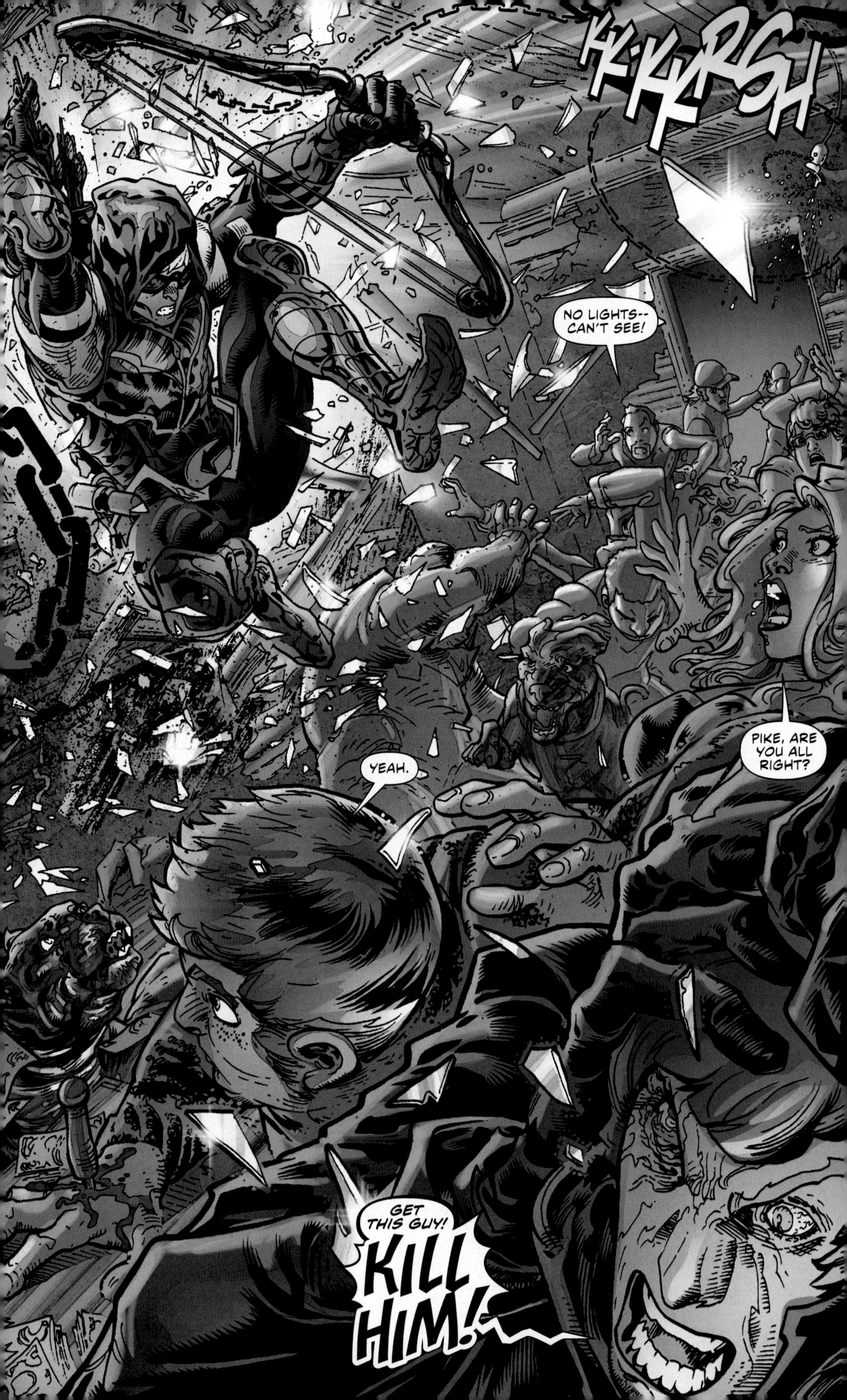
KK-KKRSH
NO LIGHTS-- CAN'T SEE!
PIKE, ARE YOU ALL RIGHT?
YEAH.
GET THIS GUY!
KILL HIM!

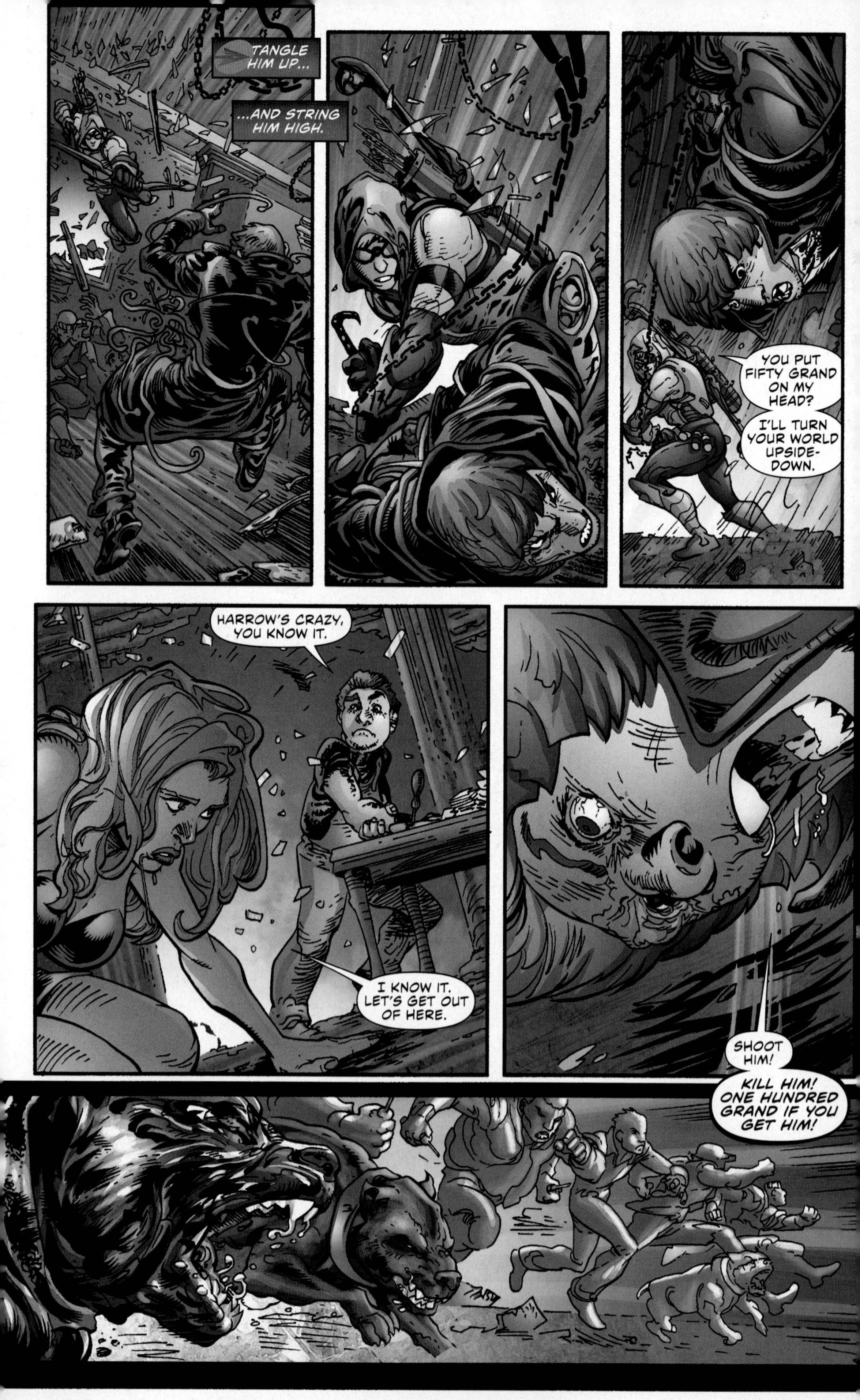
TANGLE HIM UP...
...AND STRING HIM HIGH.
YOU PUT FIFTY GRAND ON MY HEAD?
I'LL TURN YOUR WORLD UPSIDE-DOWN.
HARROW'S CRAZY, YOU KNOW IT.
I KNOW IT. LET'S GET OUT OF HERE.
SHOOT HIM!
KILL HIM! ONE HUNDRED GRAND IF YOU GET HIM!

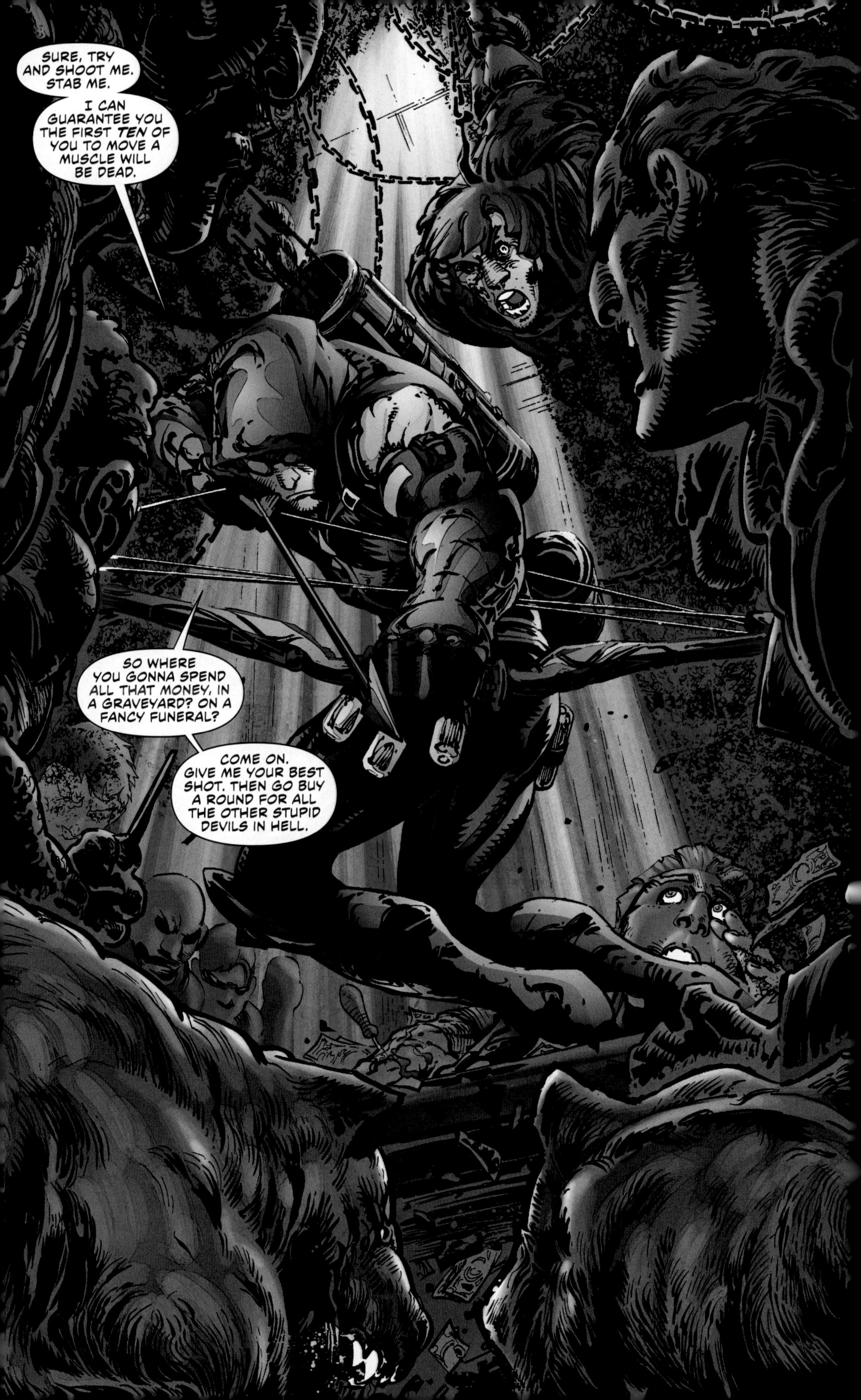
SURE, TRY AND SHOOT ME. STAB ME.
I CAN GUARANTEE YOU THE FIRST *TEN* OF YOU TO MOVE A MUSCLE WILL BE DEAD.
SO WHERE YOU GONNA SPEND ALL THAT MONEY, IN A GRAVEYARD? ON A FANCY FUNERAL?
COME ON. GIVE ME YOUR BEST SHOT. THEN GO BUY A ROUND FOR ALL THE OTHER STUPID DEVILS IN HELL.

HARROW PART 2: BATTLE FOR SEATTLE

ANN NOCENTI writer FREDDIE WILLIAMS II artist cover by BILL SIENKIEWICZ with HI-FI

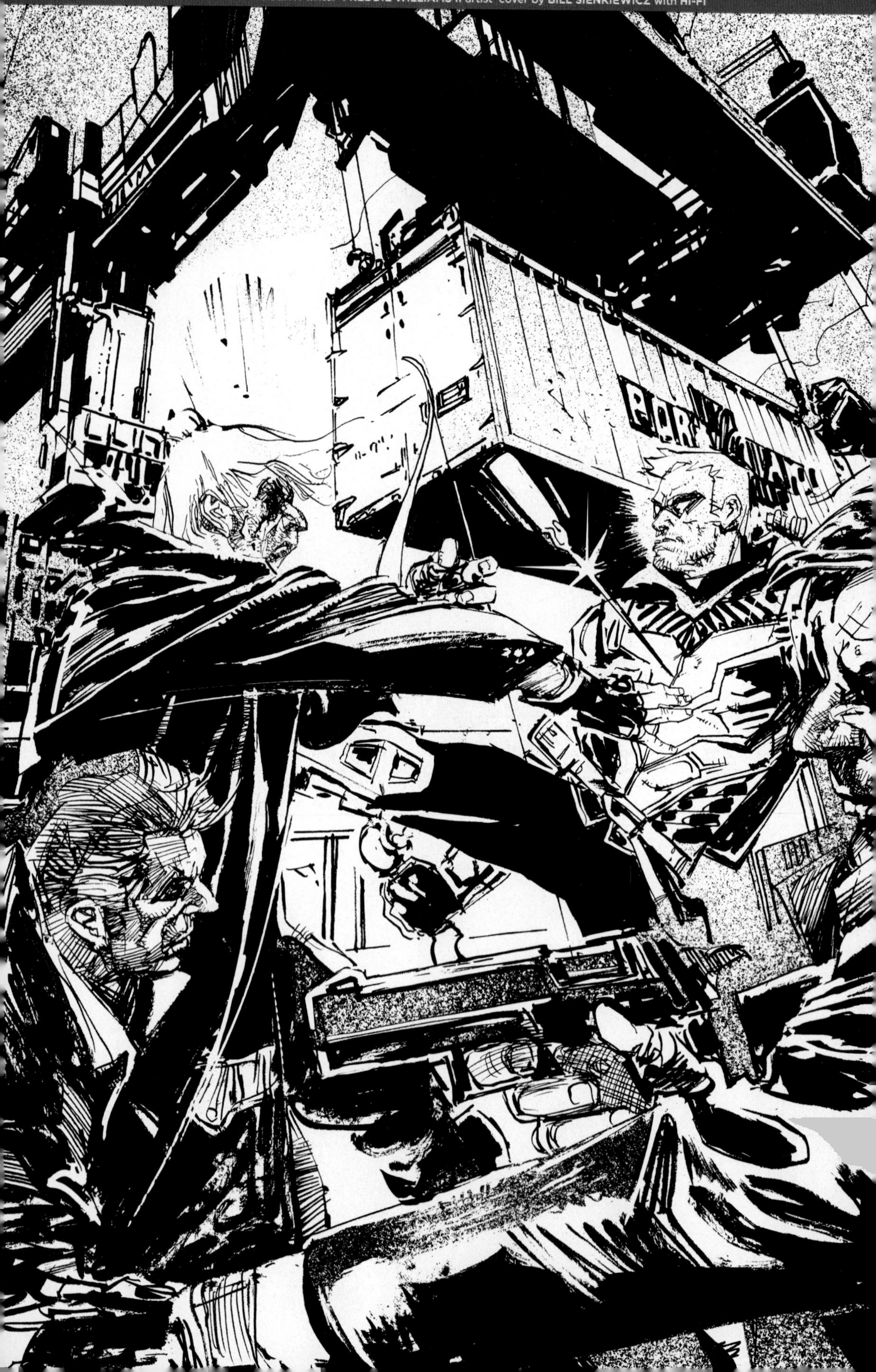

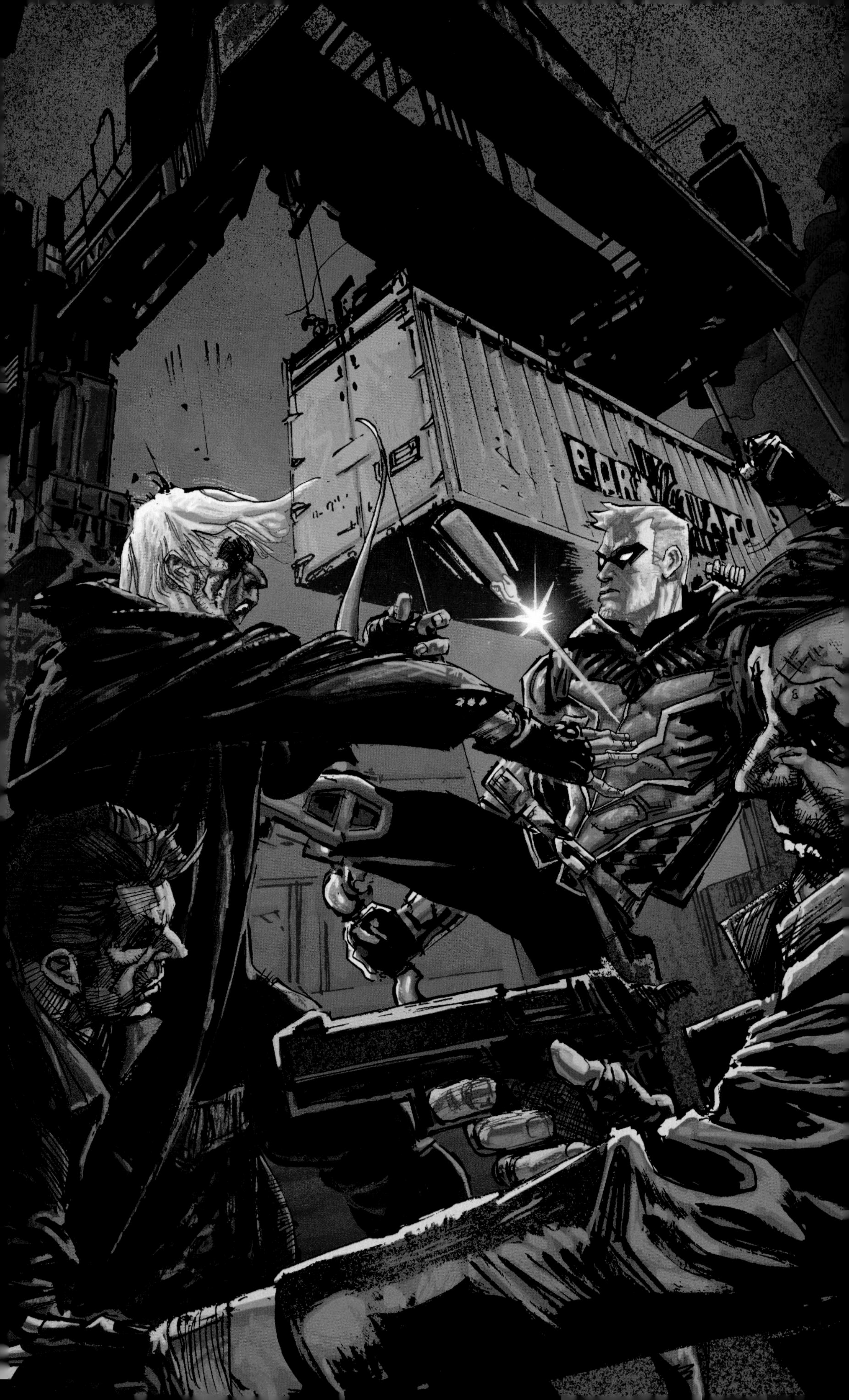

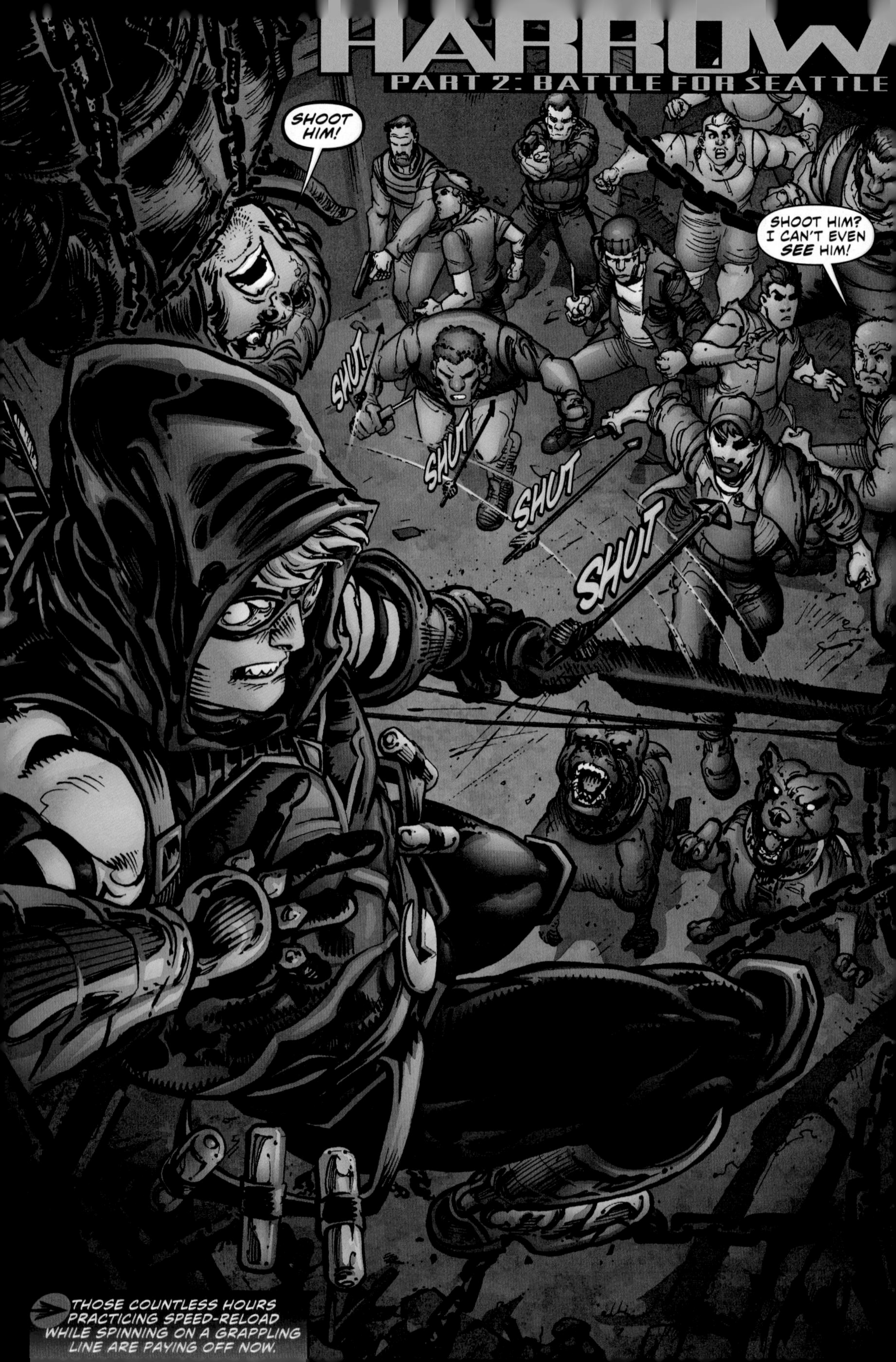
HARROW
PART 2: BATTLE FOR SEATTLE
SHOOT HIM!
SHOOT HIM? I CAN'T EVEN SEE HIM!
SHUT
SHUT
SHUT
SHUT
THOSE COUNTLESS HOURS PRACTICING SPEED-RELOAD WHILE SPINNING ON A GRAPPLING LINE ARE PAYING OFF NOW.

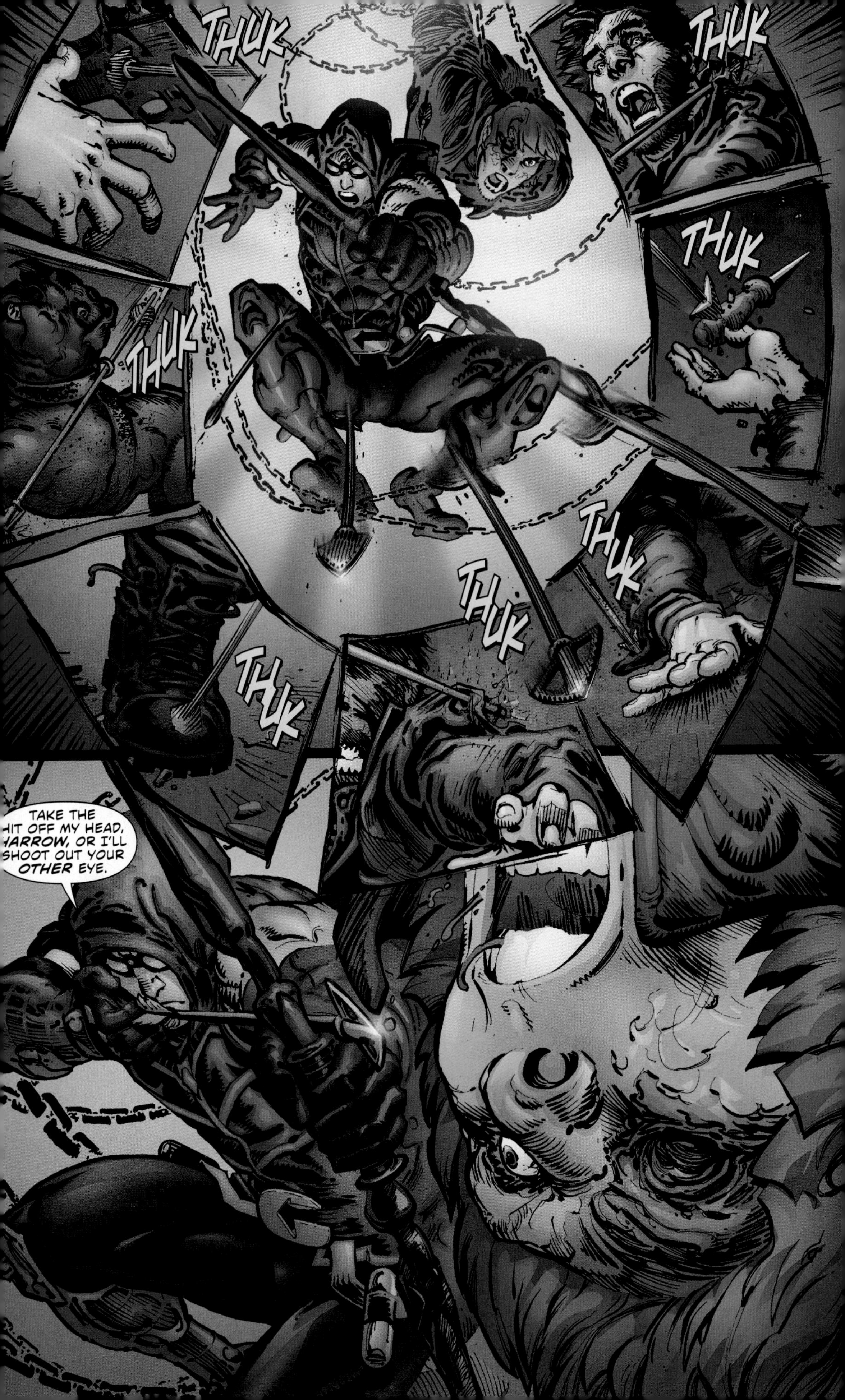
THUK
THUK
THUK
THUK
THUK
THUK
THUK
TAKE THE
HIT OFF MY HEAD,
HARROW, OR I'LL
SHOOT OUT YOUR
OTHER EYE.

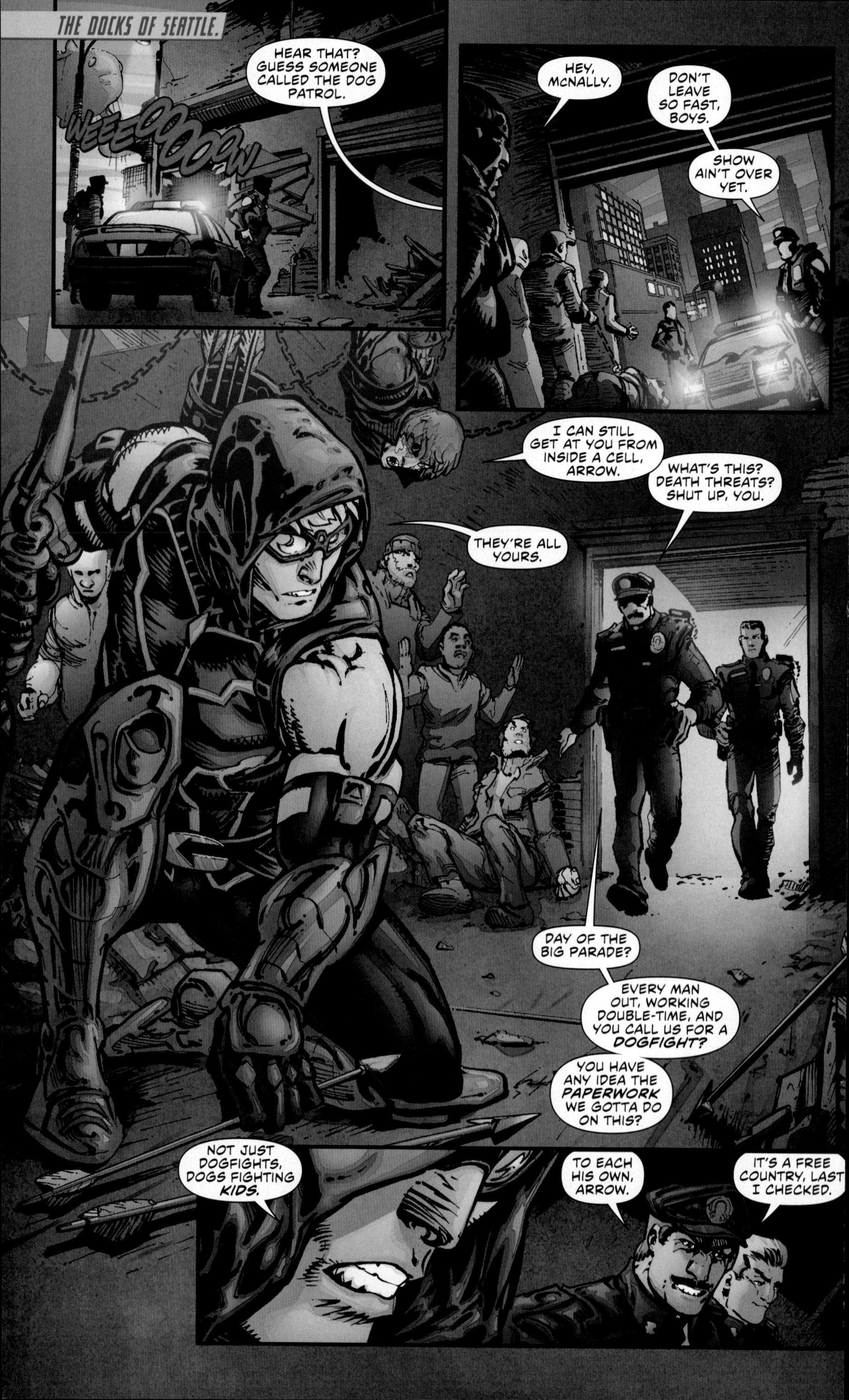
THE DOCKS OF SEATTLE.
HEAR THAT? GUESS SOMEONE CALLED THE DOG PATROL.
WEEEOOOOOOW
HEY, MCNALLY.
DON'T LEAVE SO FAST, BOYS.
SHOW AIN'T OVER YET.
I CAN STILL GET AT YOU FROM INSIDE A CELL, ARROW.
WHAT'S THIS? DEATH THREATS? SHUT UP, YOU.
THEY'RE ALL YOURS.
DAY OF THE BIG PARADE?
EVERY MAN OUT, WORKING DOUBLE-TIME, AND YOU CALL US FOR A DOGFIGHT?
YOU HAVE ANY IDEA THE PAPERWORK WE GOTTA DO ON THIS?
NOT JUST DOGFIGHTS, DOGS FIGHTING KIDS.
TO EACH HIS OWN, ARROW.
IT'S A FREE COUNTRY, LAST I CHECKED.

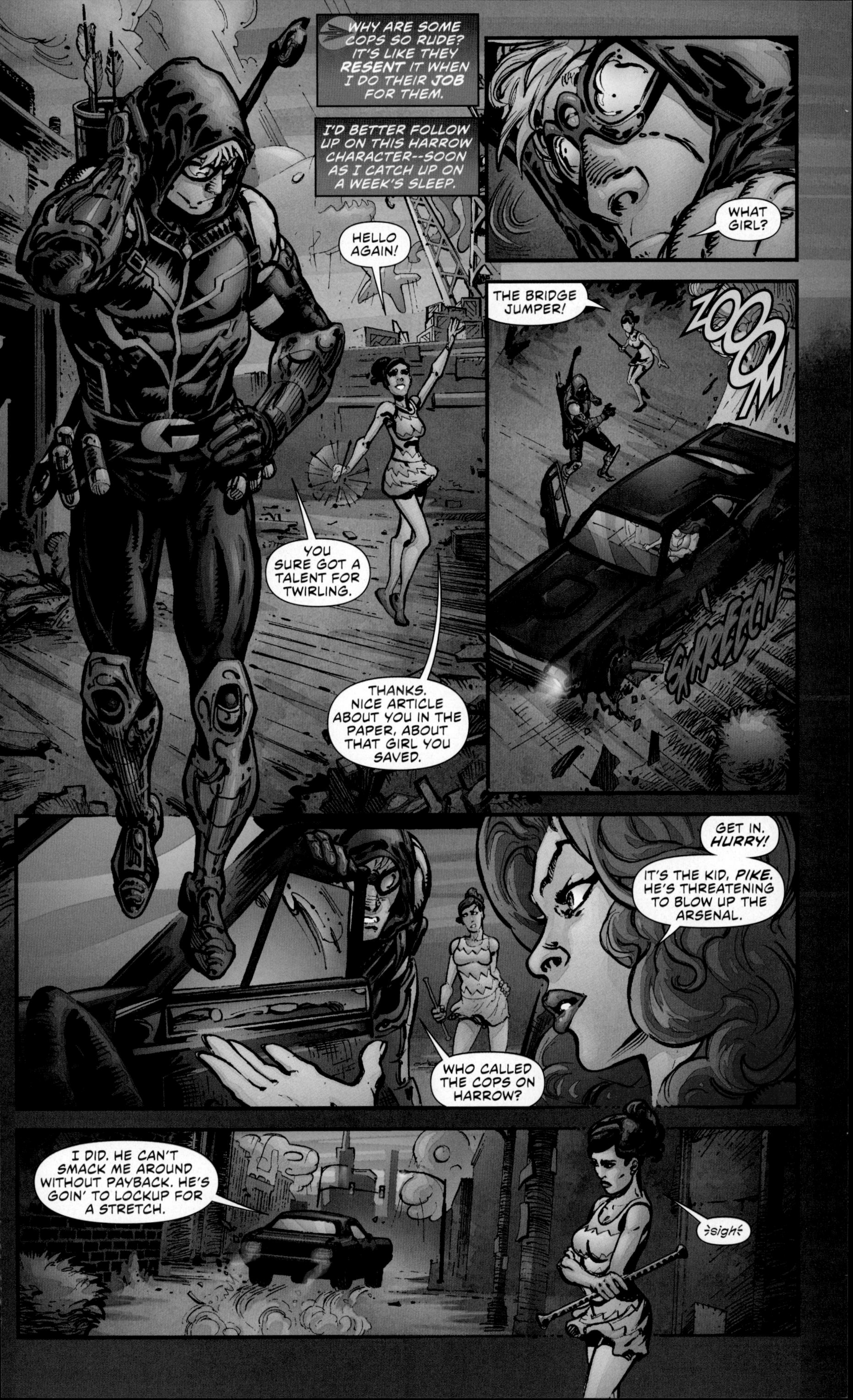

WHY ARE SOME COPS SO RUDE? IT'S LIKE THEY RESENT IT WHEN I DO THEIR JOB FOR THEM.
I'D BETTER FOLLOW UP ON THIS HARROW CHARACTER--SOON AS I CATCH UP ON A WEEK'S SLEEP.
HELLO AGAIN!
YOU SURE GOT A TALENT FOR TWIRLING.
THANKS. NICE ARTICLE ABOUT YOU IN THE PAPER, ABOUT THAT GIRL YOU SAVED.
WHAT GIRL?
THE BRIDGE JUMPER!
ZOOOM
SKREECH
GET IN. HURRY!
IT'S THE KID, PIKE. HE'S THREATENING TO BLOW UP THE ARSENAL.
WHO CALLED THE COPS ON HARROW?
I DID. HE CAN'T SMACK ME AROUND WITHOUT PAYBACK. HE'S GOIN' TO LOCKUP FOR A STRETCH.
sigh

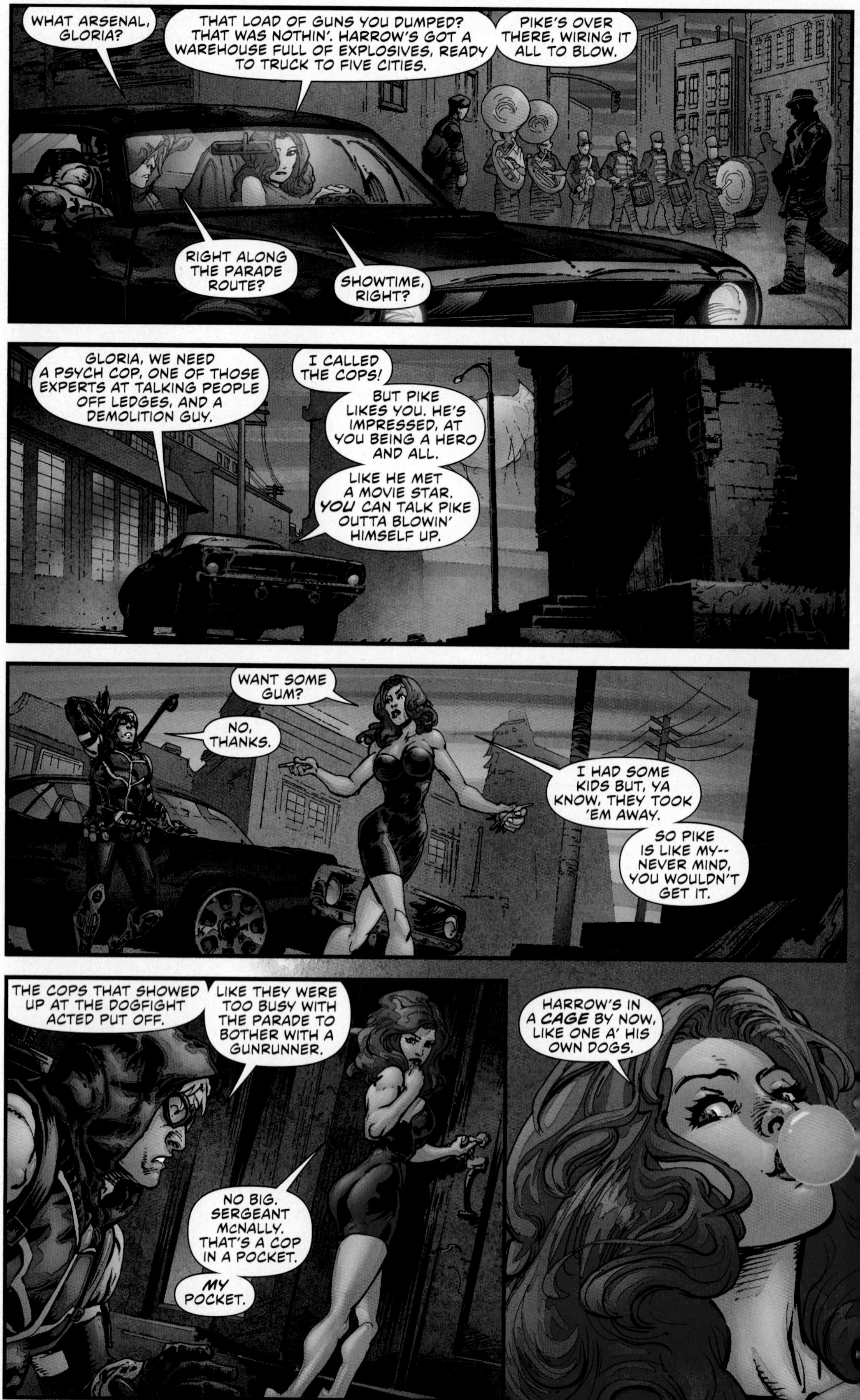

WHAT ARSENAL, GLORIA?
THAT LOAD OF GUNS YOU DUMPED? THAT WAS NOTHIN'. HARROW'S GOT A WAREHOUSE FULL OF EXPLOSIVES, READY TO TRUCK TO FIVE CITIES.
PIKE'S OVER THERE, WIRING IT ALL TO BLOW.
RIGHT ALONG THE PARADE ROUTE?
SHOWTIME, RIGHT?
GLORIA, WE NEED A PSYCH COP, ONE OF THOSE EXPERTS AT TALKING PEOPLE OFF LEDGES, AND A DEMOLITION GUY.
I CALLED THE COPS!
BUT PIKE LIKES YOU. HE'S IMPRESSED, AT YOU BEING A HERO AND ALL.
LIKE HE MET A MOVIE STAR. YOU CAN TALK PIKE OUTTA BLOWIN' HIMSELF UP.
WANT SOME GUM?
NO, THANKS.
I HAD SOME KIDS BUT, YA KNOW, THEY TOOK 'EM AWAY.
SO PIKE IS LIKE MY-- NEVER MIND, YOU WOULDN'T GET IT.
THE COPS THAT SHOWED UP AT THE DOGFIGHT ACTED PUT OFF.
LIKE THEY WERE TOO BUSY WITH THE PARADE TO BOTHER WITH A GUNRUNNER.
NO BIG. SERGEANT MCNALLY. THAT'S A COP IN A POCKET.
MY POCKET.
HARROW'S IN A CAGE BY NOW, LIKE ONE A' HIS OWN DOGS.

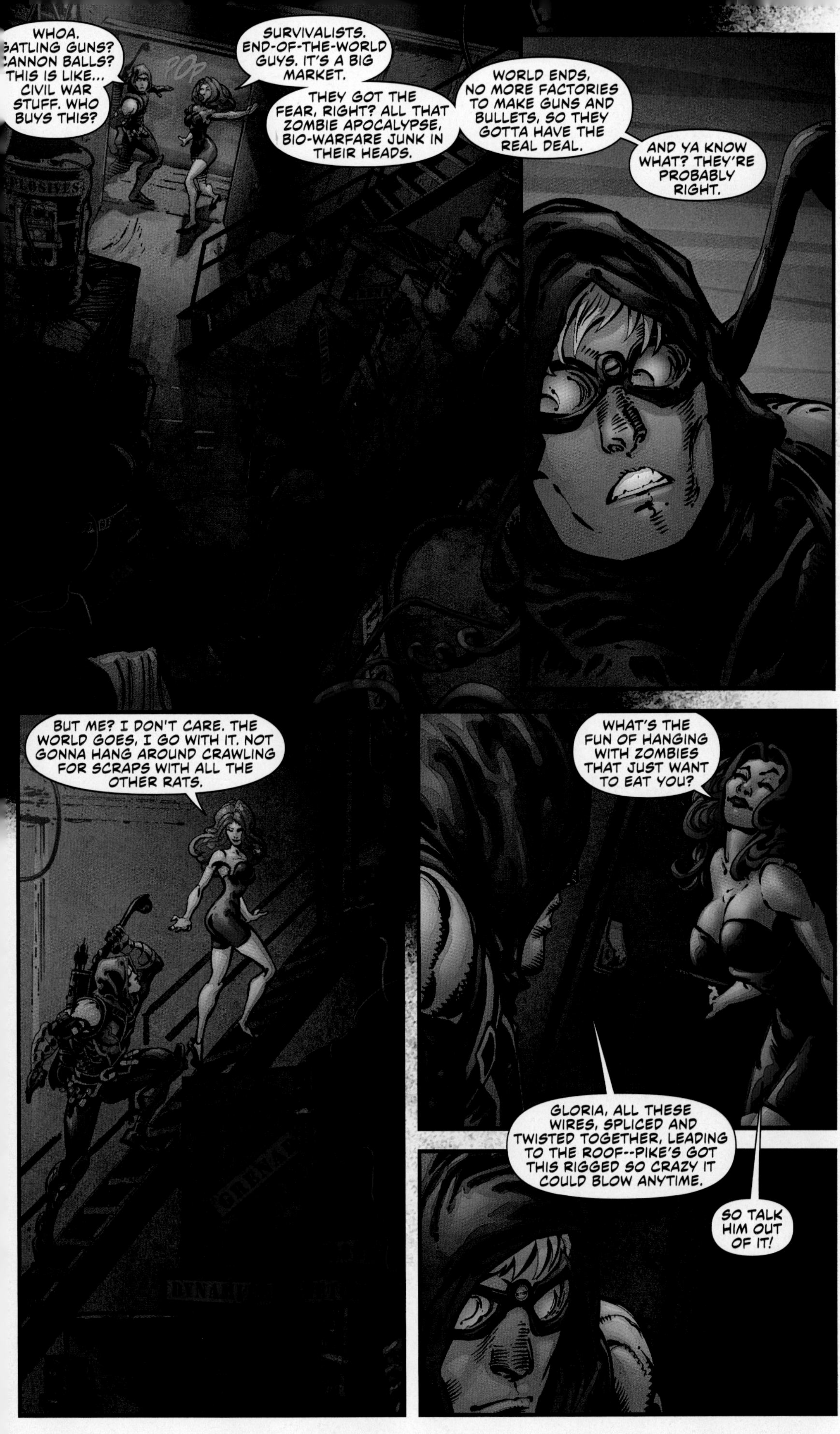
WHOA. GATLING GUNS? CANNON BALLS? THIS IS LIKE... CIVIL WAR STUFF. WHO BUYS THIS?
SURVIVALISTS. END-OF-THE-WORLD GUYS. IT'S A BIG MARKET.
THEY GOT THE FEAR, RIGHT? ALL THAT ZOMBIE APOCALYPSE, BIO-WARFARE JUNK IN THEIR HEADS.
WORLD ENDS, NO MORE FACTORIES TO MAKE GUNS AND BULLETS, SO THEY GOTTA HAVE THE REAL DEAL.
AND YA KNOW WHAT? THEY'RE PROBABLY RIGHT.
BUT ME? I DON'T CARE. THE WORLD GOES, I GO WITH IT. NOT GONNA HANG AROUND CRAWLING FOR SCRAPS WITH ALL THE OTHER RATS.
WHAT'S THE FUN OF HANGING WITH ZOMBIES THAT JUST WANT TO EAT YOU?
GLORIA, ALL THESE WIRES, SPLICED AND TWISTED TOGETHER, LEADING TO THE ROOF--PIKE'S GOT THIS RIGGED SO CRAZY IT COULD BLOW ANYTIME.
SO TALK HIM OUT OF IT!

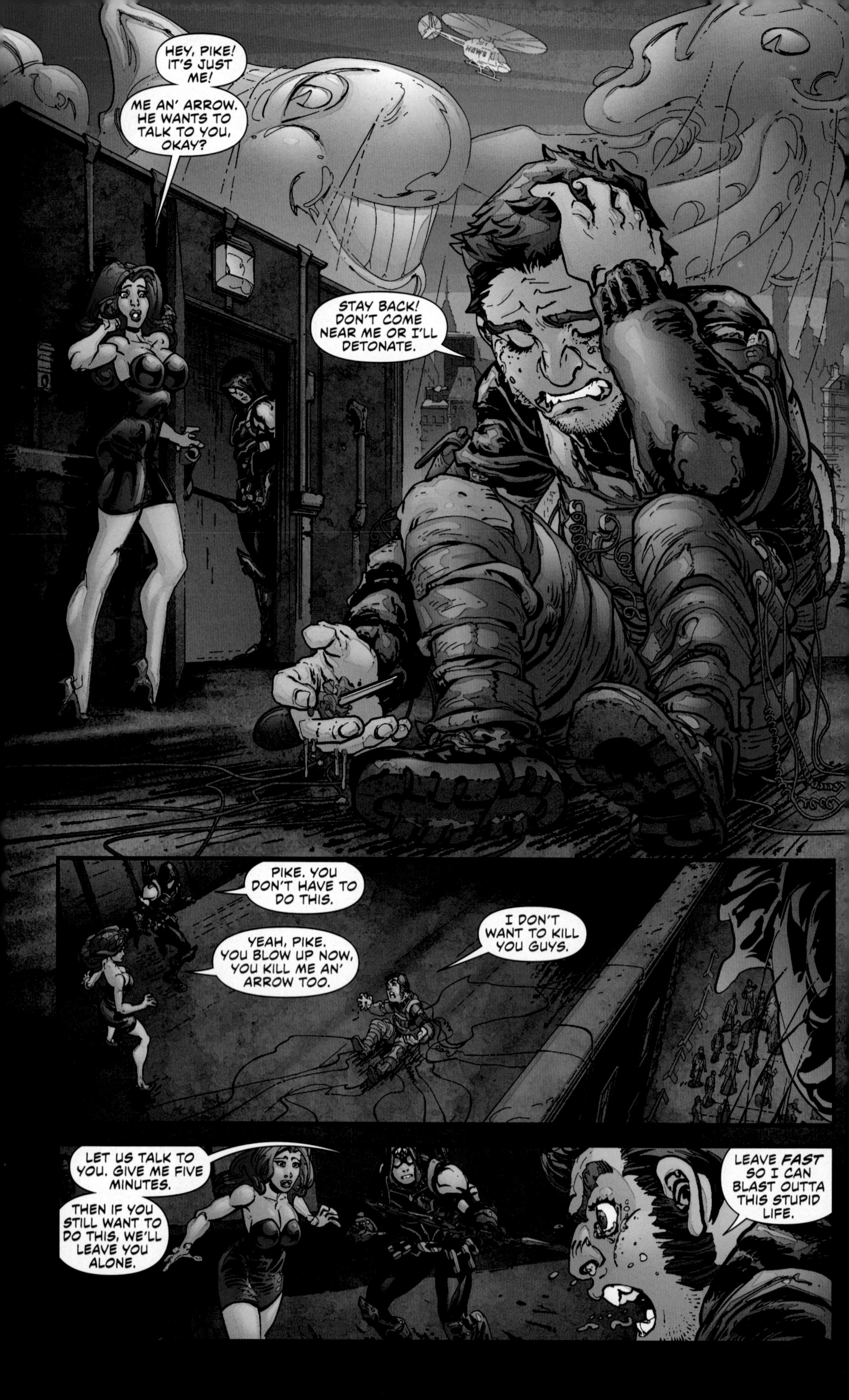
HEY, PIKE! IT'S JUST ME!
ME AN' ARROW. HE WANTS TO TALK TO YOU, OKAY?
STAY BACK! DON'T COME NEAR ME OR I'LL DETONATE.
PIKE. YOU DON'T HAVE TO DO THIS.
YEAH, PIKE. YOU BLOW UP NOW, YOU KILL ME AN' ARROW TOO.
I DON'T WANT TO KILL YOU GUYS.
LET US TALK TO YOU. GIVE ME FIVE MINUTES.
THEN IF YOU STILL WANT TO DO THIS, WE'LL LEAVE YOU ALONE.
LEAVE *FAST* SO I CAN BLAST OUTTA THIS STUPID LIFE.

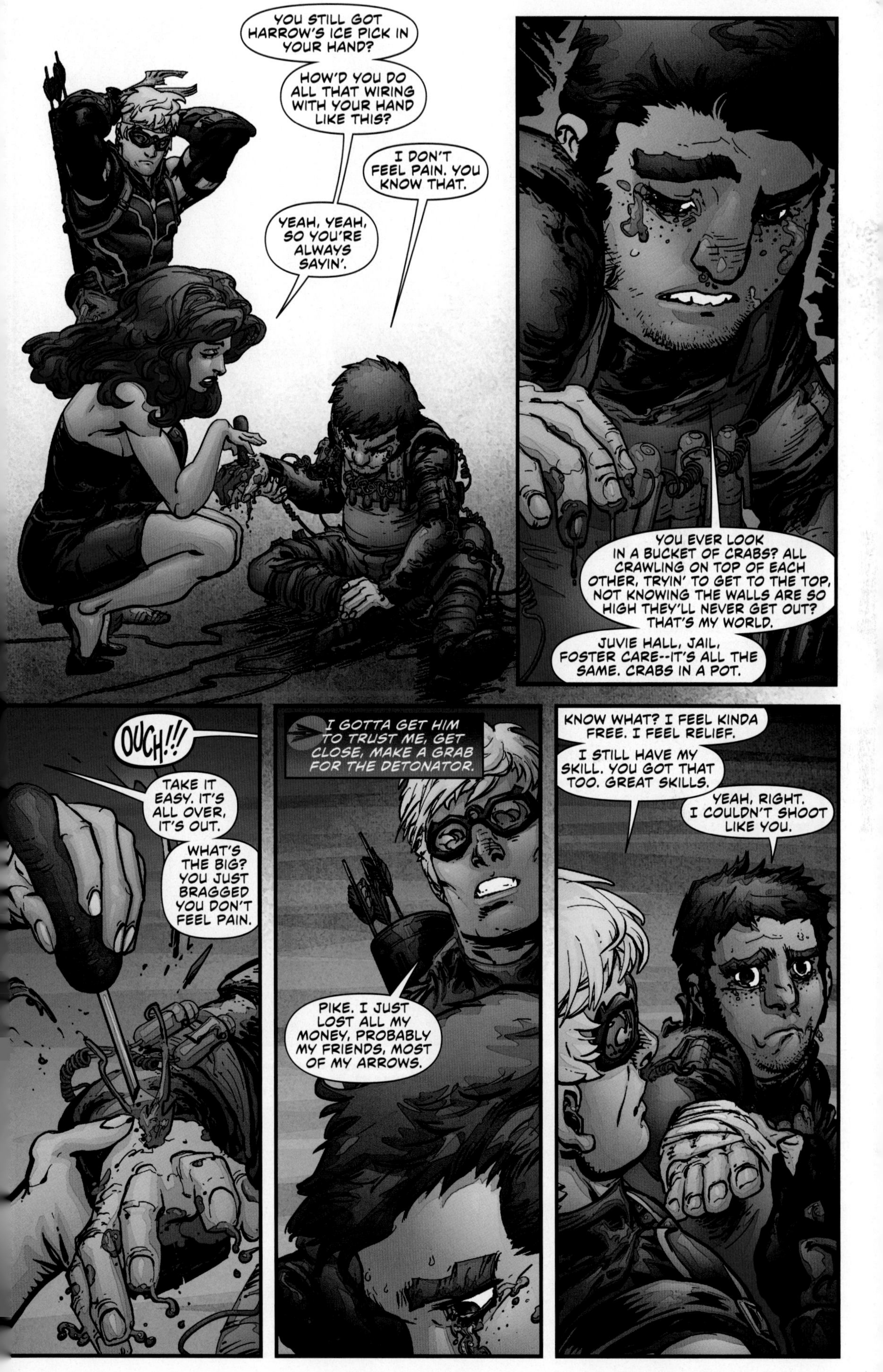
YOU STILL GOT HARROW'S ICE PICK IN YOUR HAND?
HOW'D YOU DO ALL THAT WIRING WITH YOUR HAND LIKE THIS?
I DON'T FEEL PAIN. YOU KNOW THAT.
YEAH, YEAH, SO YOU'RE ALWAYS SAYIN'.
YOU EVER LOOK IN A BUCKET OF CRABS? ALL CRAWLING ON TOP OF EACH OTHER, TRYIN' TO GET TO THE TOP, NOT KNOWING THE WALLS ARE SO HIGH THEY'LL NEVER GET OUT? THAT'S MY WORLD.
JUVIE HALL, JAIL, FOSTER CARE--IT'S ALL THE SAME. CRABS IN A POT.
OUCH!!!
TAKE IT EASY. IT'S ALL OVER, IT'S OUT.
WHAT'S THE BIG? YOU JUST BRAGGED YOU DON'T FEEL PAIN.
I GOTTA GET HIM TO TRUST ME, GET CLOSE, MAKE A GRAB FOR THE DETONATOR.
PIKE. I JUST LOST ALL MY MONEY, PROBABLY MY FRIENDS, MOST OF MY ARROWS.
KNOW WHAT? I FEEL KINDA FREE. I FEEL RELIEF.
I STILL HAVE MY SKILL. YOU GOT THAT TOO. GREAT SKILLS.
YEAH, RIGHT. I COULDN'T SHOOT LIKE YOU.

WHY NOT? YOU'RE STRONG ENOUGH.

HE GOES FOR THIS, HE'LL LET GO OF THAT DETONATOR.

WHATTA YA DOIN', ARROW? HE COULD SHOOT YOU.

HE'S NOT GOING TO SHOOT ME. YOU NOCK THE ARROW LIKE THIS. THEN PULL BACK THE BOWSTRING--

FIND YOUR TARGET.

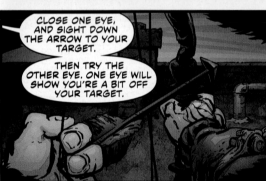

CLOSE ONE EYE, AND SIGHT DOWN THE ARROW TO YOUR TARGET.

THEN TRY THE OTHER EYE. ONE EYE WILL SHOW YOU'RE A BIT OFF YOUR TARGET.

SEE THAT? THAT'S HOW YOU TELL IF YOU'RE A RIGHTY OR LEFTY.

YOU FIGURE OUT WHICH EYE?

YEAH! I THINK I'M A LEFTY!

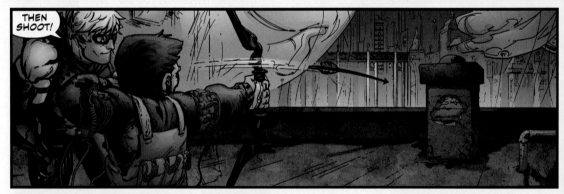

THEN SHOOT!

THUK

WAS IT GOOD?

IT WAS PERFECT!

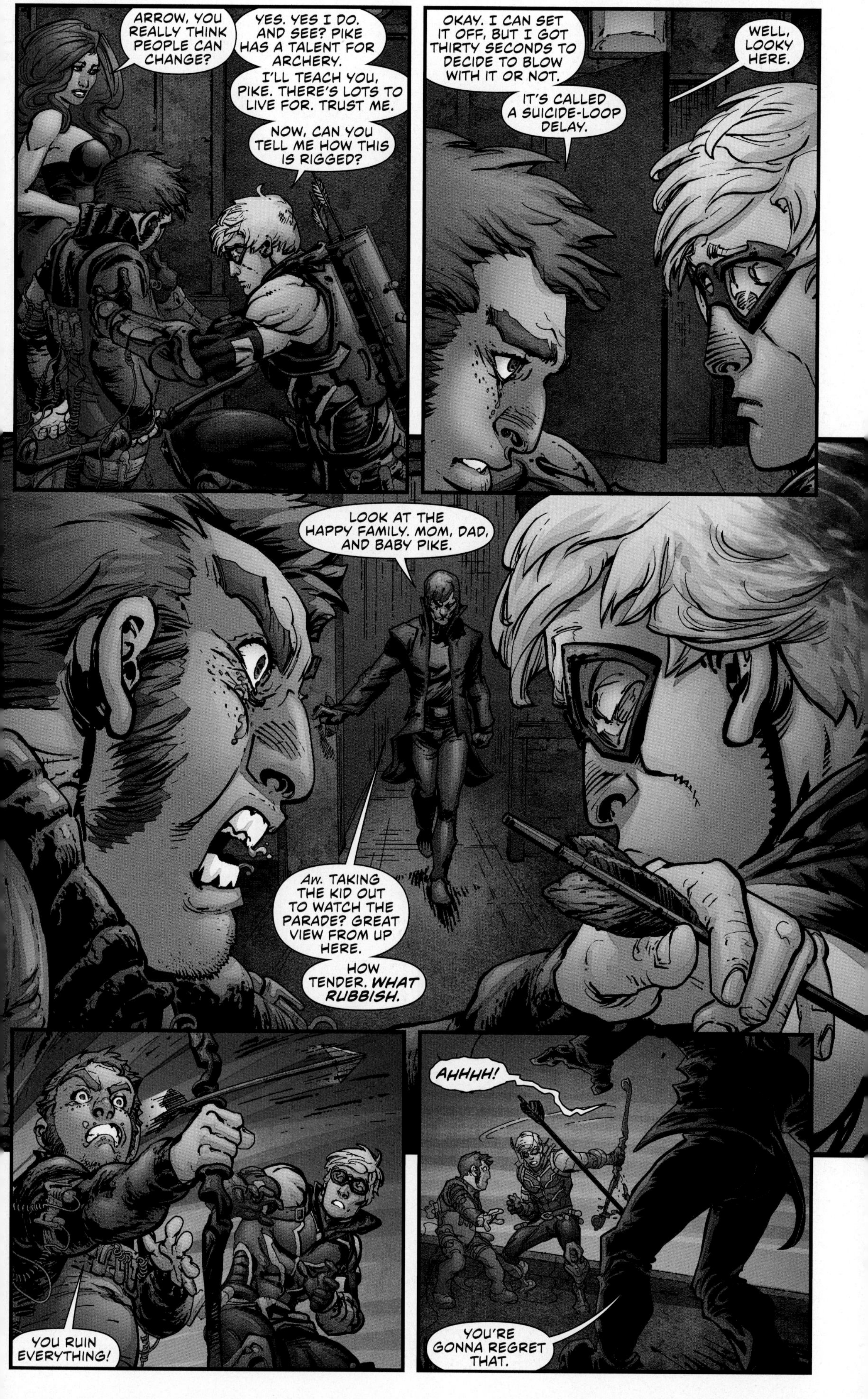

ARROW, YOU REALLY THINK PEOPLE CAN CHANGE?
YES. YES I DO. AND SEE? PIKE HAS A TALENT FOR ARCHERY.
I'LL TEACH YOU, PIKE. THERE'S LOTS TO LIVE FOR. TRUST ME.
NOW, CAN YOU TELL ME HOW THIS IS RIGGED?
OKAY. I CAN SET IT OFF, BUT I GOT THIRTY SECONDS TO DECIDE TO BLOW WITH IT OR NOT.
IT'S CALLED A SUICIDE-LOOP DELAY.
WELL, LOOKY HERE.
LOOK AT THE HAPPY FAMILY. MOM, DAD, AND BABY PIKE.
AW. TAKING THE KID OUT TO WATCH THE PARADE? GREAT VIEW FROM UP HERE.
HOW TENDER. WHAT RUBBISH.
YOU RUIN EVERYTHING!
AHHHH!
YOU'RE GONNA REGRET THAT.

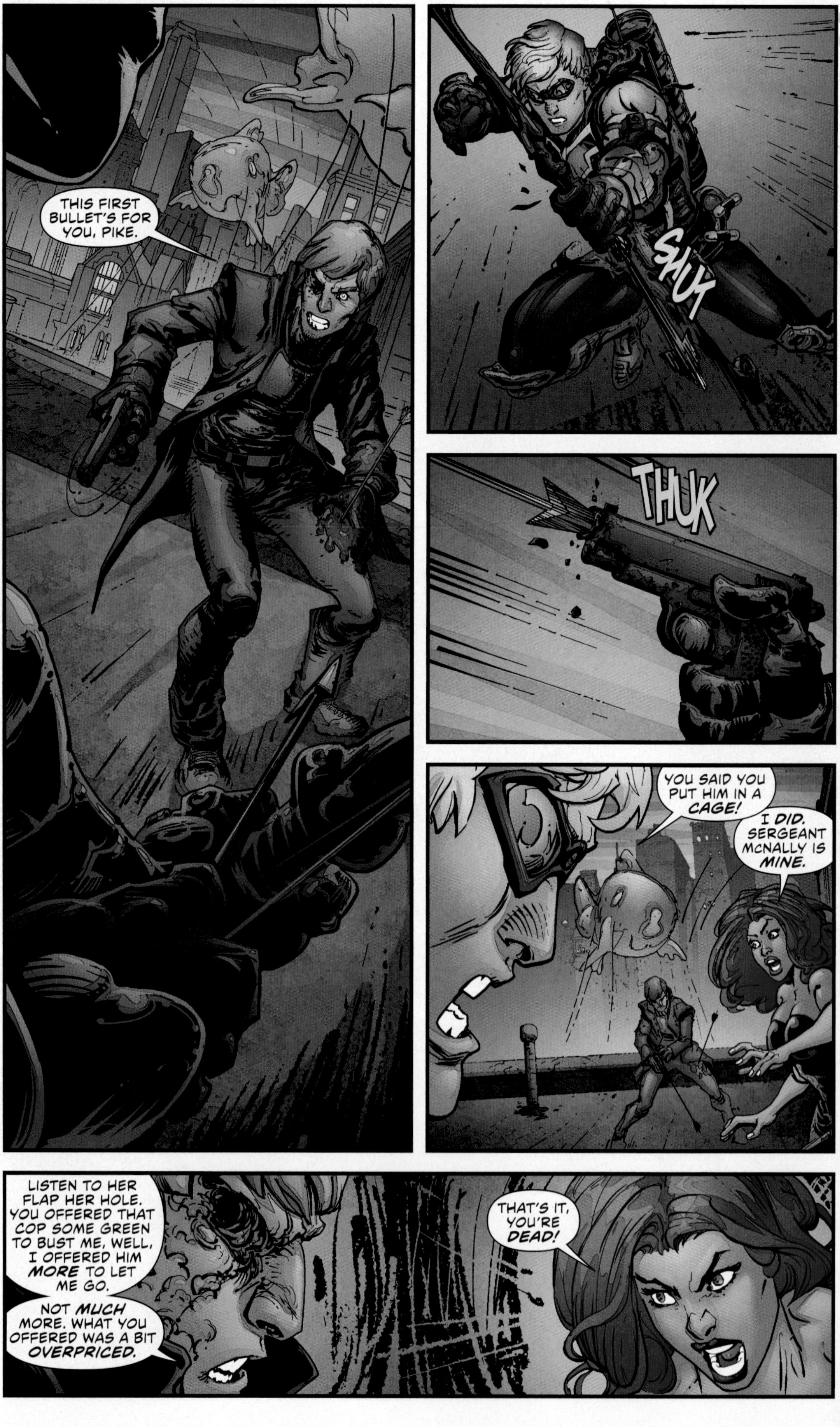
THIS FIRST BULLET'S FOR YOU, PIKE.
SHUK
THUK
YOU SAID YOU PUT HIM IN A CAGE!
I DID. SERGEANT McNALLY IS MINE.
LISTEN TO HER FLAP HER HOLE. YOU OFFERED THAT COP SOME GREEN TO BUST ME, WELL, I OFFERED HIM MORE TO LET ME GO.
NOT MUCH MORE. WHAT YOU OFFERED WAS A BIT OVERPRICED.
THAT'S IT, YOU'RE DEAD!

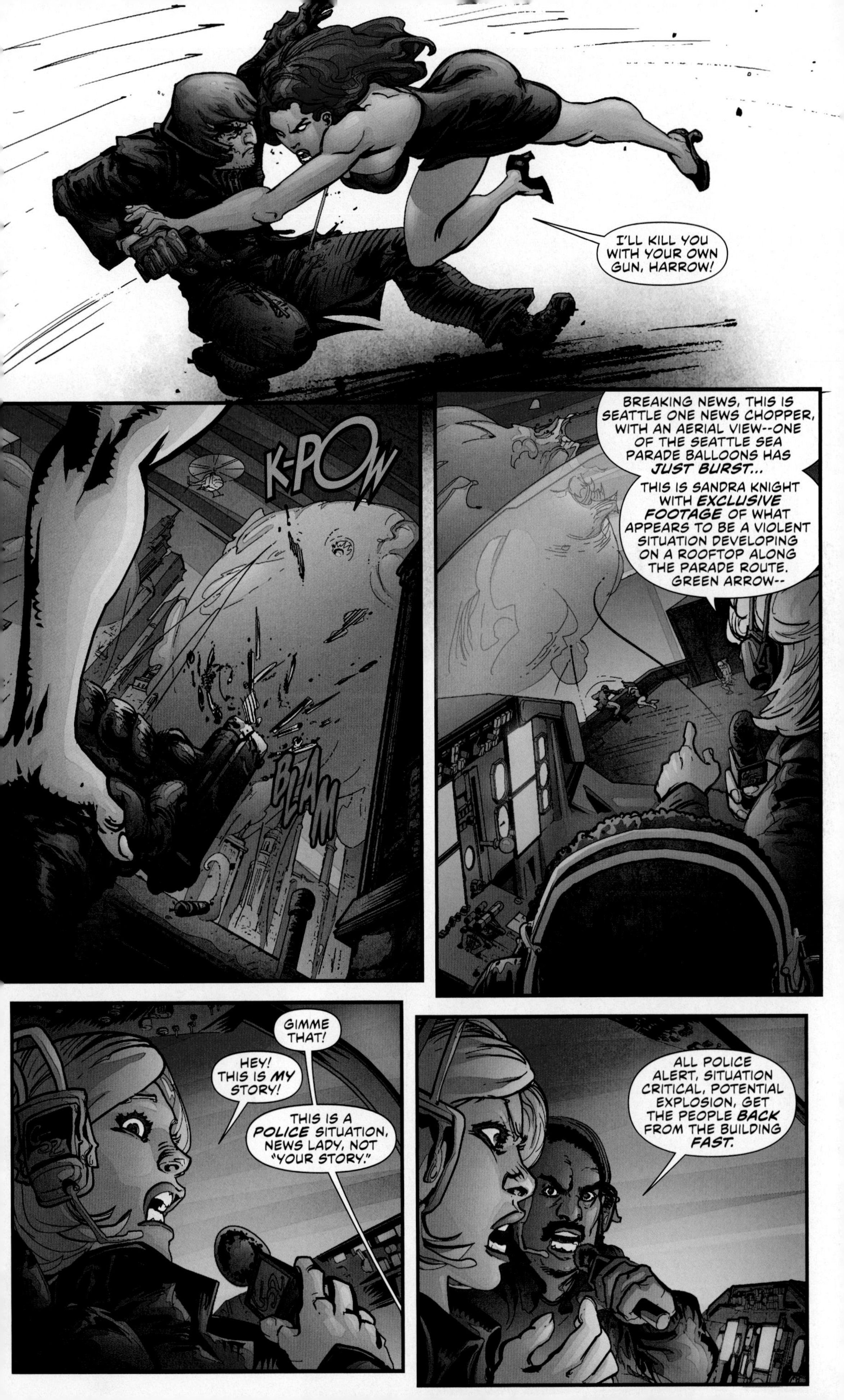
I'LL KILL YOU WITH YOUR OWN GUN, HARROW!
K-POW
BLAM
BREAKING NEWS, THIS IS SEATTLE ONE NEWS CHOPPER, WITH AN AERIAL VIEW--ONE OF THE SEATTLE SEA PARADE BALLOONS HAS JUST BURST...
THIS IS SANDRA KNIGHT WITH EXCLUSIVE FOOTAGE OF WHAT APPEARS TO BE A VIOLENT SITUATION DEVELOPING ON A ROOFTOP ALONG THE PARADE ROUTE. GREEN ARROW--
GIMME THAT!
HEY! THIS IS MY STORY!
THIS IS A POLICE SITUATION, NEWS LADY, NOT "YOUR STORY."
ALL POLICE ALERT, SITUATION CRITICAL, POTENTIAL EXPLOSION, GET THE PEOPLE BACK FROM THE BUILDING FAST.

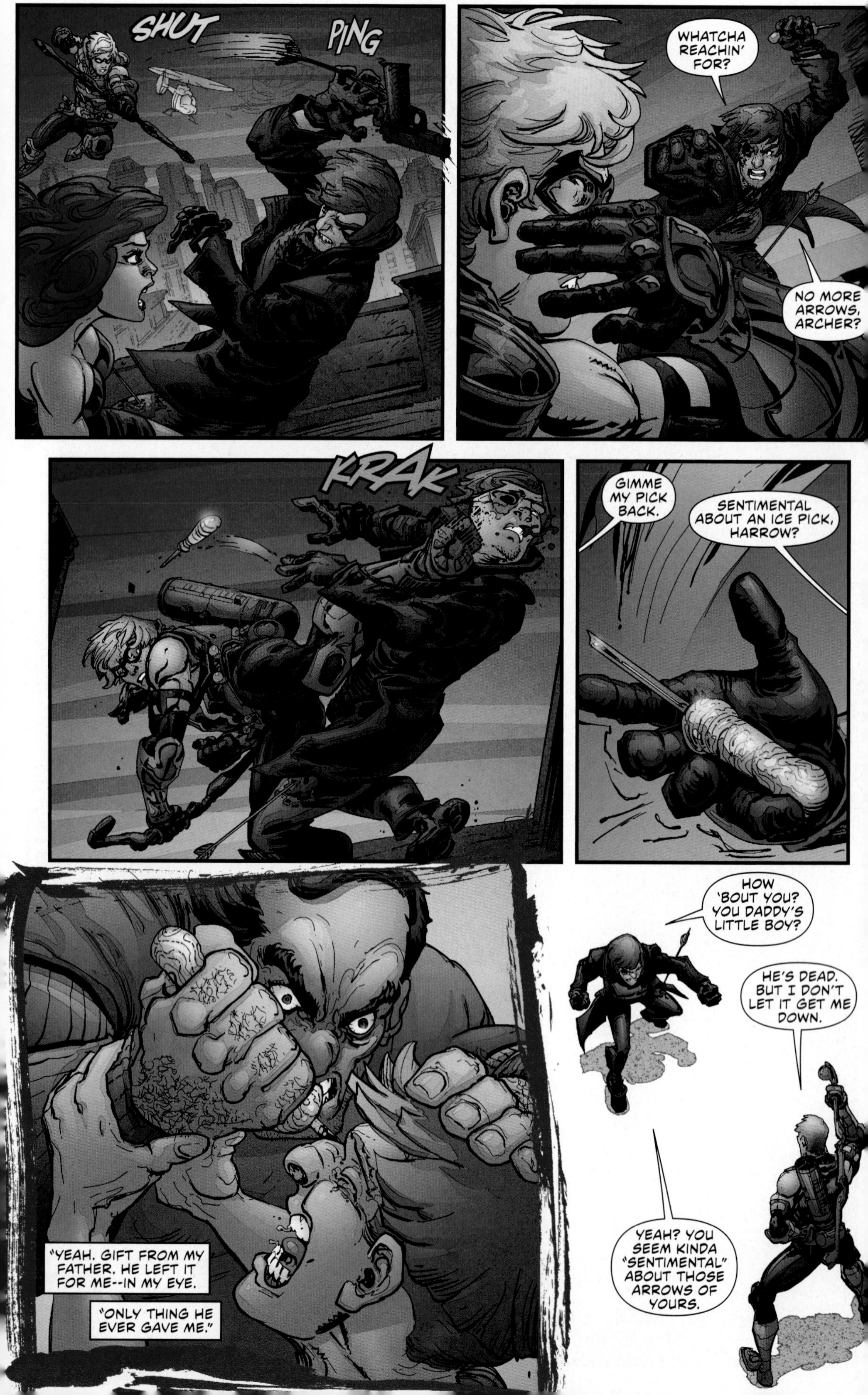
SHUT
PING
WHATCHA REACHIN' FOR?
NO MORE ARROWS, ARCHER?
KRAK
GIMME MY PICK BACK.
SENTIMENTAL ABOUT AN ICE PICK, HARROW?
"YEAH. GIFT FROM MY FATHER. HE LEFT IT FOR ME--IN MY EYE.
"ONLY THING HE EVER GAVE ME."
HOW 'BOUT YOU? YOU DADDY'S LITTLE BOY?
HE'S DEAD. BUT I DON'T LET IT GET ME DOWN.
YEAH? YOU SEEM KINDA "SENTIMENTAL" ABOUT THOSE ARROWS OF YOURS.

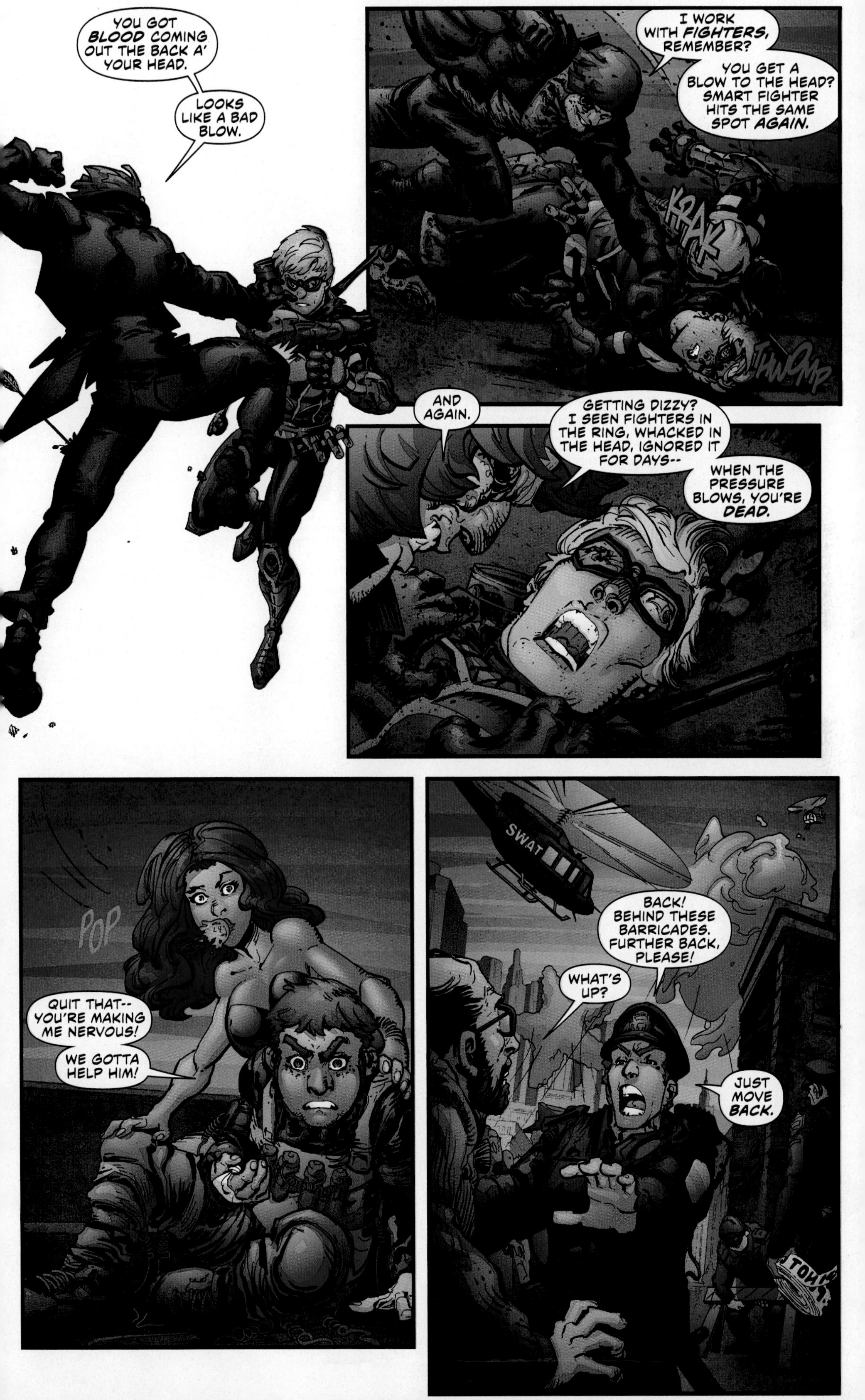
YOU GOT BLOOD COMING OUT THE BACK A' YOUR HEAD.
LOOKS LIKE A BAD BLOW.
I WORK WITH FIGHTERS, REMEMBER?
YOU GET A BLOW TO THE HEAD? SMART FIGHTER HITS THE SAME SPOT AGAIN.
KRAK
THWOMP
AND AGAIN.
GETTING DIZZY? I SEEN FIGHTERS IN THE RING, WHACKED IN THE HEAD, IGNORED IT FOR DAYS--
WHEN THE PRESSURE BLOWS, YOU'RE DEAD.
POP
QUIT THAT-- YOU'RE MAKING ME NERVOUS!
WE GOTTA HELP HIM!
SWAT
BACK! BEHIND THESE BARRICADES. FURTHER BACK, PLEASE!
WHAT'S UP?
JUST MOVE BACK.

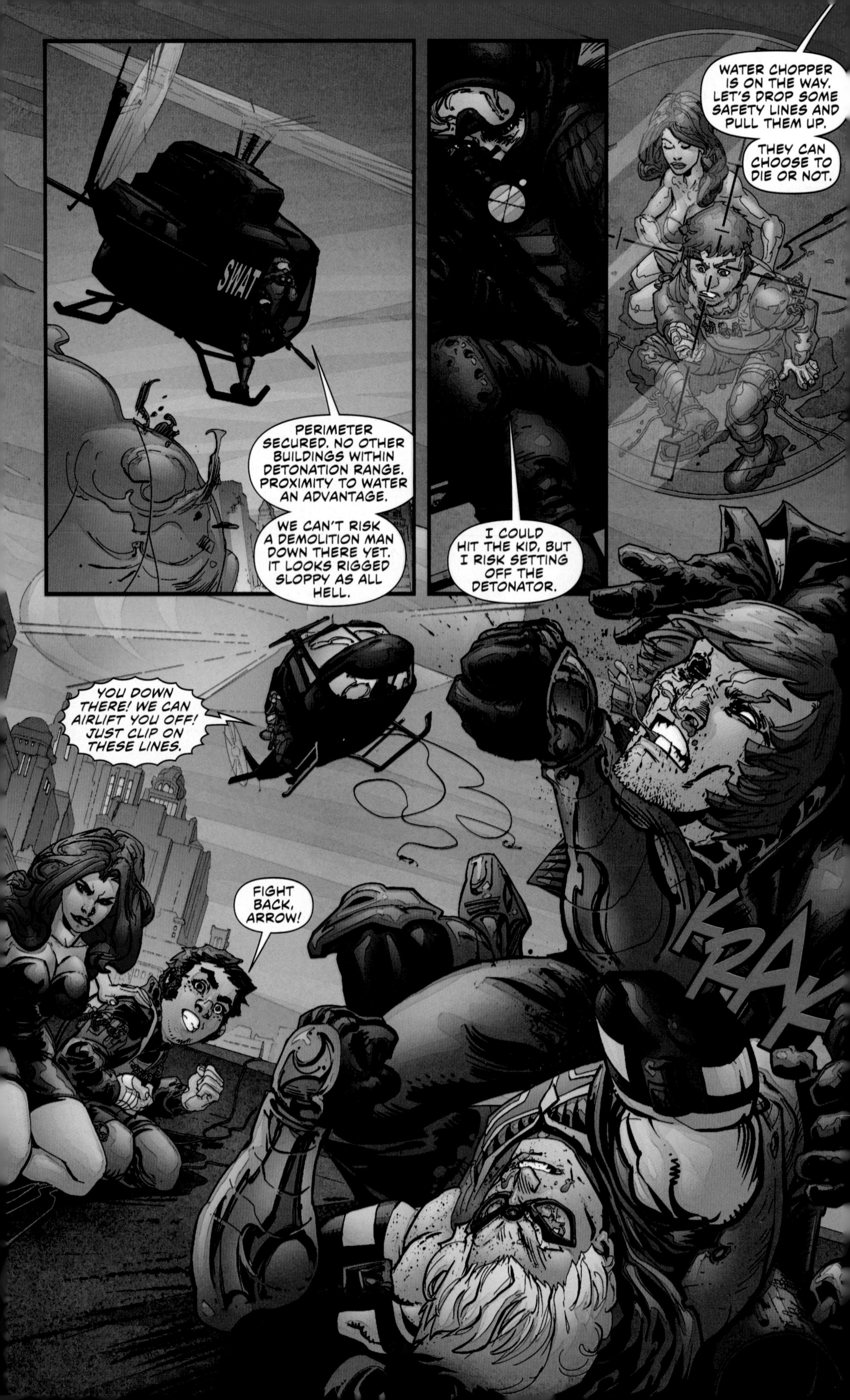
PERIMETER SECURED. NO OTHER BUILDINGS WITHIN DETONATION RANGE. PROXIMITY TO WATER AN ADVANTAGE.
WE CAN'T RISK A DEMOLITION MAN DOWN THERE YET. IT LOOKS RIGGED SLOPPY AS ALL HELL.
I COULD HIT THE KID, BUT I RISK SETTING OFF THE DETONATOR.
WATER CHOPPER IS ON THE WAY. LET'S DROP SOME SAFETY LINES AND PULL THEM UP.
THEY CAN CHOOSE TO DIE OR NOT.
YOU DOWN THERE! WE CAN AIRLIFT YOU OFF! JUST CLIP ON THESE LINES.
FIGHT BACK, ARROW!
KRAK

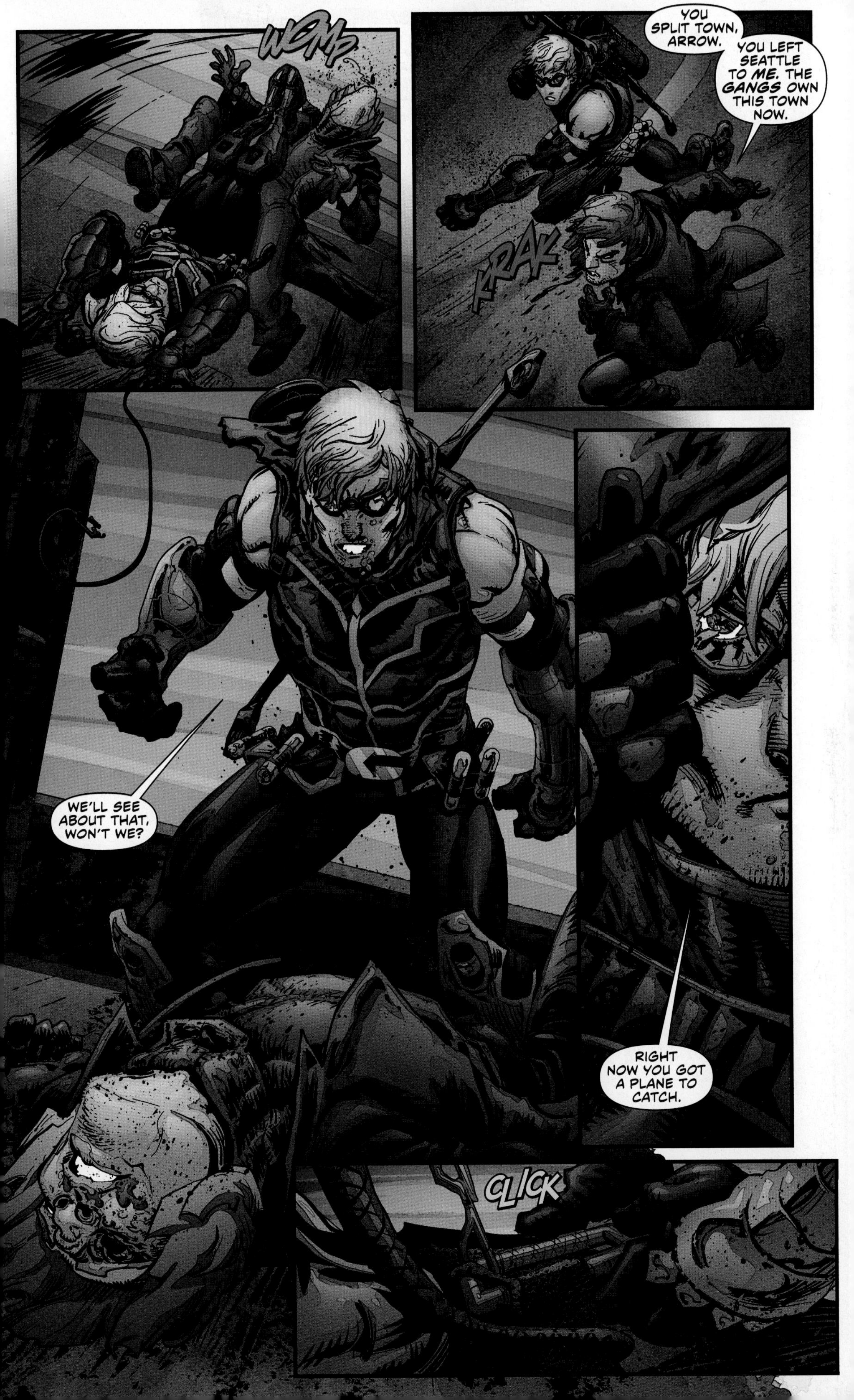
WOMP
YOU SPLIT TOWN, ARROW.
YOU LEFT SEATTLE TO ME. THE GANGS OWN THIS TOWN NOW.
KRAK
WE'LL SEE ABOUT THAT, WON'T WE?
RIGHT NOW YOU GOT A PLANE TO CATCH.
CLICK

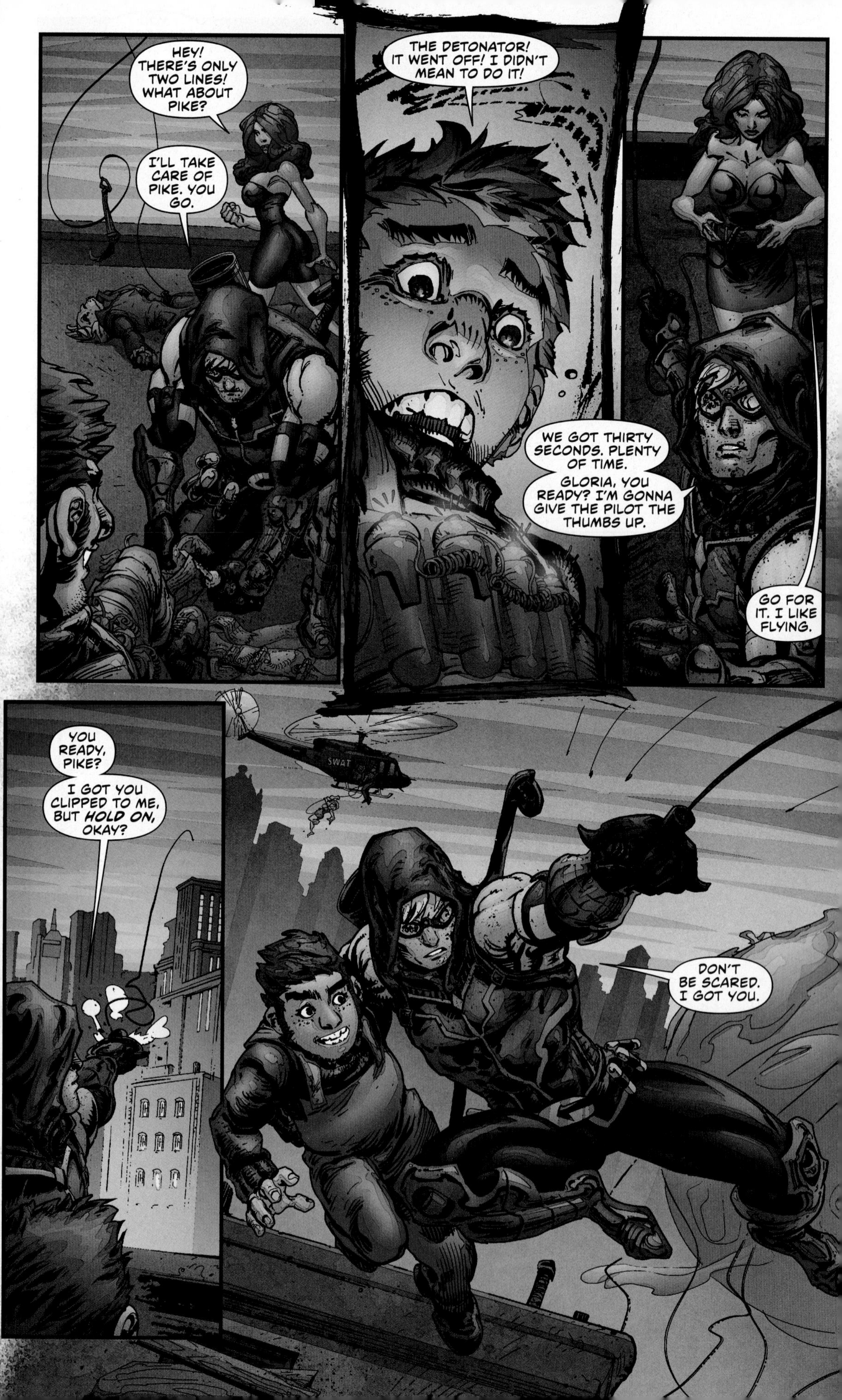
HEY! THERE'S ONLY TWO LINES! WHAT ABOUT PIKE?
I'LL TAKE CARE OF PIKE. YOU GO.
THE DETONATOR! IT WENT OFF! I DIDN'T MEAN TO DO IT!
WE GOT THIRTY SECONDS. PLENTY OF TIME.
GLORIA, YOU READY? I'M GONNA GIVE THE PILOT THE THUMBS UP.
GO FOR IT. I LIKE FLYING.
YOU READY, PIKE?
I GOT YOU CLIPPED TO ME, BUT *HOLD ON*, OKAY?
SWAT
DON'T BE SCARED. I GOT YOU.

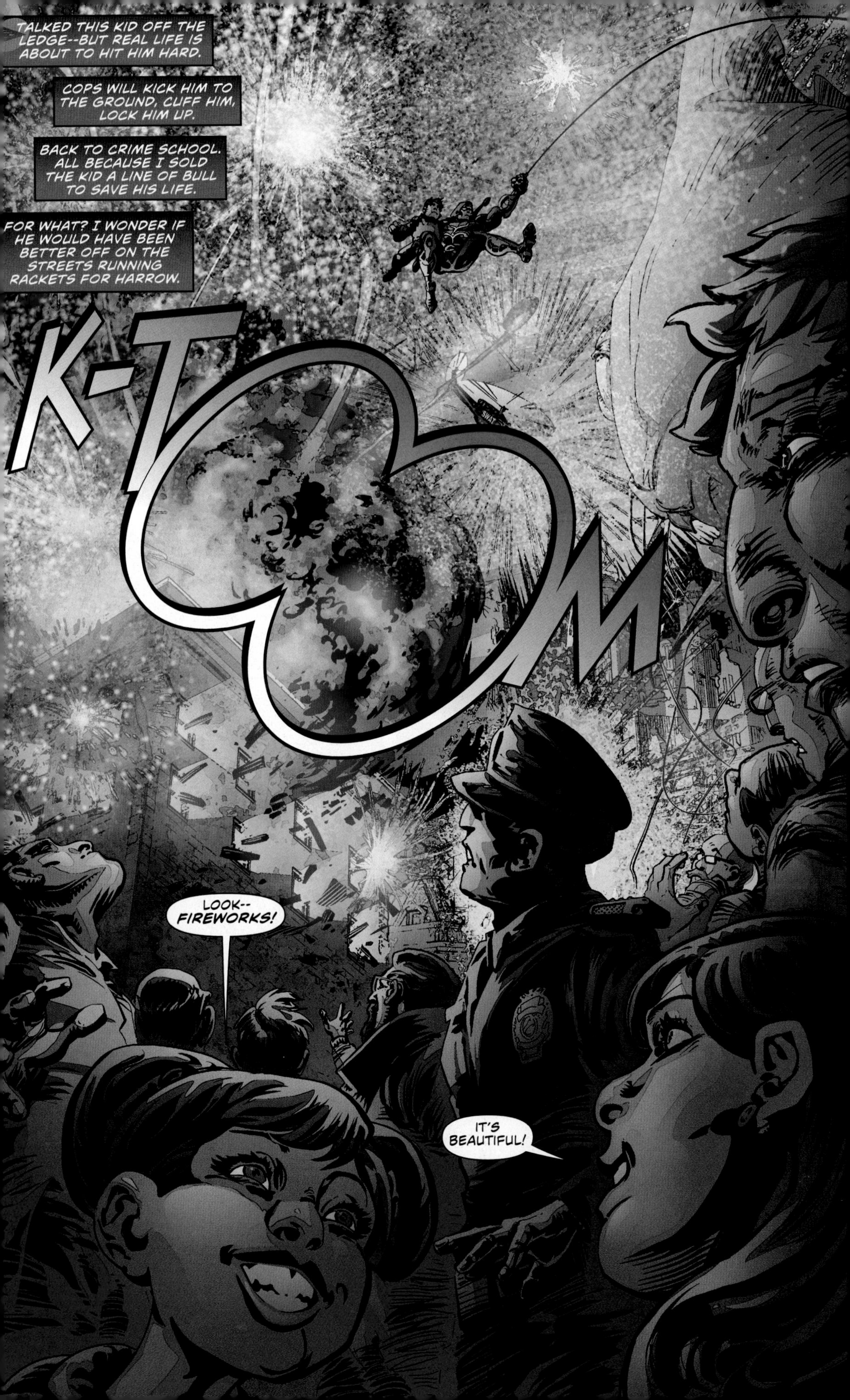
TALKED THIS KID OFF THE LEDGE--BUT REAL LIFE IS ABOUT TO HIT HIM HARD.
COPS WILL KICK HIM TO THE GROUND, CUFF HIM, LOCK HIM UP.
BACK TO CRIME SCHOOL. ALL BECAUSE I SOLD THE KID A LINE OF BULL TO SAVE HIS LIFE.
FOR WHAT? I WONDER IF HE WOULD HAVE BEEN BETTER OFF ON THE STREETS RUNNING RACKETS FOR HARROW.
K-TOOM
LOOK-- FIREWORKS!
IT'S BEAUTIFUL!

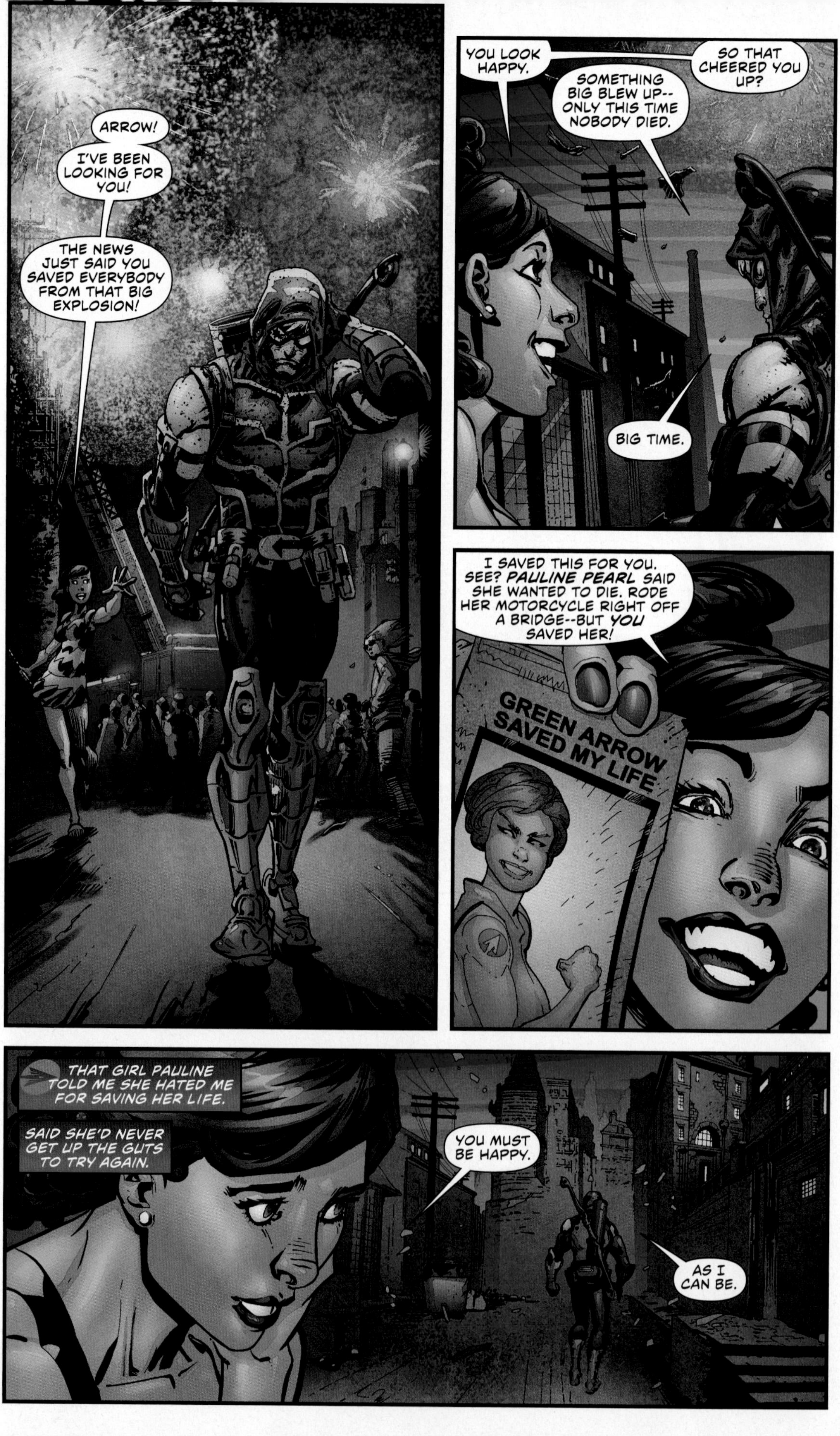
ARROW!
I'VE BEEN LOOKING FOR YOU!
THE NEWS JUST SAID YOU SAVED EVERYBODY FROM THAT BIG EXPLOSION!
YOU LOOK HAPPY.
SOMETHING BIG BLEW UP-- ONLY THIS TIME NOBODY DIED.
SO THAT CHEERED YOU UP?
BIG TIME.
I SAVED THIS FOR YOU. SEE? PAULINE PEARL SAID SHE WANTED TO DIE. RODE HER MOTORCYCLE RIGHT OFF A BRIDGE--BUT YOU SAVED HER!
GREEN ARROW SAVED MY LIFE
THAT GIRL PAULINE TOLD ME SHE HATED ME FOR SAVING HER LIFE.
SAID SHE'D NEVER GET UP THE GUTS TO TRY AGAIN.
YOU MUST BE HAPPY.
AS I CAN BE.

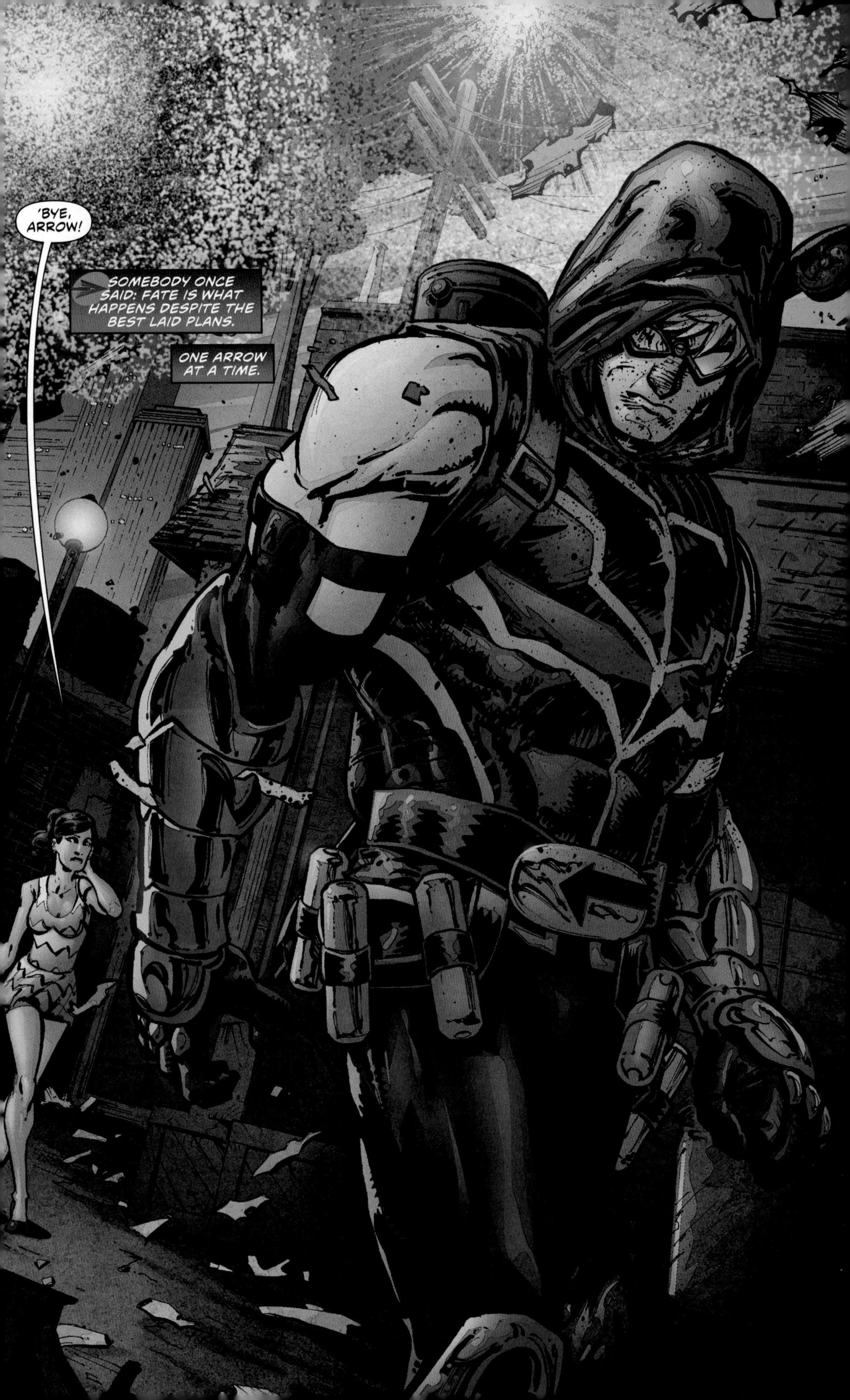
'BYE, ARROW!
SOMEBODY ONCE SAID: FATE IS WHAT HAPPENS DESPITE THE BEST LAID PLANS.
ONE ARROW AT A TIME.

JUSTICE LEAGUE TEAM-UP: GREEN ARROW

GEOFF JOHNS writer CARLOS D'ANDA, IVAN REIS & JOE PRADO artists cover by JIM LEE, SCOTT WILLIAMS & ALEX SINCLAIR

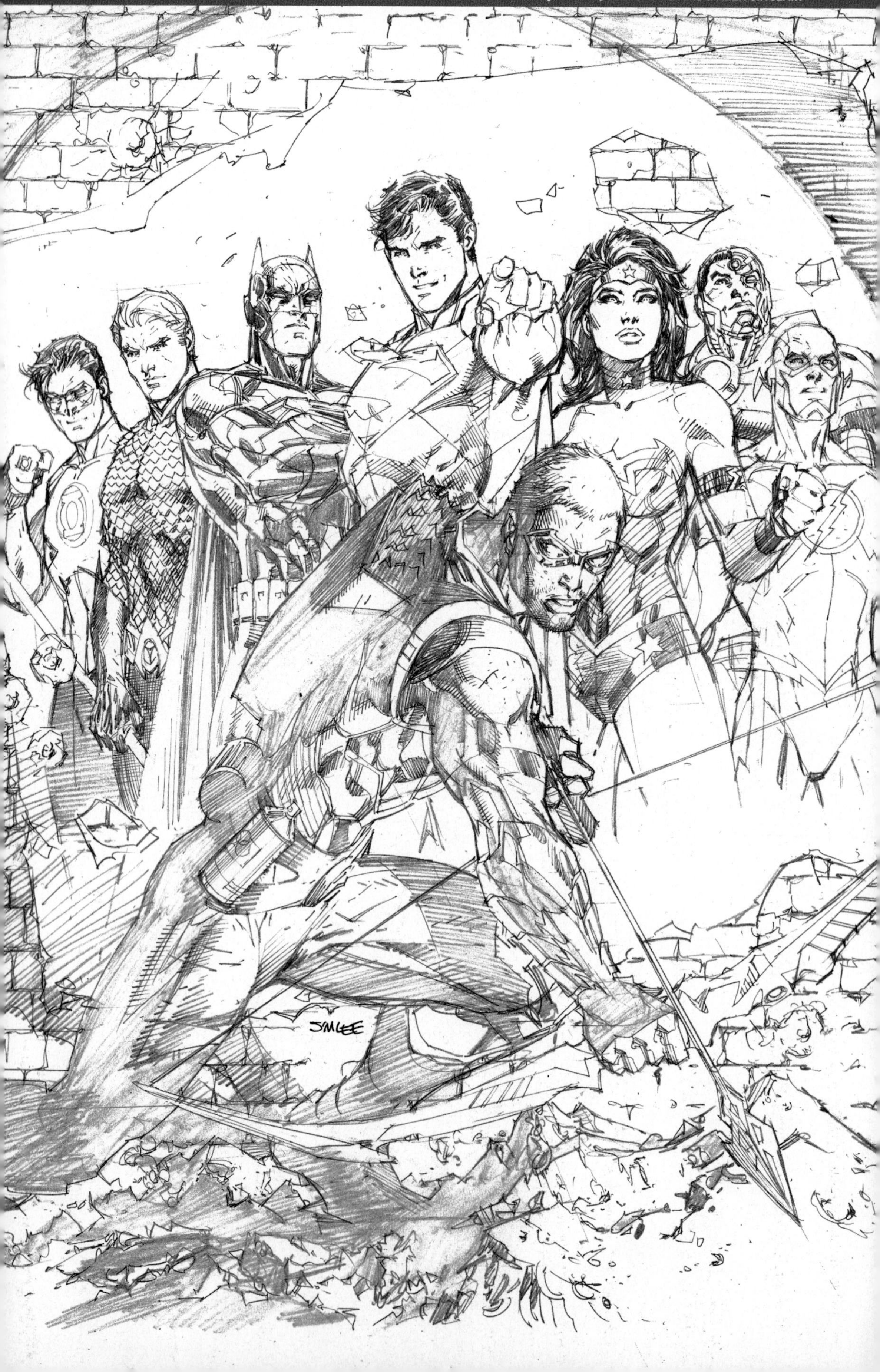
JIM LEE

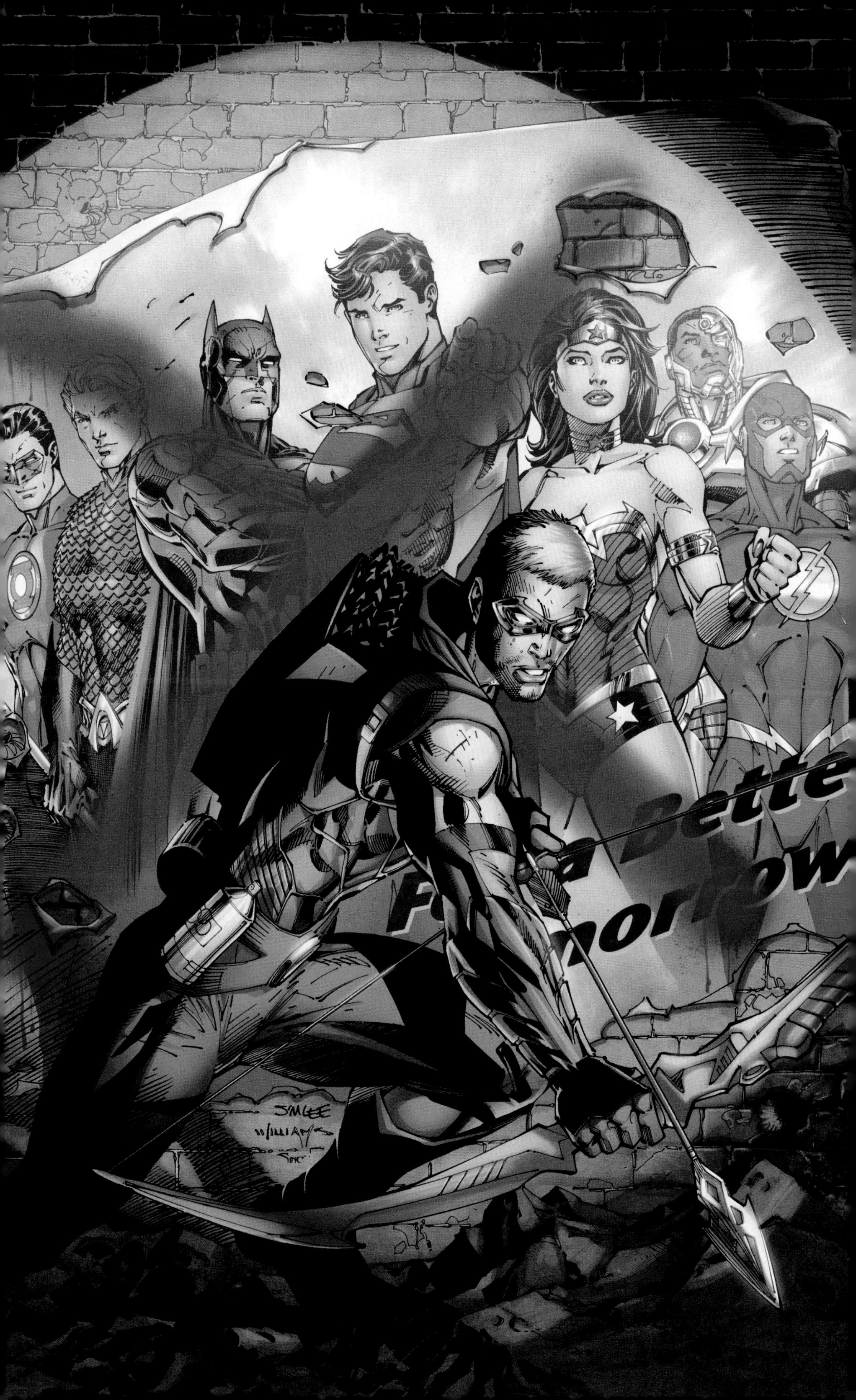

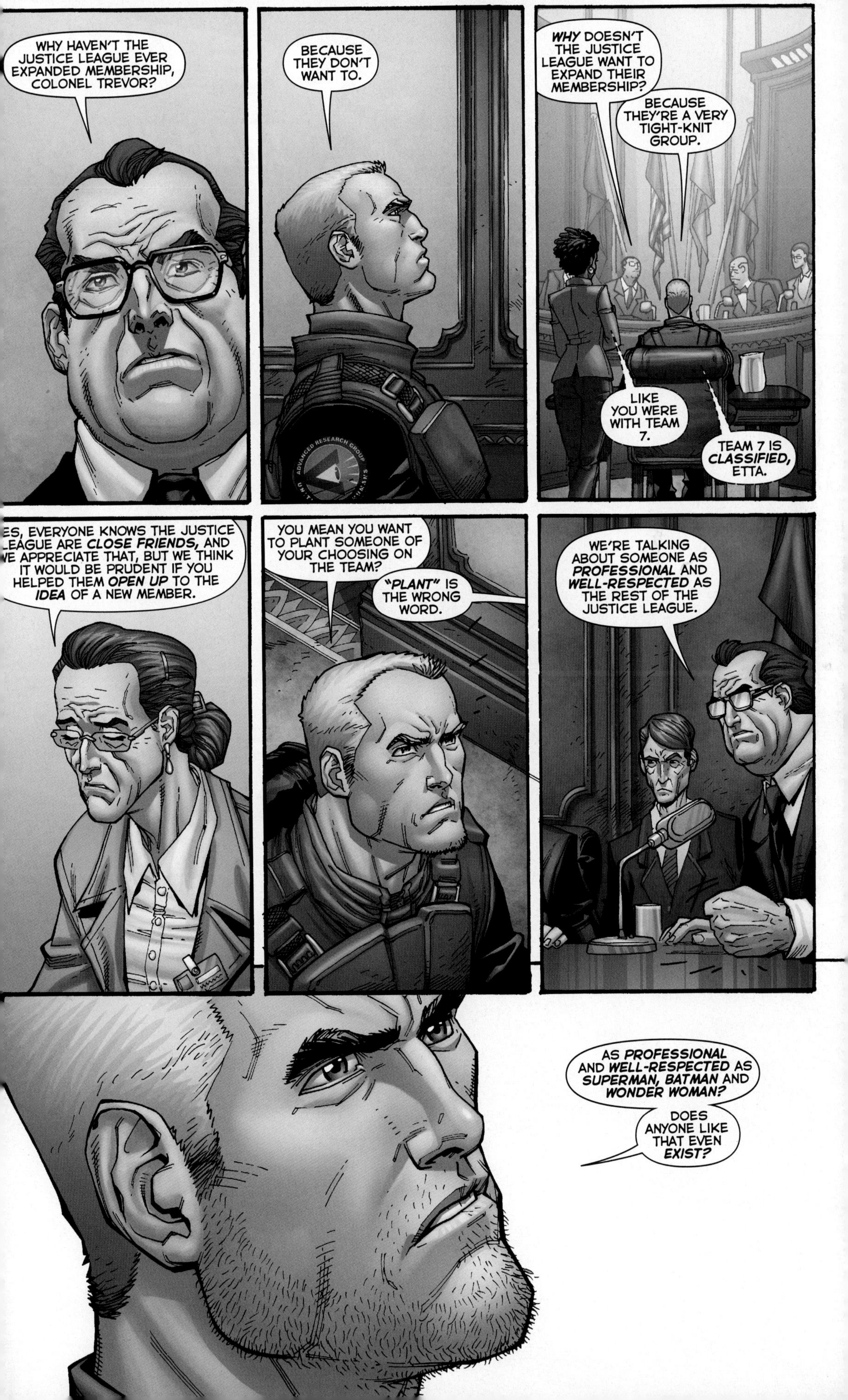
WHY HAVEN'T THE JUSTICE LEAGUE EVER EXPANDED MEMBERSHIP, COLONEL TREVOR?
BECAUSE THEY DON'T WANT TO.
WHY DOESN'T THE JUSTICE LEAGUE WANT TO EXPAND THEIR MEMBERSHIP?
BECAUSE THEY'RE A VERY TIGHT-KNIT GROUP.
LIKE YOU WERE WITH TEAM 7.
TEAM 7 IS *CLASSIFIED,* ETTA.
ES, EVERYONE KNOWS THE JUSTICE EAGUE ARE *CLOSE FRIENDS,* AND E APPRECIATE THAT, BUT WE THINK IT WOULD BE PRUDENT IF YOU HELPED THEM *OPEN UP* TO THE *IDEA* OF A NEW MEMBER.
YOU MEAN YOU WANT TO PLANT SOMEONE OF YOUR CHOOSING ON THE TEAM?
"PLANT" IS THE WRONG WORD.
WE'RE TALKING ABOUT SOMEONE AS *PROFESSIONAL* AND *WELL-RESPECTED* AS THE REST OF THE JUSTICE LEAGUE.
AS *PROFESSIONAL* AND *WELL-RESPECTED* AS *SUPERMAN, BATMAN* AND *WONDER WOMAN?*
DOES ANYONE LIKE THAT EVEN *EXIST?*

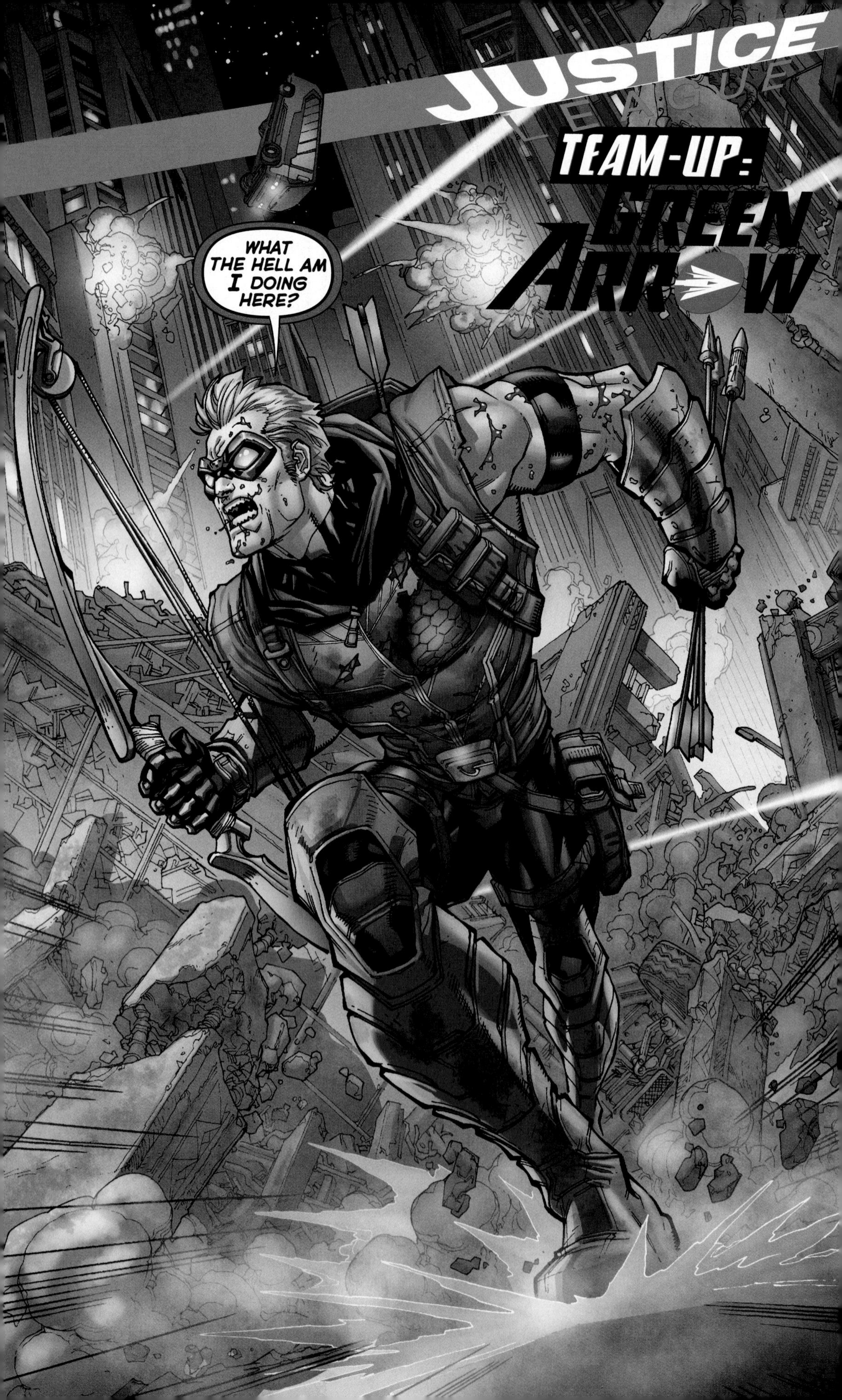
JUSTICE LEAGUE
TEAM-UP: GREEN ARROW
WHAT THE HELL AM I DOING HERE?

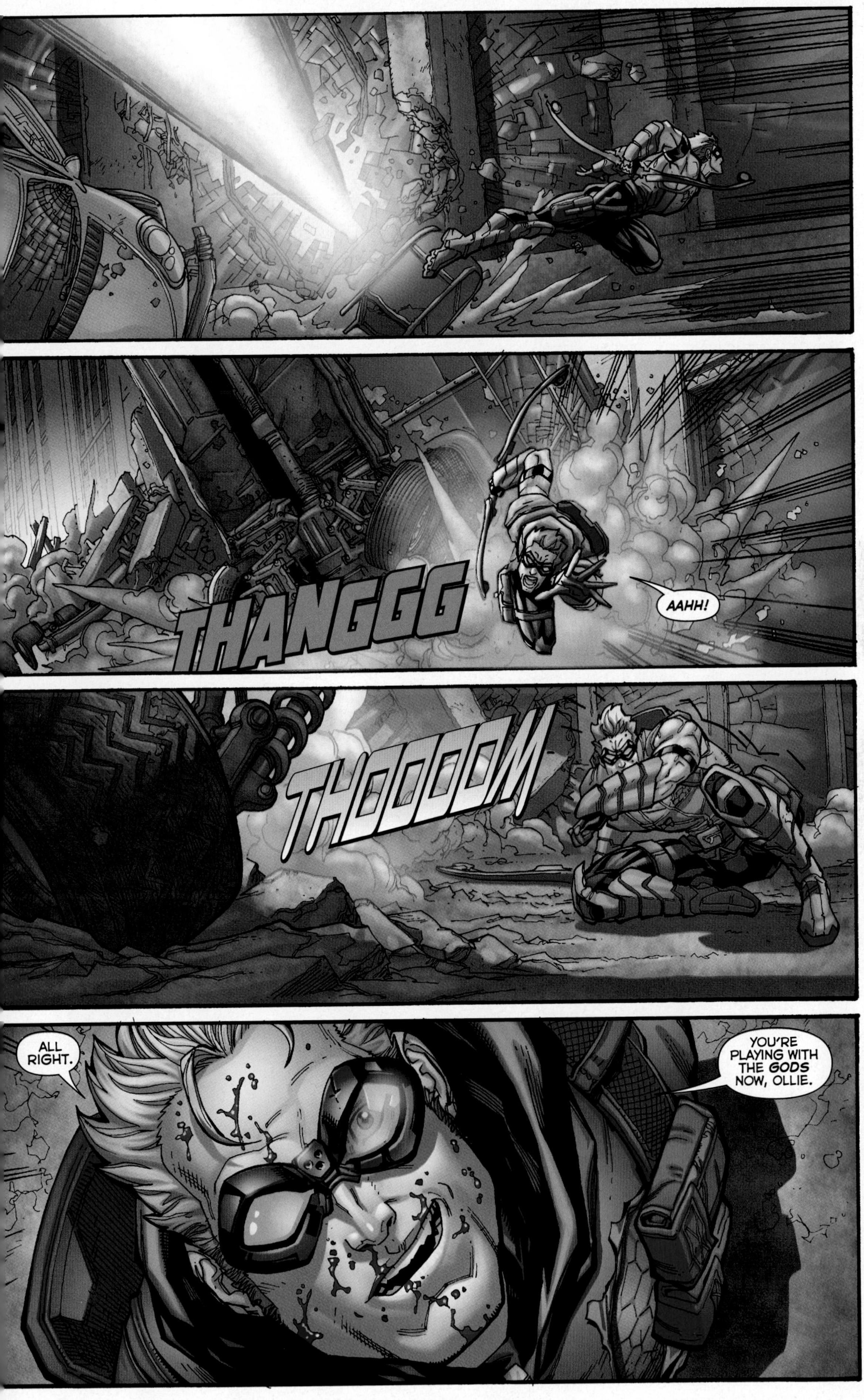
THANGGG
AAHH!
THOOOOM
ALL RIGHT.
YOU'RE PLAYING WITH THE GODS NOW, OLLIE.

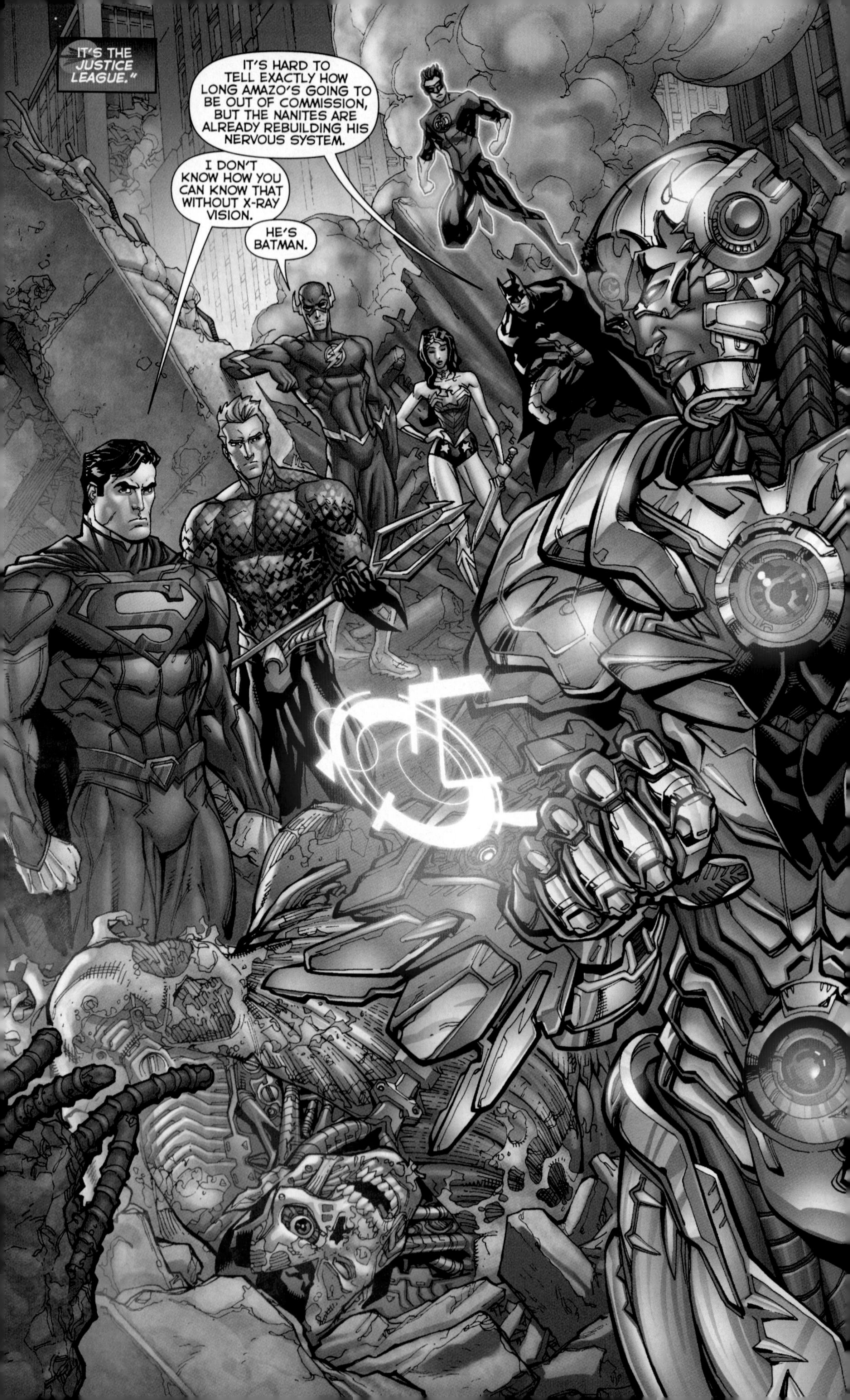
IT'S THE JUSTICE LEAGUE."
IT'S HARD TO TELL EXACTLY HOW LONG AMAZO'S GOING TO BE OUT OF COMMISSION, BUT THE NANITES ARE ALREADY REBUILDING HIS NERVOUS SYSTEM.
I DON'T KNOW HOW YOU CAN KNOW THAT WITHOUT X-RAY VISION.
HE'S BATMAN.

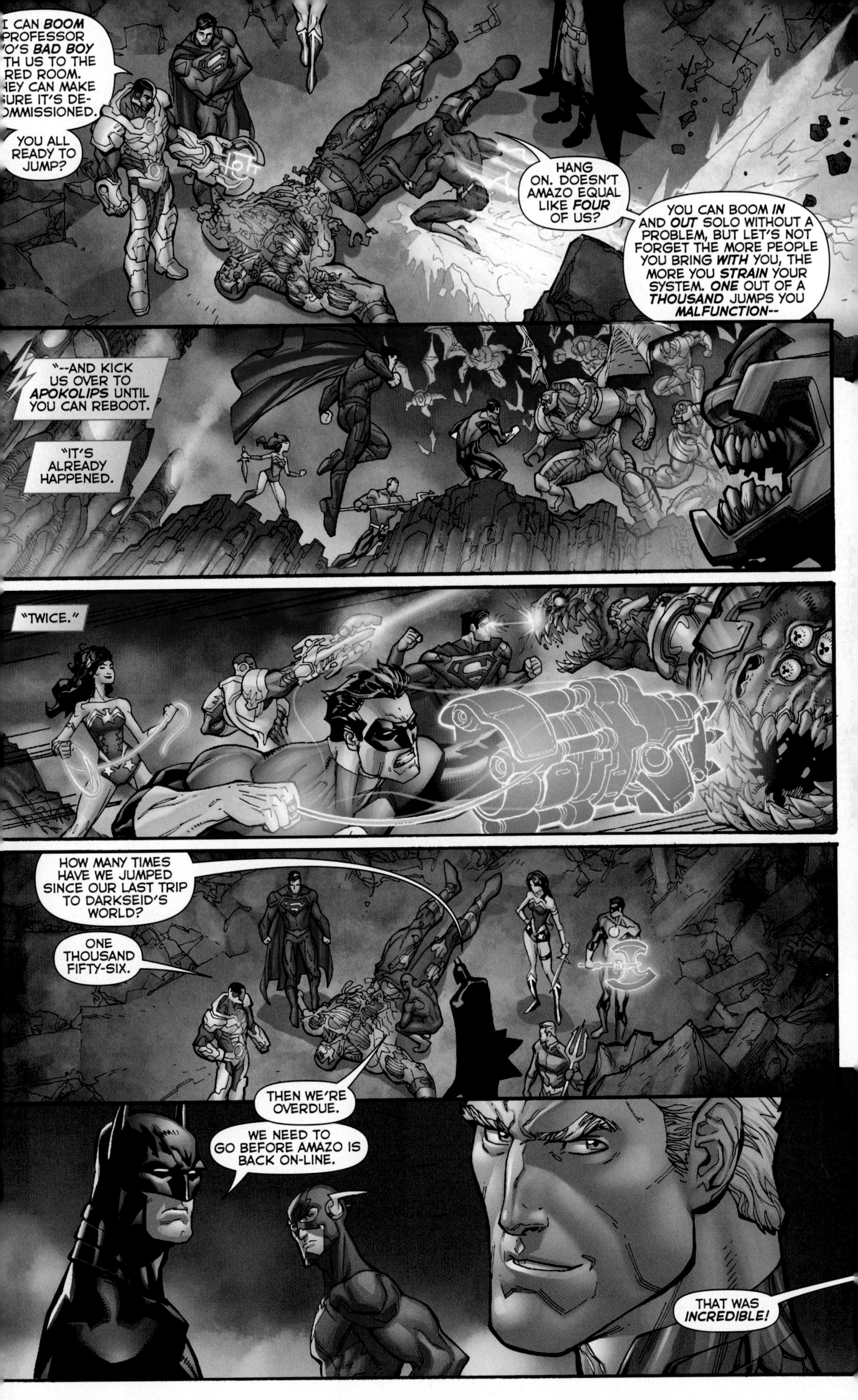
I CAN BOOM PROFESSOR O'S BAD BOY TH US TO THE RED ROOM. HEY CAN MAKE URE IT'S DE- OMMISSIONED.
YOU ALL READY TO JUMP?
HANG ON. DOESN'T AMAZO EQUAL LIKE FOUR OF US?
YOU CAN BOOM IN AND OUT SOLO WITHOUT A PROBLEM, BUT LET'S NOT FORGET THE MORE PEOPLE YOU BRING WITH YOU, THE MORE YOU STRAIN YOUR SYSTEM. ONE OUT OF A THOUSAND JUMPS YOU MALFUNCTION--
"--AND KICK US OVER TO APOKOLIPS UNTIL YOU CAN REBOOT.
"IT'S ALREADY HAPPENED.
"TWICE."
HOW MANY TIMES HAVE WE JUMPED SINCE OUR LAST TRIP TO DARKSEID'S WORLD?
ONE THOUSAND FIFTY-SIX.
THEN WE'RE OVERDUE.
WE NEED TO GO BEFORE AMAZO IS BACK ON-LINE.
THAT WAS INCREDIBLE!

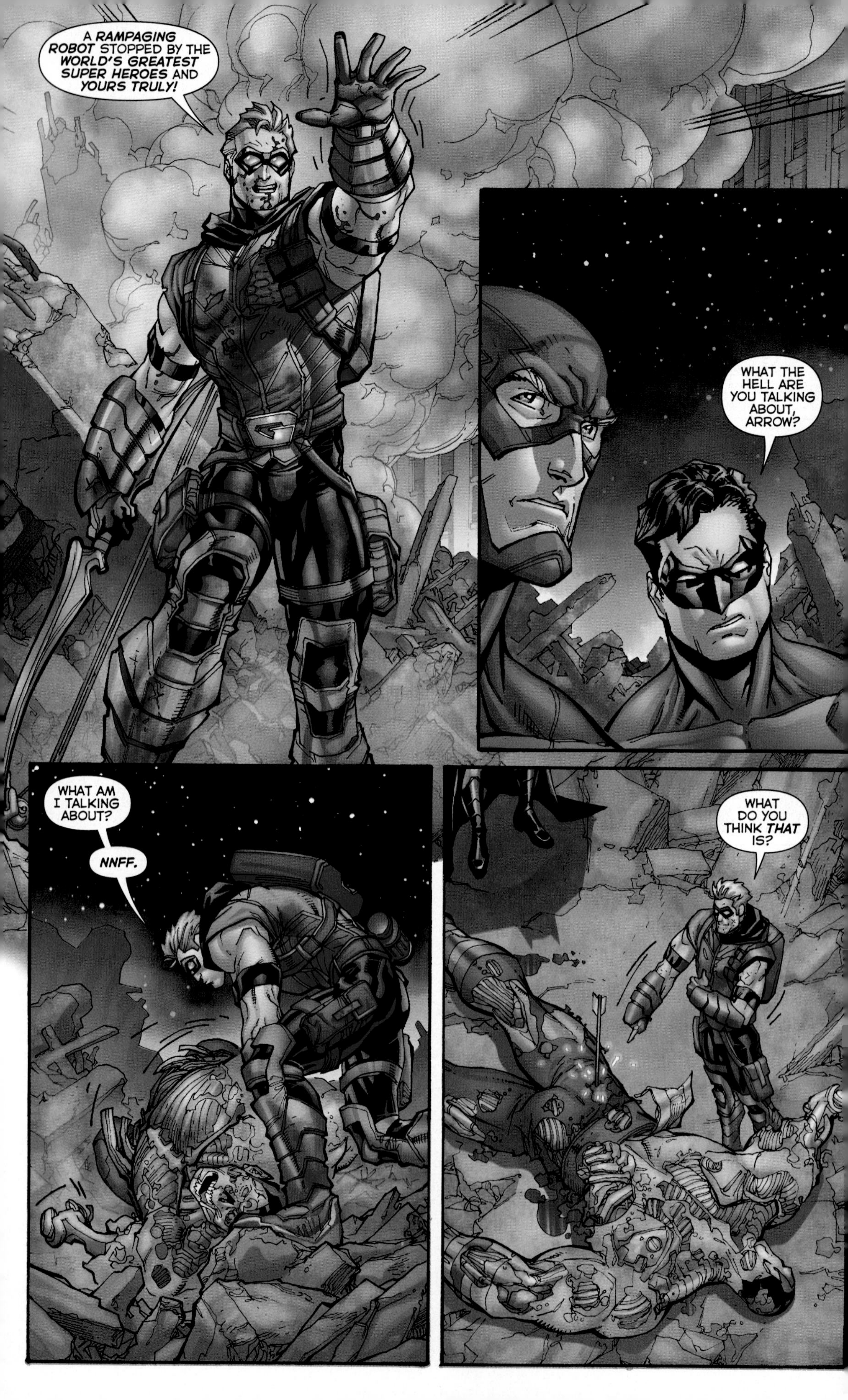
A *RAMPAGING ROBOT* STOPPED BY THE *WORLD'S GREATEST SUPER HEROES* AND *YOURS TRULY!*
WHAT THE HELL ARE YOU TALKING ABOUT, ARROW?
WHAT AM I TALKING ABOUT?
NNFF.
WHAT DO YOU THINK *THAT* IS?

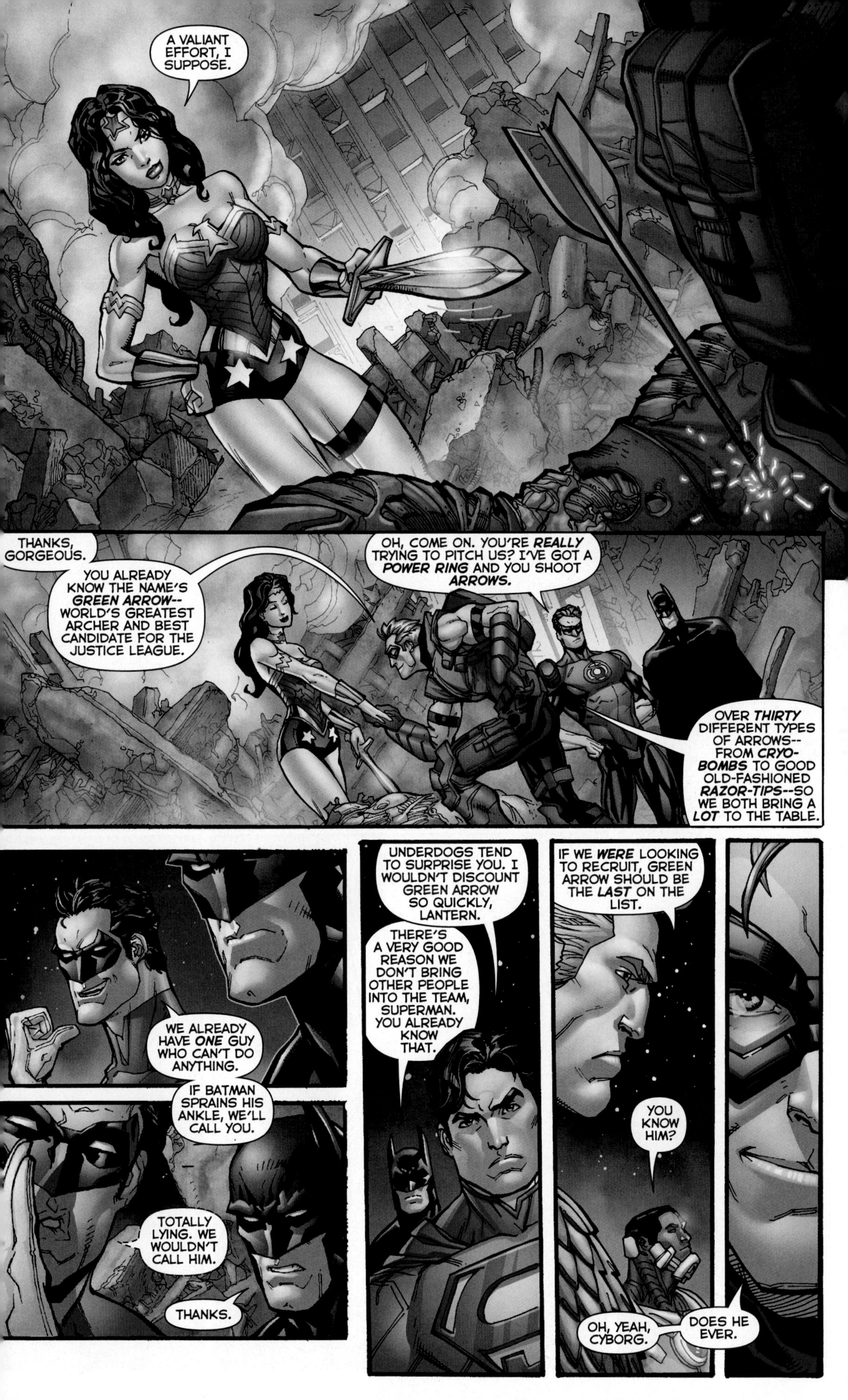

A VALIANT EFFORT, I SUPPOSE.
THANKS, GORGEOUS.
YOU ALREADY KNOW THE NAME'S GREEN ARROW-- WORLD'S GREATEST ARCHER AND BEST CANDIDATE FOR THE JUSTICE LEAGUE.
OH, COME ON. YOU'RE REALLY TRYING TO PITCH US? I'VE GOT A POWER RING AND YOU SHOOT ARROWS.
OVER THIRTY DIFFERENT TYPES OF ARROWS-- FROM CRYO-BOMBS TO GOOD OLD-FASHIONED RAZOR-TIPS--SO WE BOTH BRING A LOT TO THE TABLE.
WE ALREADY HAVE ONE GUY WHO CAN'T DO ANYTHING.
IF BATMAN SPRAINS HIS ANKLE, WE'LL CALL YOU.
TOTALLY LYING. WE WOULDN'T CALL HIM.
THANKS.
UNDERDOGS TEND TO SURPRISE YOU. I WOULDN'T DISCOUNT GREEN ARROW SO QUICKLY, LANTERN.
THERE'S A VERY GOOD REASON WE DON'T BRING OTHER PEOPLE INTO THE TEAM, SUPERMAN. YOU ALREADY KNOW THAT.
IF WE WERE LOOKING TO RECRUIT, GREEN ARROW SHOULD BE THE LAST ON THE LIST.
YOU KNOW HIM?
OH, YEAH, CYBORG.
DOES HE EVER.

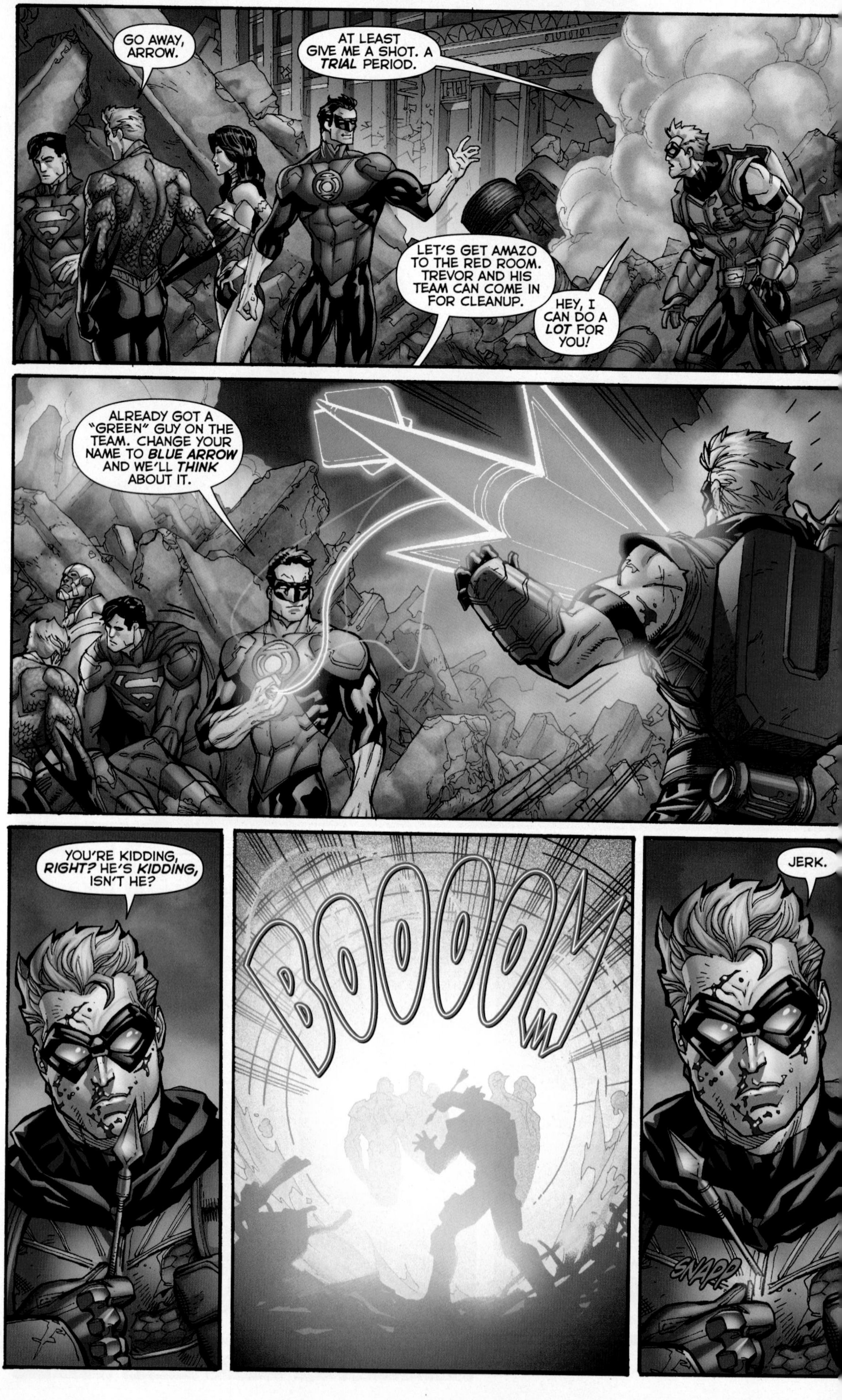
GO AWAY, ARROW.
AT LEAST GIVE ME A SHOT. A TRIAL PERIOD.
LET'S GET AMAZO TO THE RED ROOM. TREVOR AND HIS TEAM CAN COME IN FOR CLEANUP.
HEY, I CAN DO A LOT FOR YOU!
ALREADY GOT A "GREEN" GUY ON THE TEAM. CHANGE YOUR NAME TO BLUE ARROW AND WE'LL THINK ABOUT IT.
YOU'RE KIDDING, RIGHT? HE'S KIDDING, ISN'T HE?
BOOOOM
JERK.
SNAPP

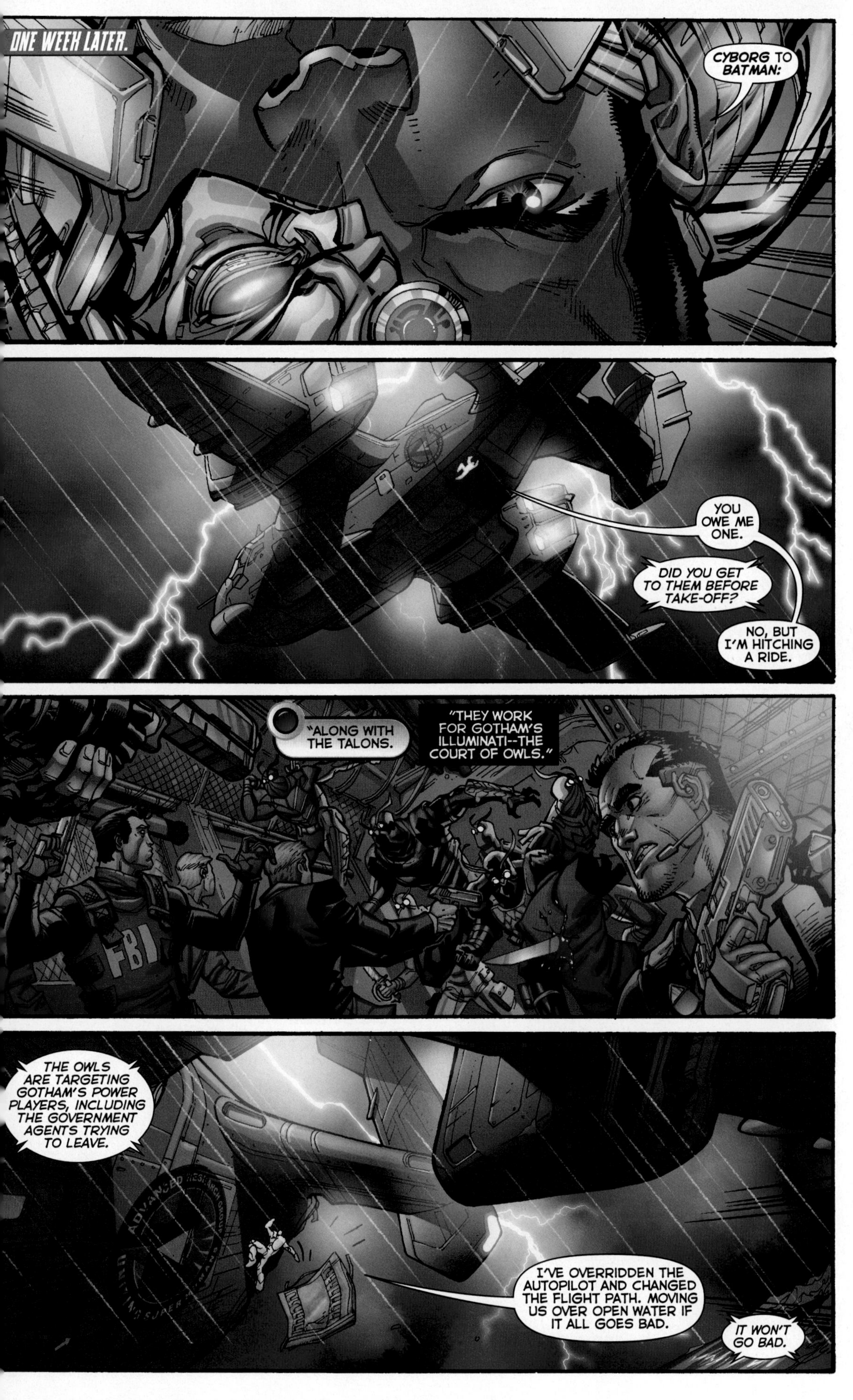
ONE WEEK LATER.
CYBORG TO BATMAN:
YOU OWE ME ONE.
DID YOU GET TO THEM BEFORE TAKE-OFF?
NO, BUT I'M HITCHING A RIDE.
"ALONG WITH THE TALONS.
"THEY WORK FOR GOTHAM'S ILLUMINATI--THE COURT OF OWLS."
FBI
THE OWLS ARE TARGETING GOTHAM'S POWER PLAYERS, INCLUDING THE GOVERNMENT AGENTS TRYING TO LEAVE.
I'VE OVERRIDDEN THE AUTOPILOT AND CHANGED THE FLIGHT PATH. MOVING US OVER OPEN WATER IF IT ALL GOES BAD.
IT WON'T GO BAD.

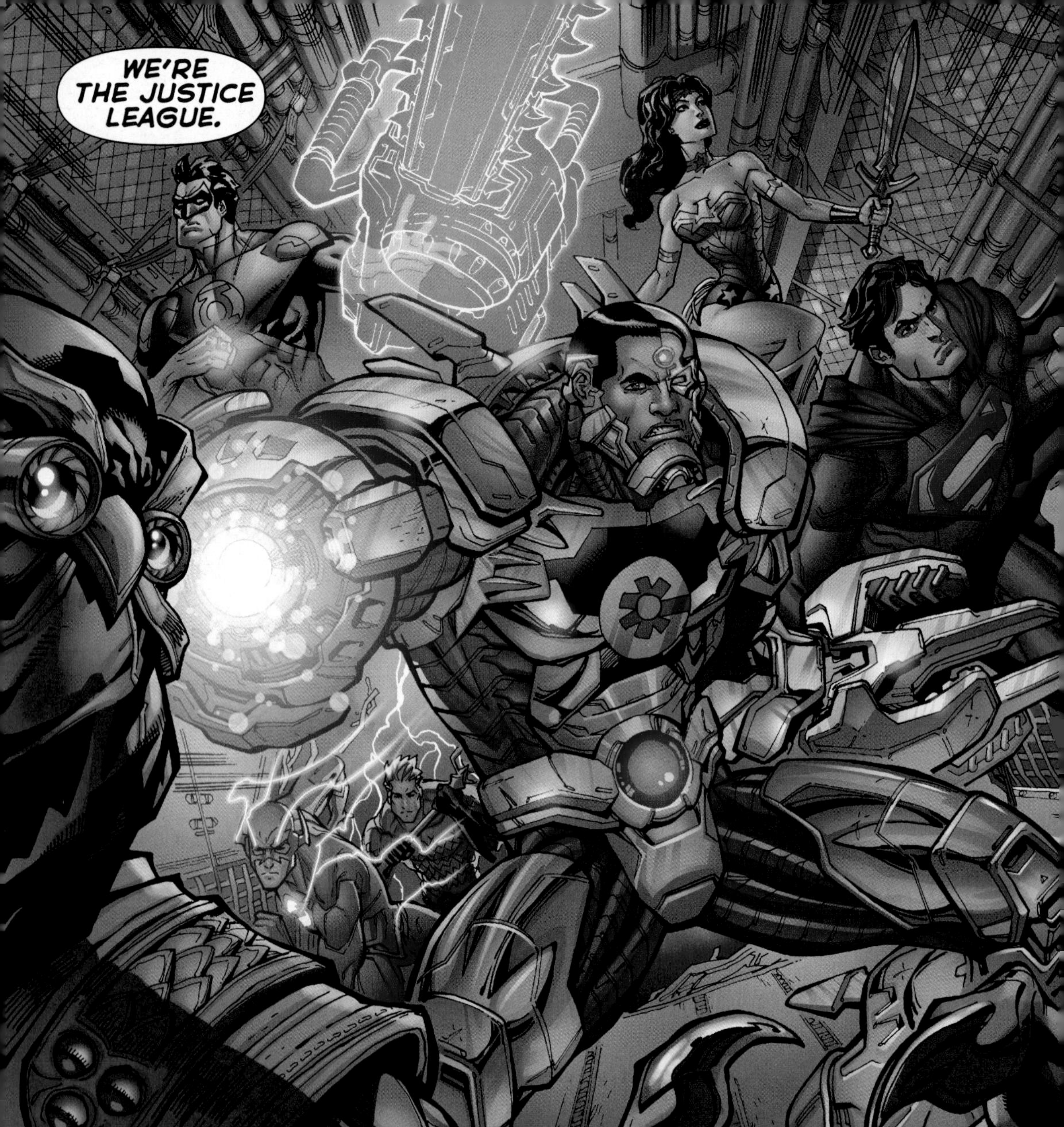
WE'RE THE JUSTICE LEAGUE.

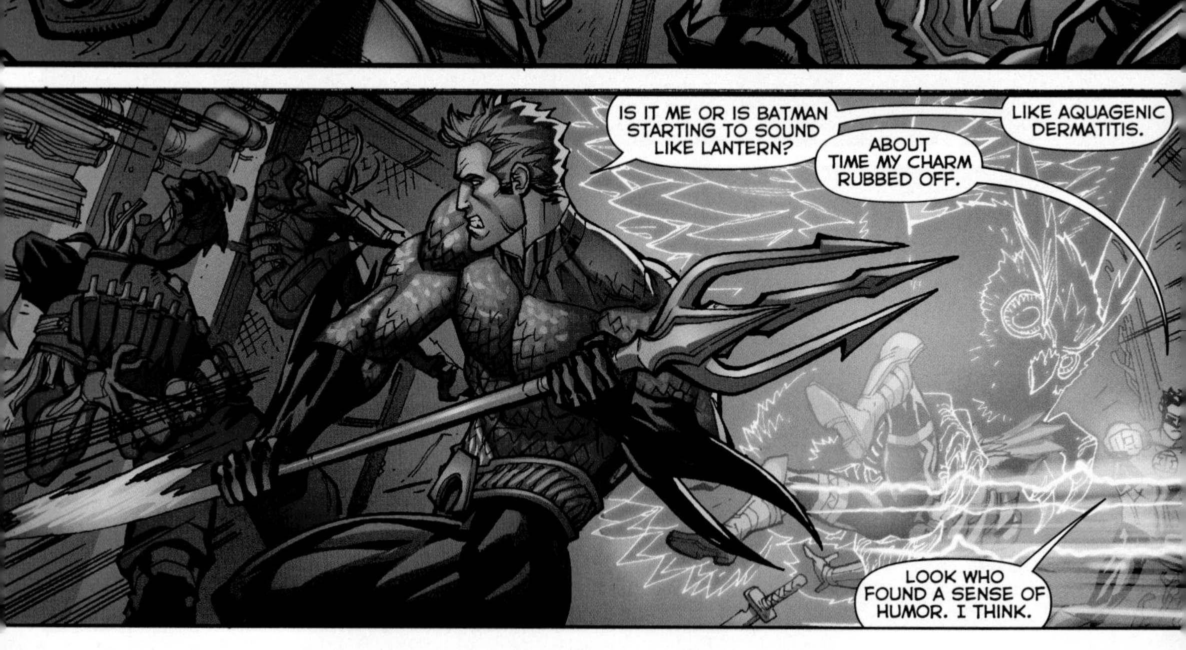
IS IT ME OR IS BATMAN STARTING TO SOUND LIKE LANTERN?
LIKE AQUAGENIC DERMATITIS.
ABOUT TIME MY CHARM RUBBED OFF.
LOOK WHO FOUND A SENSE OF HUMOR. I THINK.

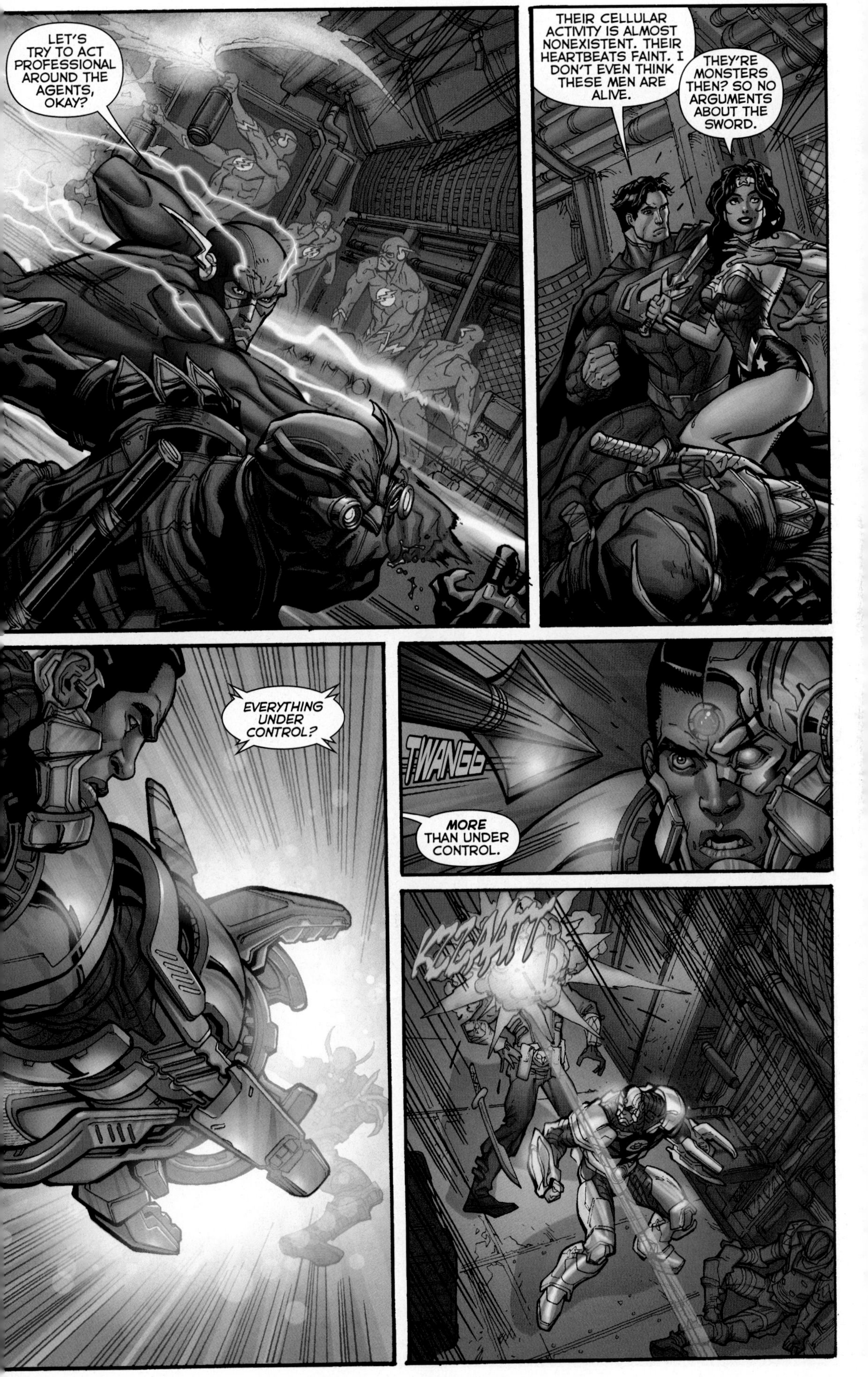
LET'S TRY TO ACT PROFESSIONAL AROUND THE AGENTS, OKAY?
THEIR CELLULAR ACTIVITY IS ALMOST NONEXISTENT. THEIR HEARTBEATS FAINT. I DON'T EVEN THINK THESE MEN ARE ALIVE.
THEY'RE MONSTERS THEN? SO NO ARGUMENTS ABOUT THE SWORD.
EVERYTHING UNDER CONTROL?
TWANGG
MORE THAN UNDER CONTROL.
KZZAAT

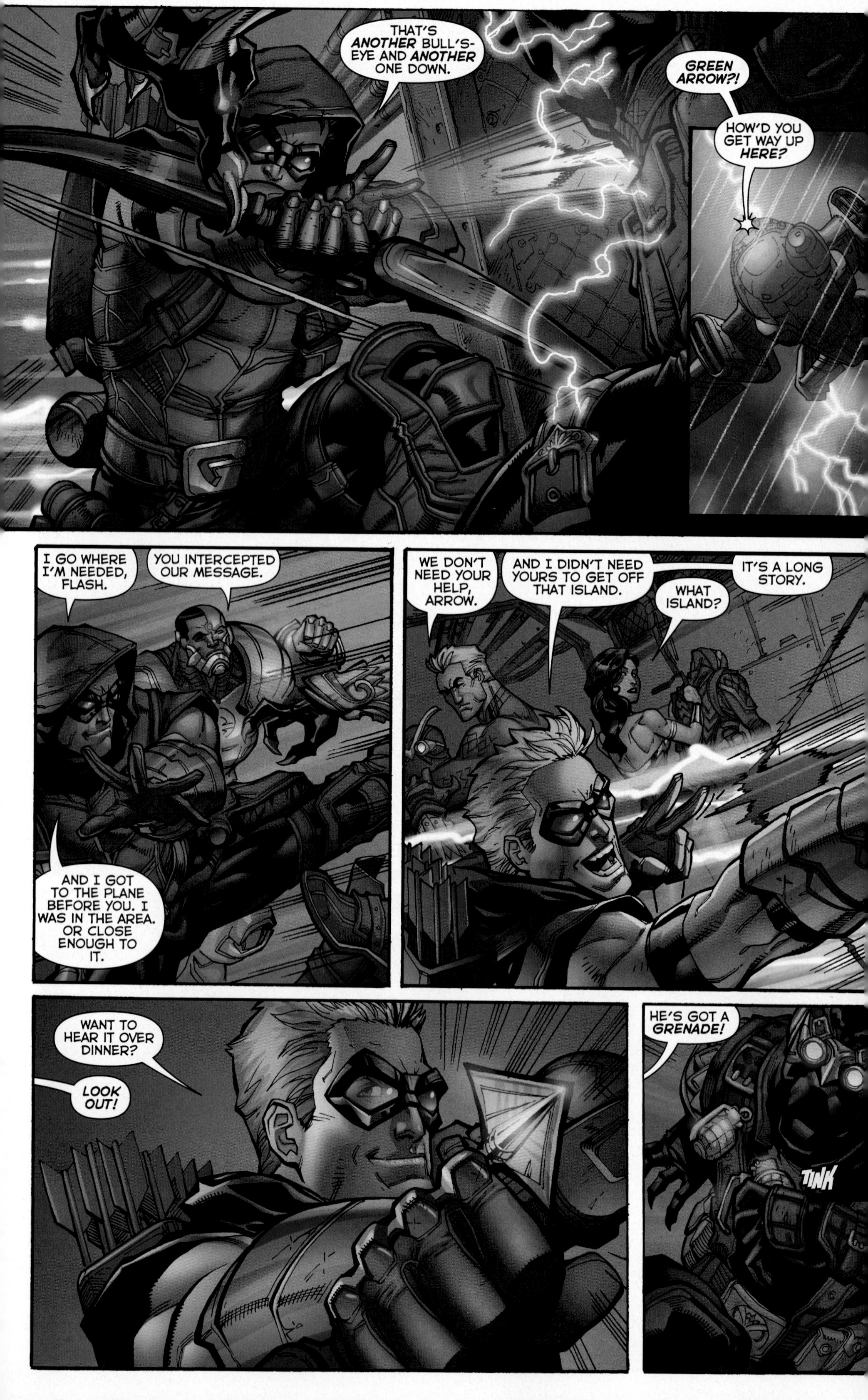

THAT'S ANOTHER BULL'S-EYE AND ANOTHER ONE DOWN.
GREEN ARROW?!
HOW'D YOU GET WAY UP HERE?
I GO WHERE I'M NEEDED, FLASH.
YOU INTERCEPTED OUR MESSAGE.
AND I GOT TO THE PLANE BEFORE YOU. I WAS IN THE AREA. OR CLOSE ENOUGH TO IT.
WE DON'T NEED YOUR HELP, ARROW.
AND I DIDN'T NEED YOURS TO GET OFF THAT ISLAND.
IT'S A LONG STORY.
WHAT ISLAND?
WANT TO HEAR IT OVER DINNER?
LOOK OUT!
HE'S GOT A GRENADE!
TINK

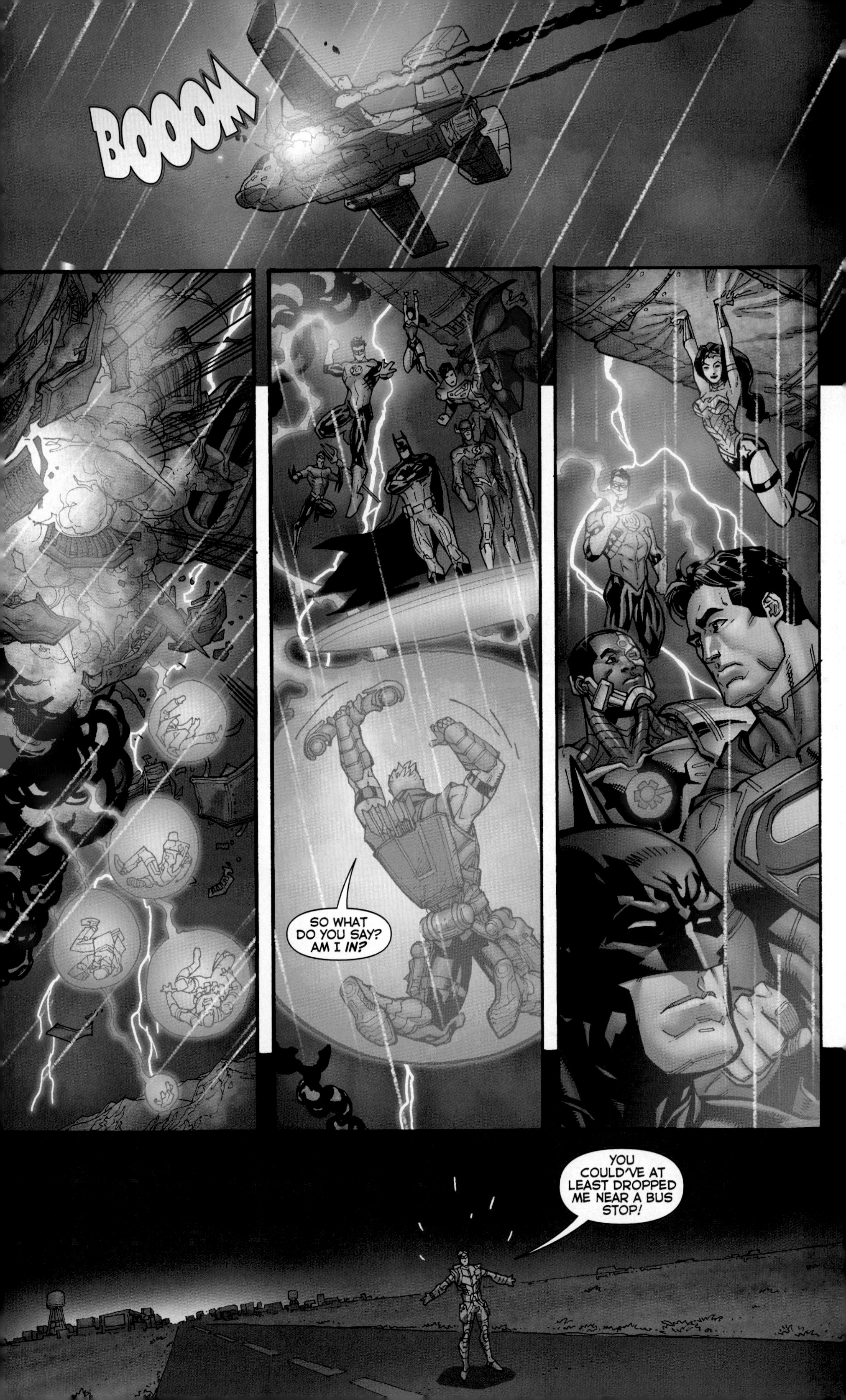
BOOOM
SO WHAT DO YOU SAY? AM I *IN?*
YOU COULD'VE AT LEAST DROPPED ME NEAR A BUS STOP!

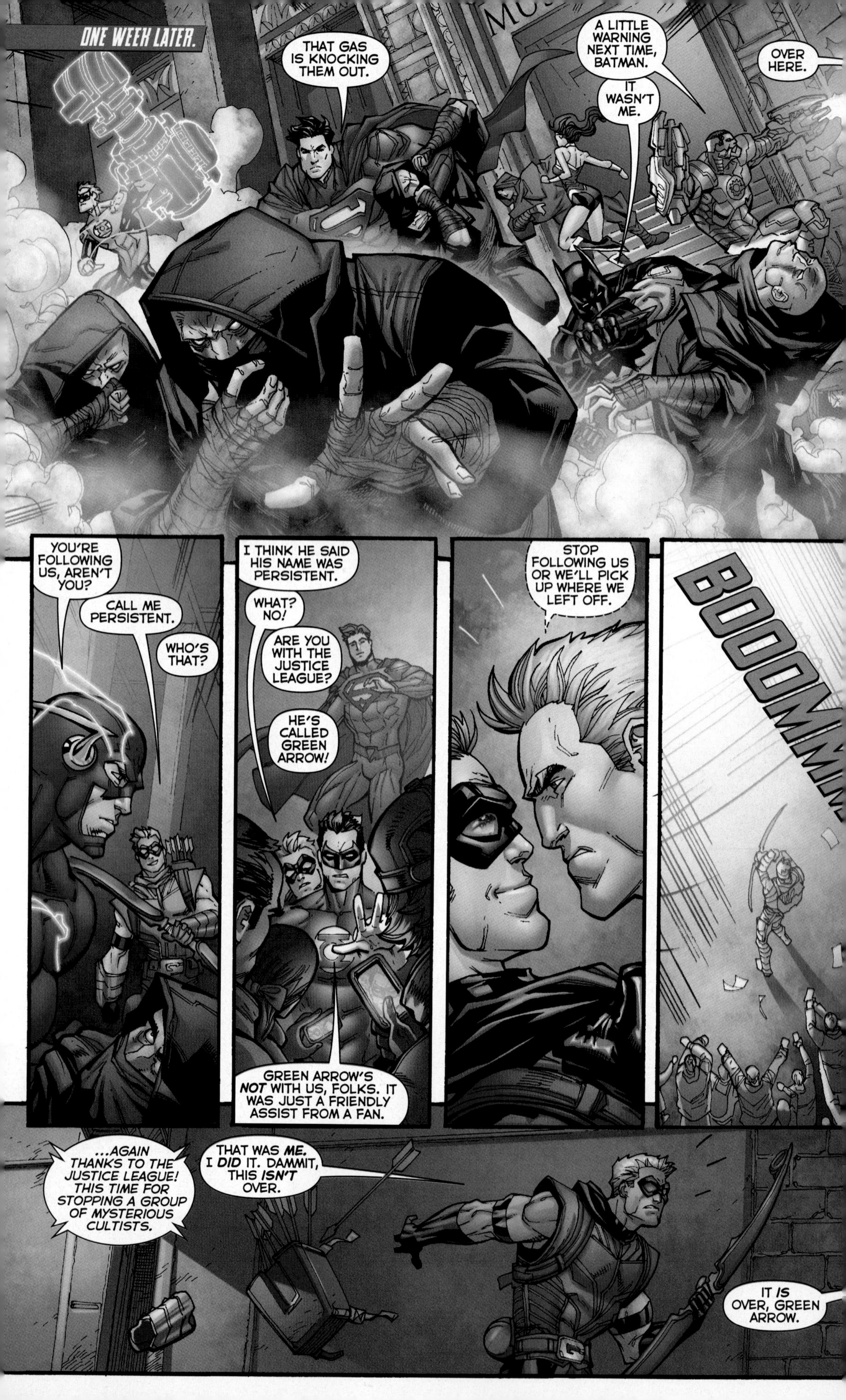
ONE WEEK LATER.
THAT GAS IS KNOCKING THEM OUT.
A LITTLE WARNING NEXT TIME, BATMAN.
IT WASN'T ME.
OVER HERE.
YOU'RE FOLLOWING US, AREN'T YOU?
CALL ME PERSISTENT.
WHO'S THAT?
I THINK HE SAID HIS NAME WAS PERSISTENT.
WHAT? NO!
ARE YOU WITH THE JUSTICE LEAGUE?
HE'S CALLED GREEN ARROW!
GREEN ARROW'S NOT WITH US, FOLKS. IT WAS JUST A FRIENDLY ASSIST FROM A FAN.
STOP FOLLOWING US OR WE'LL PICK UP WHERE WE LEFT OFF.
BOOOMMM
...AGAIN THANKS TO THE JUSTICE LEAGUE! THIS TIME FOR STOPPING A GROUP OF MYSTERIOUS CULTISTS.
THAT WAS ME. I DID IT. DAMMIT, THIS ISN'T OVER.
IT IS OVER, GREEN ARROW.

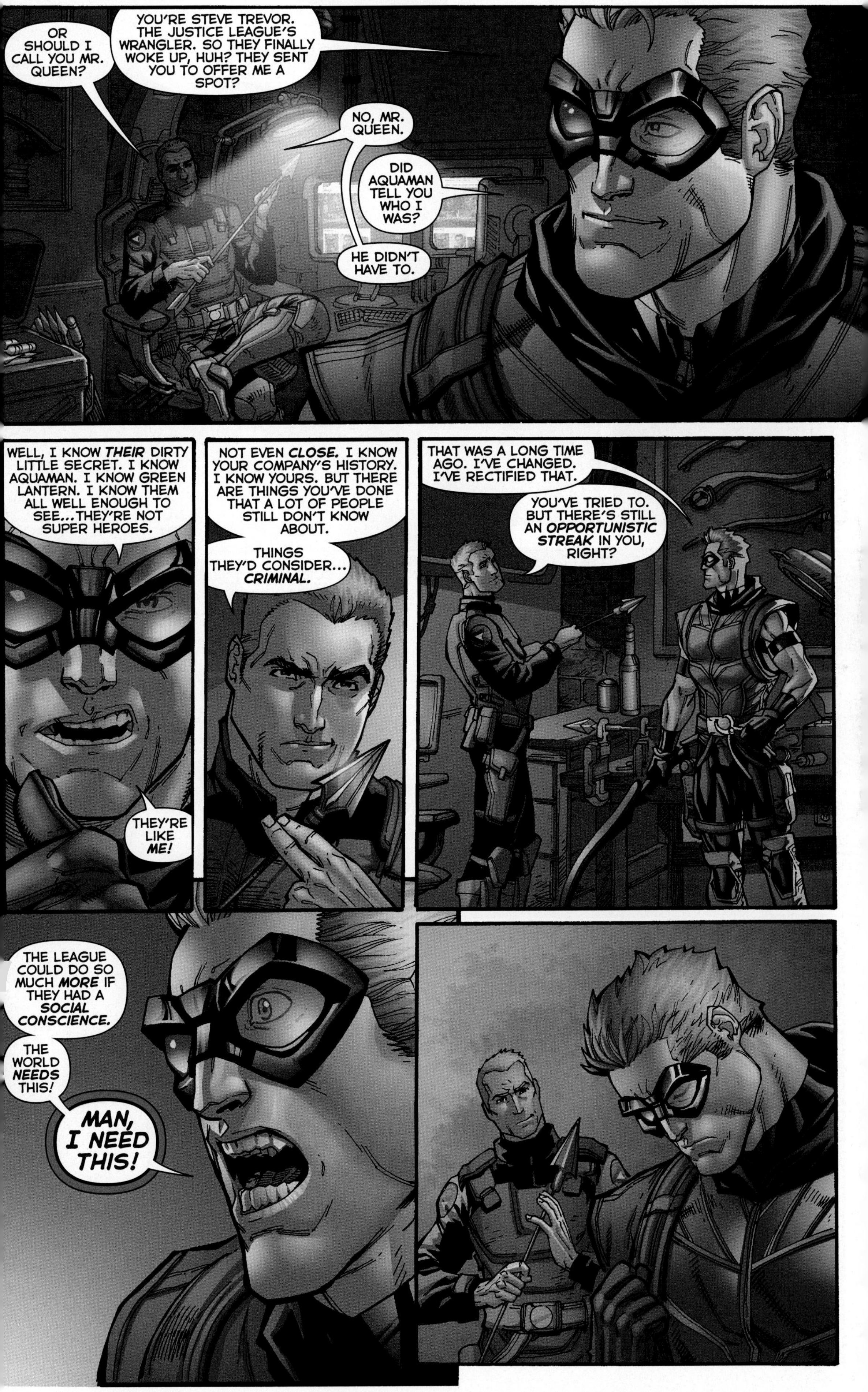
OR SHOULD I CALL YOU MR. QUEEN?
YOU'RE STEVE TREVOR. THE JUSTICE LEAGUE'S WRANGLER. SO THEY FINALLY WOKE UP, HUH? THEY SENT YOU TO OFFER ME A SPOT?
NO, MR. QUEEN.
DID AQUAMAN TELL YOU WHO I WAS?
HE DIDN'T HAVE TO.
WELL, I KNOW *THEIR* DIRTY LITTLE SECRET. I KNOW AQUAMAN. I KNOW GREEN LANTERN. I KNOW THEM ALL WELL ENOUGH TO SEE...THEY'RE NOT SUPER HEROES.
THEY'RE LIKE *ME!*
NOT EVEN *CLOSE.* I KNOW YOUR COMPANY'S HISTORY. I KNOW YOURS. BUT THERE ARE THINGS YOU'VE DONE THAT A LOT OF PEOPLE STILL DON'T KNOW ABOUT.
THINGS THEY'D CONSIDER... *CRIMINAL.*
THAT WAS A LONG TIME AGO. I'VE CHANGED. I'VE RECTIFIED THAT.
YOU'VE TRIED TO. BUT THERE'S STILL AN *OPPORTUNISTIC STREAK* IN YOU, RIGHT?
THE LEAGUE COULD DO SO MUCH *MORE* IF THEY HAD A *SOCIAL CONSCIENCE.*
THE WORLD *NEEDS* THIS!
MAN, I NEED THIS!

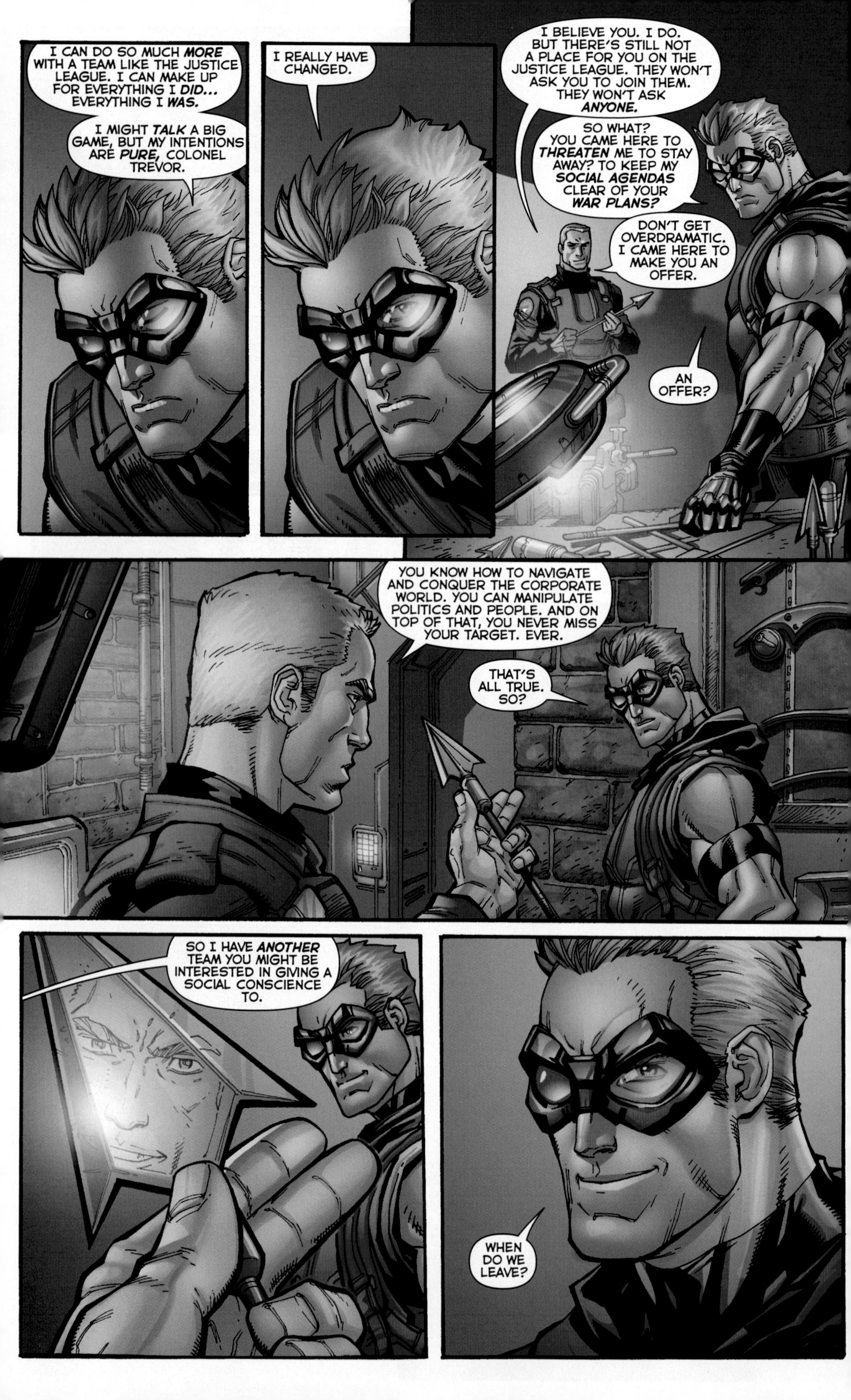
I CAN DO SO MUCH MORE WITH A TEAM LIKE THE JUSTICE LEAGUE. I CAN MAKE UP FOR EVERYTHING I DID... EVERYTHING I WAS.
I MIGHT TALK A BIG GAME, BUT MY INTENTIONS ARE PURE, COLONEL TREVOR.
I REALLY HAVE CHANGED.
I BELIEVE YOU. I DO. BUT THERE'S STILL NOT A PLACE FOR YOU ON THE JUSTICE LEAGUE. THEY WON'T ASK YOU TO JOIN THEM. THEY WON'T ASK ANYONE.
SO WHAT? YOU CAME HERE TO THREATEN ME TO STAY AWAY? TO KEEP MY SOCIAL AGENDAS CLEAR OF YOUR WAR PLANS?
DON'T GET OVERDRAMATIC. I CAME HERE TO MAKE YOU AN OFFER.
AN OFFER?
YOU KNOW HOW TO NAVIGATE AND CONQUER THE CORPORATE WORLD. YOU CAN MANIPULATE POLITICS AND PEOPLE. AND ON TOP OF THAT, YOU NEVER MISS YOUR TARGET. EVER.
THAT'S ALL TRUE. SO?
SO I HAVE ANOTHER TEAM YOU MIGHT BE INTERESTED IN GIVING A SOCIAL CONSCIENCE TO.
WHEN DO WE LEAVE?

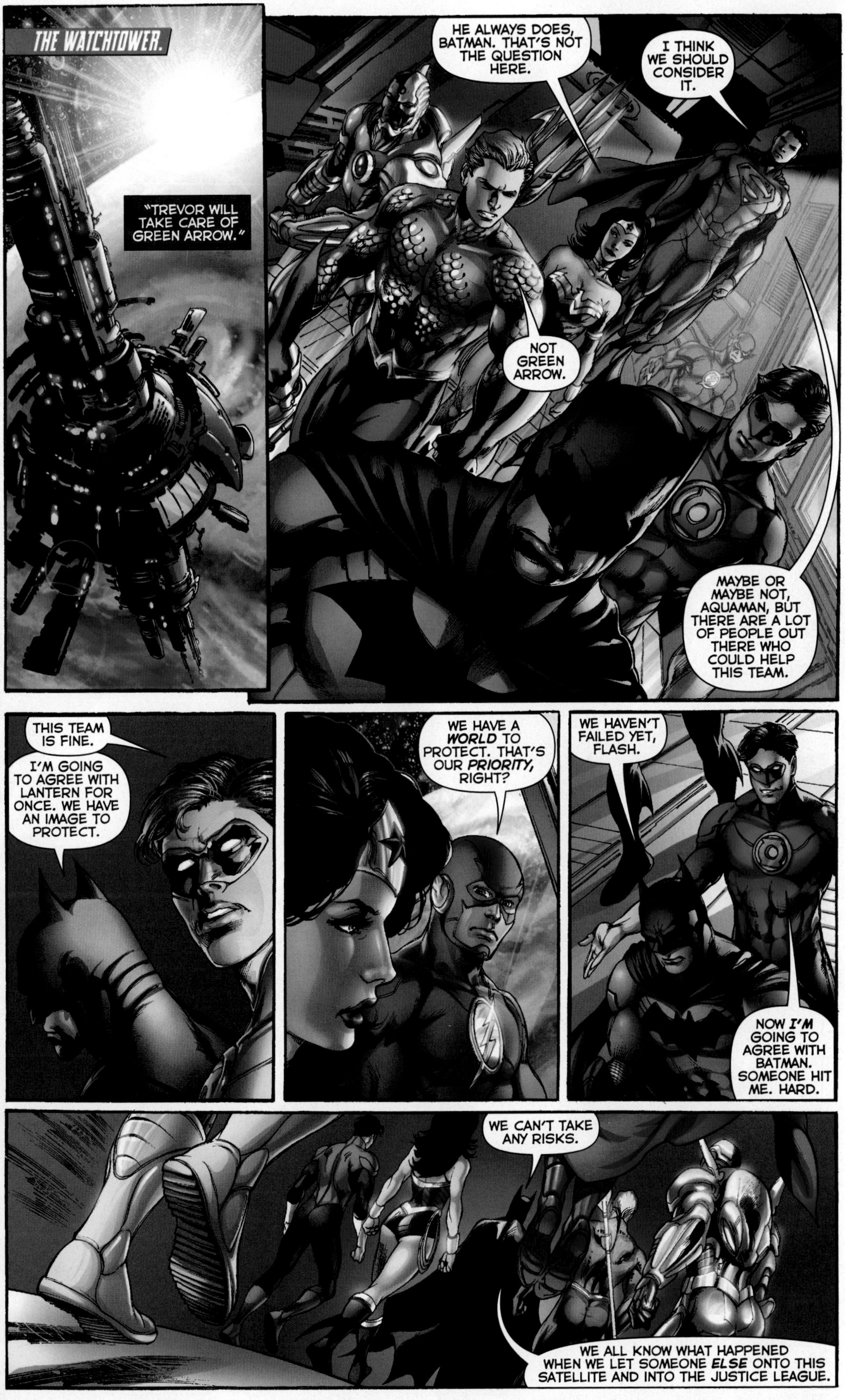
THE WATCHTOWER.
"TREVOR WILL TAKE CARE OF GREEN ARROW."
HE ALWAYS DOES, BATMAN. THAT'S NOT THE QUESTION HERE.
I THINK WE SHOULD CONSIDER IT.
NOT GREEN ARROW.
MAYBE OR MAYBE NOT, AQUAMAN, BUT THERE ARE A LOT OF PEOPLE OUT THERE WHO COULD HELP THIS TEAM.
THIS TEAM IS FINE.
I'M GOING TO AGREE WITH LANTERN FOR ONCE. WE HAVE AN IMAGE TO PROTECT.
WE HAVE A *WORLD* TO PROTECT. THAT'S OUR *PRIORITY,* RIGHT?
WE HAVEN'T FAILED YET, FLASH.
NOW *I'M* GOING TO AGREE WITH BATMAN. SOMEONE HIT ME. HARD.
WE CAN'T TAKE ANY RISKS.
WE ALL KNOW WHAT HAPPENED WHEN WE LET SOMEONE *ELSE* ONTO THIS SATELLITE AND INTO THE JUSTICE LEAGUE.

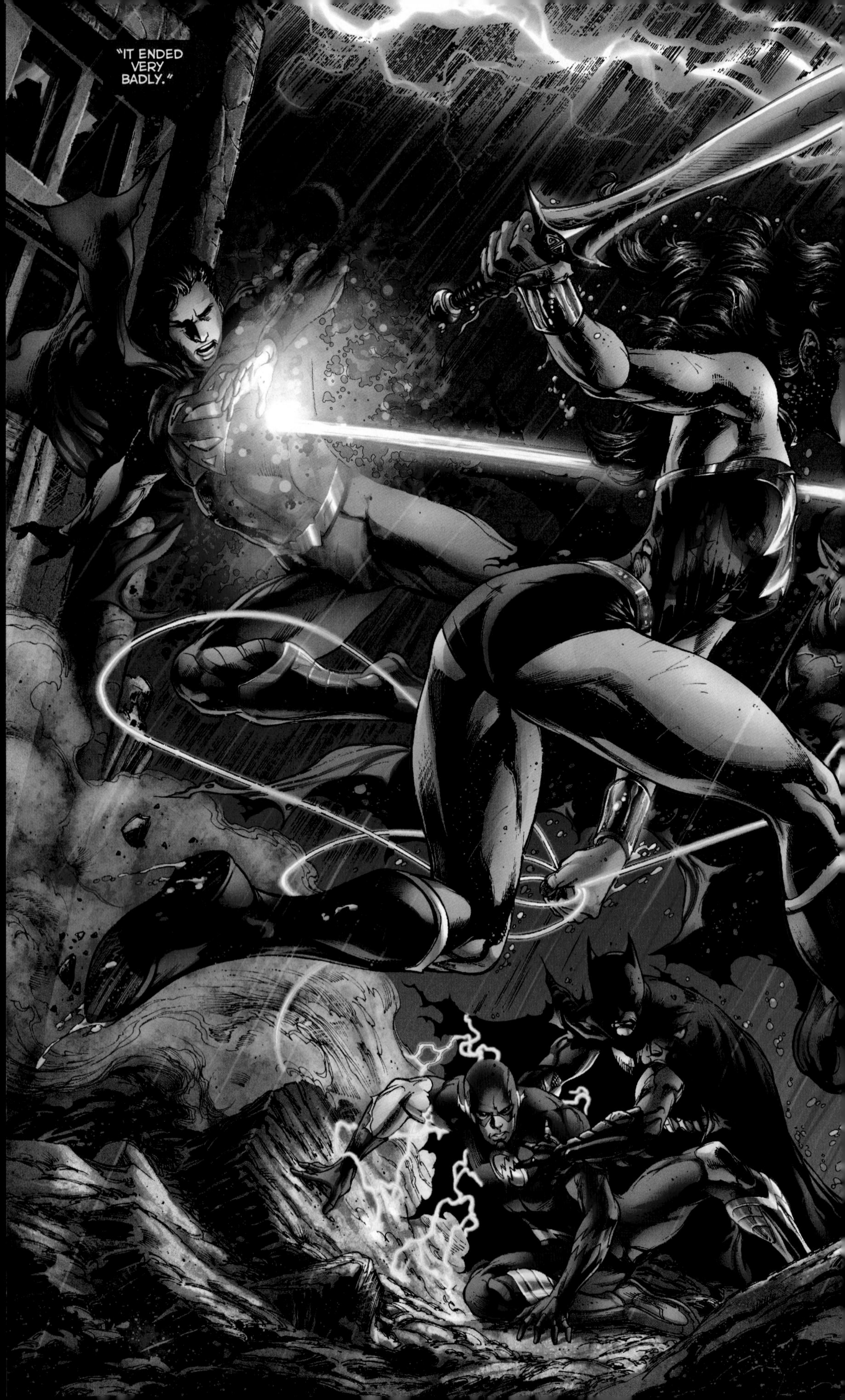
"IT ENDED VERY BADLY."

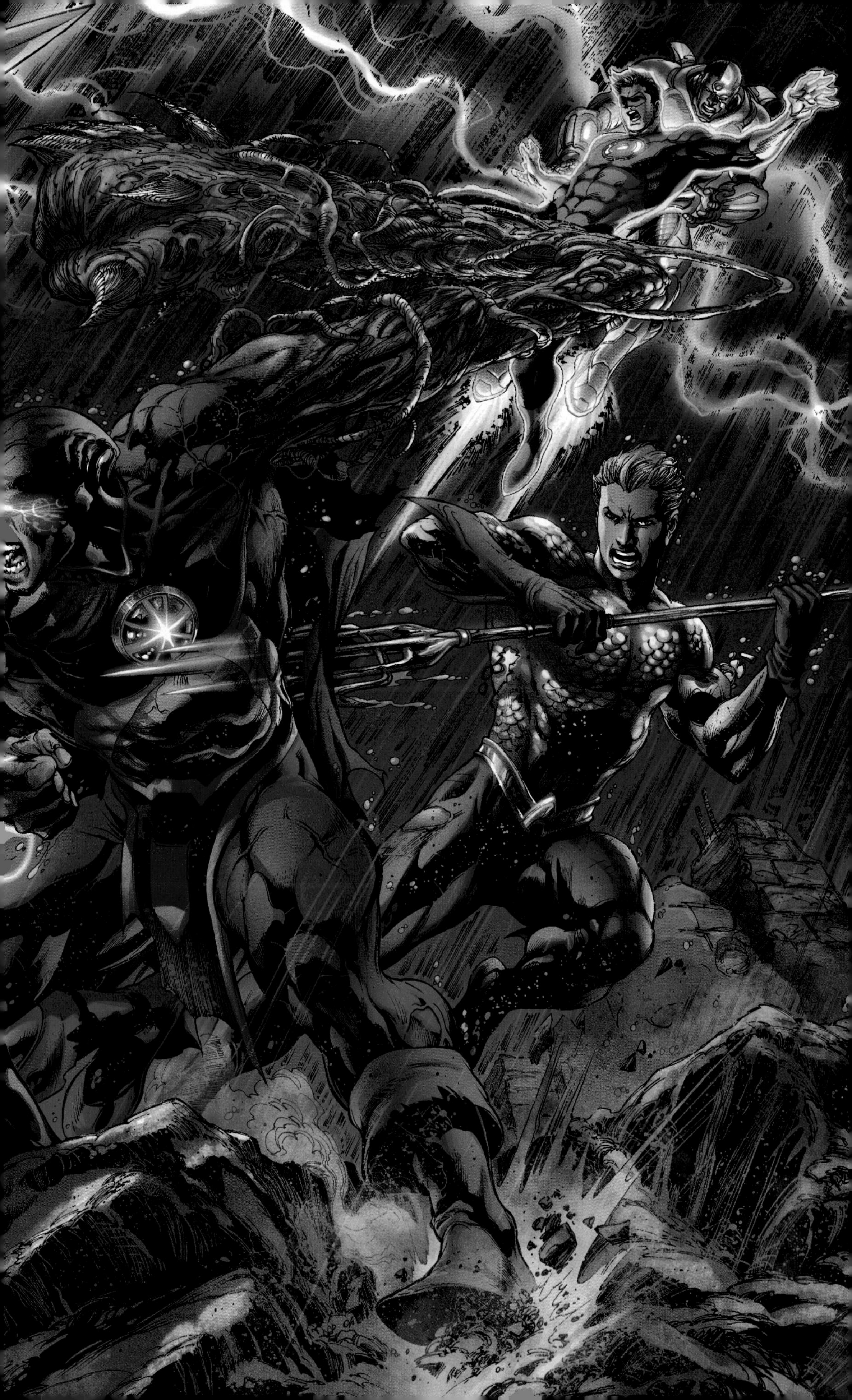

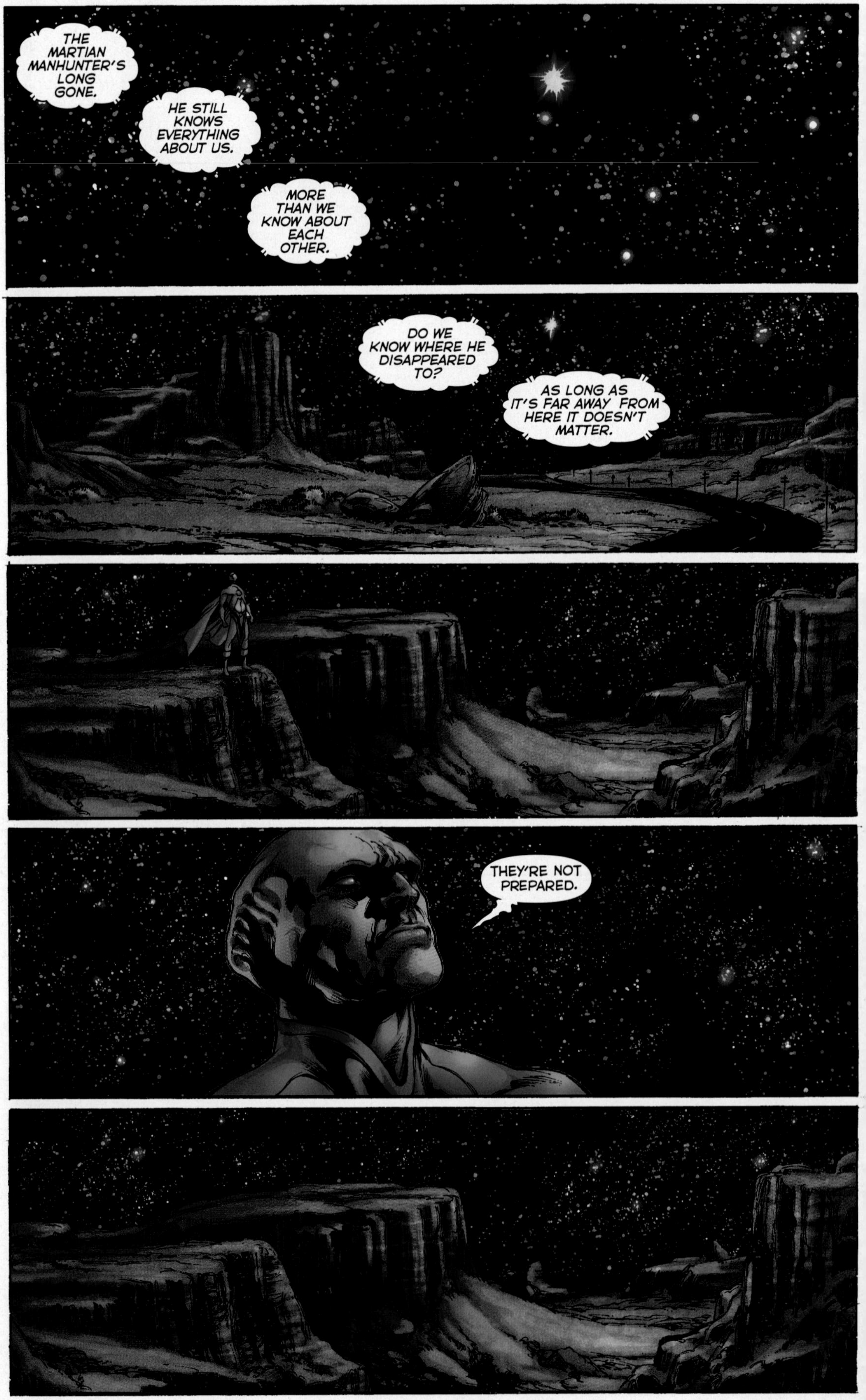
THE MARTIAN MANHUNTER'S LONG GONE.
HE STILL KNOWS EVERYTHING ABOUT US.
MORE THAN WE KNOW ABOUT EACH OTHER.
DO WE KNOW WHERE HE DISAPPEARED TO?
AS LONG AS IT'S FAR AWAY FROM HERE IT DOESN'T MATTER.
THEY'RE NOT PREPARED.

ON THE OUTS

GEOFF JOHNS & JEFF LEMIRE writers BRAD WALKER penciller DREW HENNESSY inker

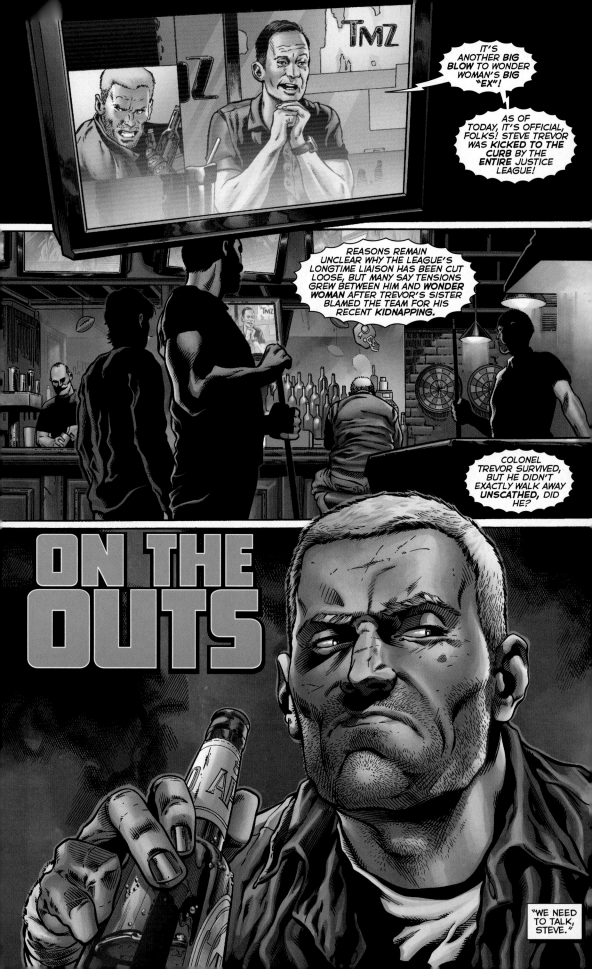

TMZ

IT'S ANOTHER BIG BLOW TO WONDER WOMAN'S BIG "EX"!

AS OF TODAY, IT'S OFFICIAL, FOLKS! STEVE TREVOR WAS KICKED TO THE CURB BY THE ENTIRE JUSTICE LEAGUE!

REASONS REMAIN UNCLEAR WHY THE LEAGUE'S LONGTIME LIAISON HAS BEEN CUT LOOSE, BUT MANY SAY TENSIONS GREW BETWEEN HIM AND WONDER WOMAN AFTER TREVOR'S SISTER BLAMED THE TEAM FOR HIS RECENT KIDNAPPING.

COLONEL TREVOR SURVIVED, BUT HE DIDN'T EXACTLY WALK AWAY UNSCATHED, DID HE?

ON THE OUTS

"WE NEED TO TALK, STEVE."

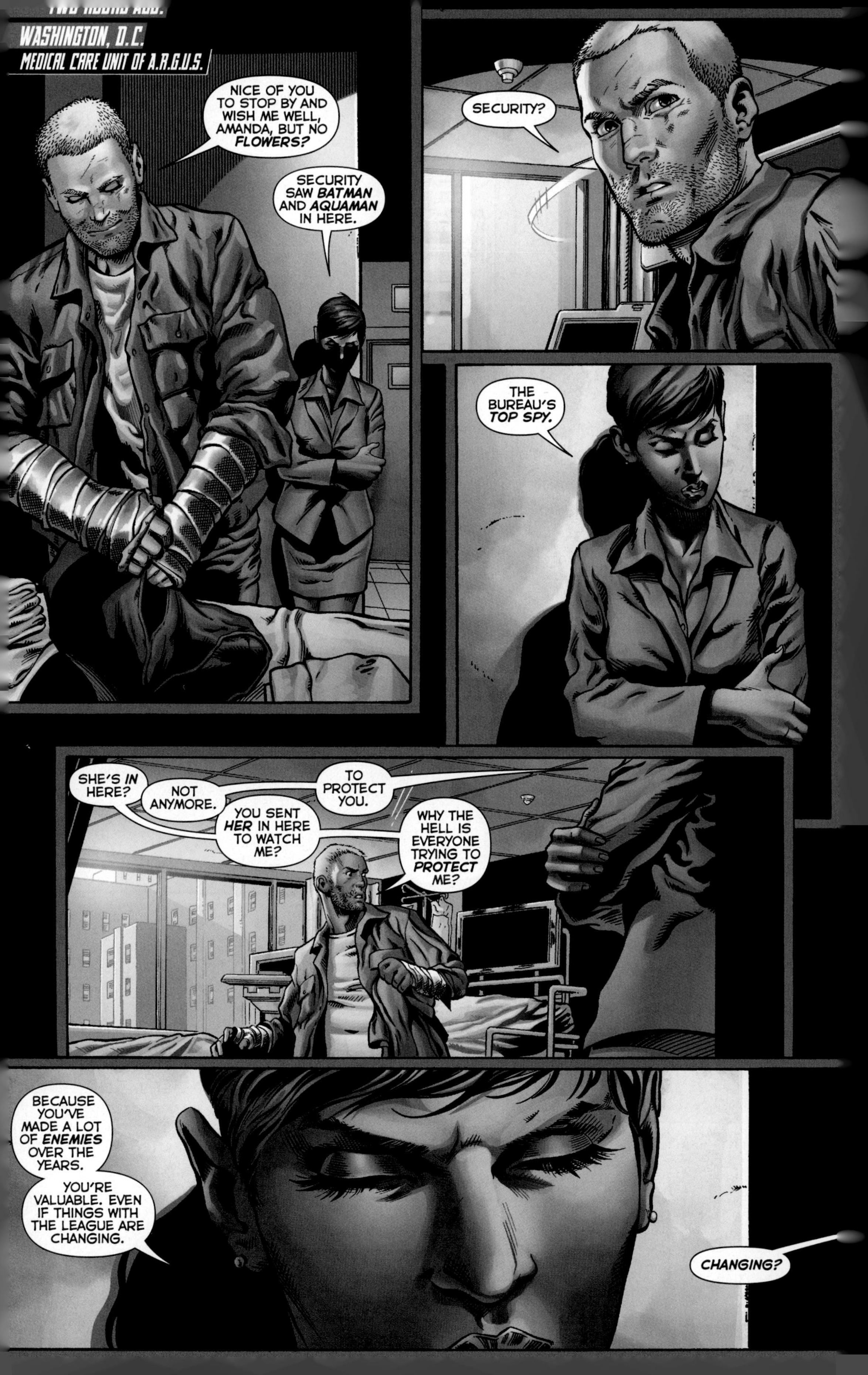
WASHINGTON, D.C.
MEDICAL CARE UNIT OF A.R.G.U.S.
NICE OF YOU TO STOP BY AND WISH ME WELL, AMANDA, BUT NO FLOWERS?
SECURITY SAW BATMAN AND AQUAMAN IN HERE.
SECURITY?
THE BUREAU'S TOP SPY.
SHE'S IN HERE?
NOT ANYMORE.
TO PROTECT YOU.
YOU SENT HER IN HERE TO WATCH ME?
WHY THE HELL IS EVERYONE TRYING TO PROTECT ME?
BECAUSE YOU'VE MADE A LOT OF ENEMIES OVER THE YEARS.
YOU'RE VALUABLE. EVEN IF THINGS WITH THE LEAGUE ARE CHANGING.
CHANGING?

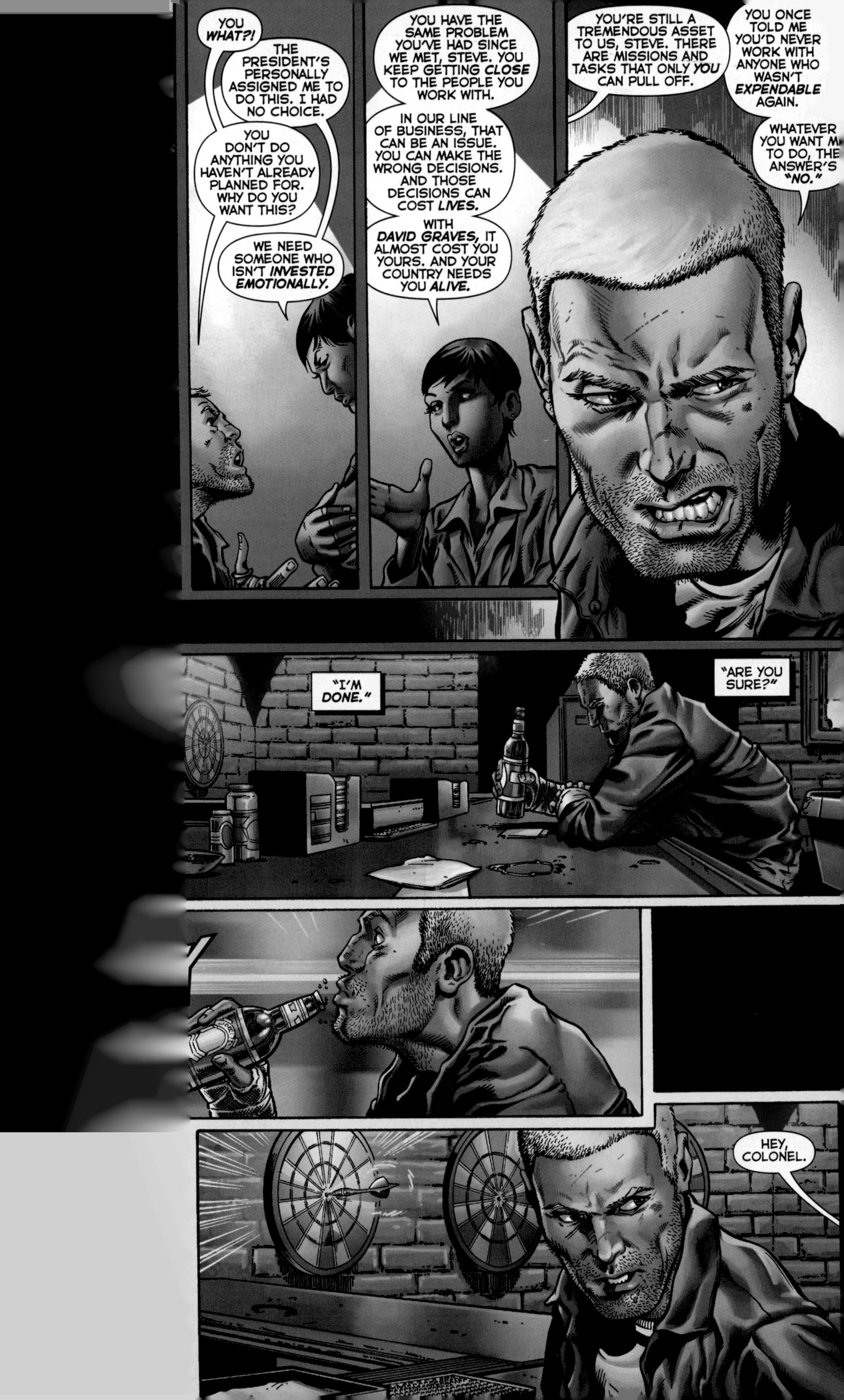
YOU WHAT?!
THE PRESIDENT'S PERSONALLY ASSIGNED ME TO DO THIS. I HAD NO CHOICE.
YOU DON'T DO ANYTHING YOU HAVEN'T ALREADY PLANNED FOR. WHY DO YOU WANT THIS?
WE NEED SOMEONE WHO ISN'T INVESTED EMOTIONALLY.
YOU HAVE THE SAME PROBLEM YOU'VE HAD SINCE WE MET, STEVE. YOU KEEP GETTING CLOSE TO THE PEOPLE YOU WORK WITH.
IN OUR LINE OF BUSINESS, THAT CAN BE AN ISSUE. YOU CAN MAKE THE WRONG DECISIONS. AND THOSE DECISIONS CAN COST LIVES.
WITH DAVID GRAVES, IT ALMOST COST YOU YOURS. AND YOUR COUNTRY NEEDS YOU ALIVE.
YOU'RE STILL A TREMENDOUS ASSET TO US, STEVE. THERE ARE MISSIONS AND TASKS THAT ONLY YOU CAN PULL OFF.
YOU ONCE TOLD ME YOU'D NEVER WORK WITH ANYONE WHO WASN'T EXPENDABLE AGAIN.
WHATEVER YOU WANT M TO DO, THE ANSWER'S "NO."
"I'M DONE."
"ARE YOU SURE?"
HEY, COLONEL.

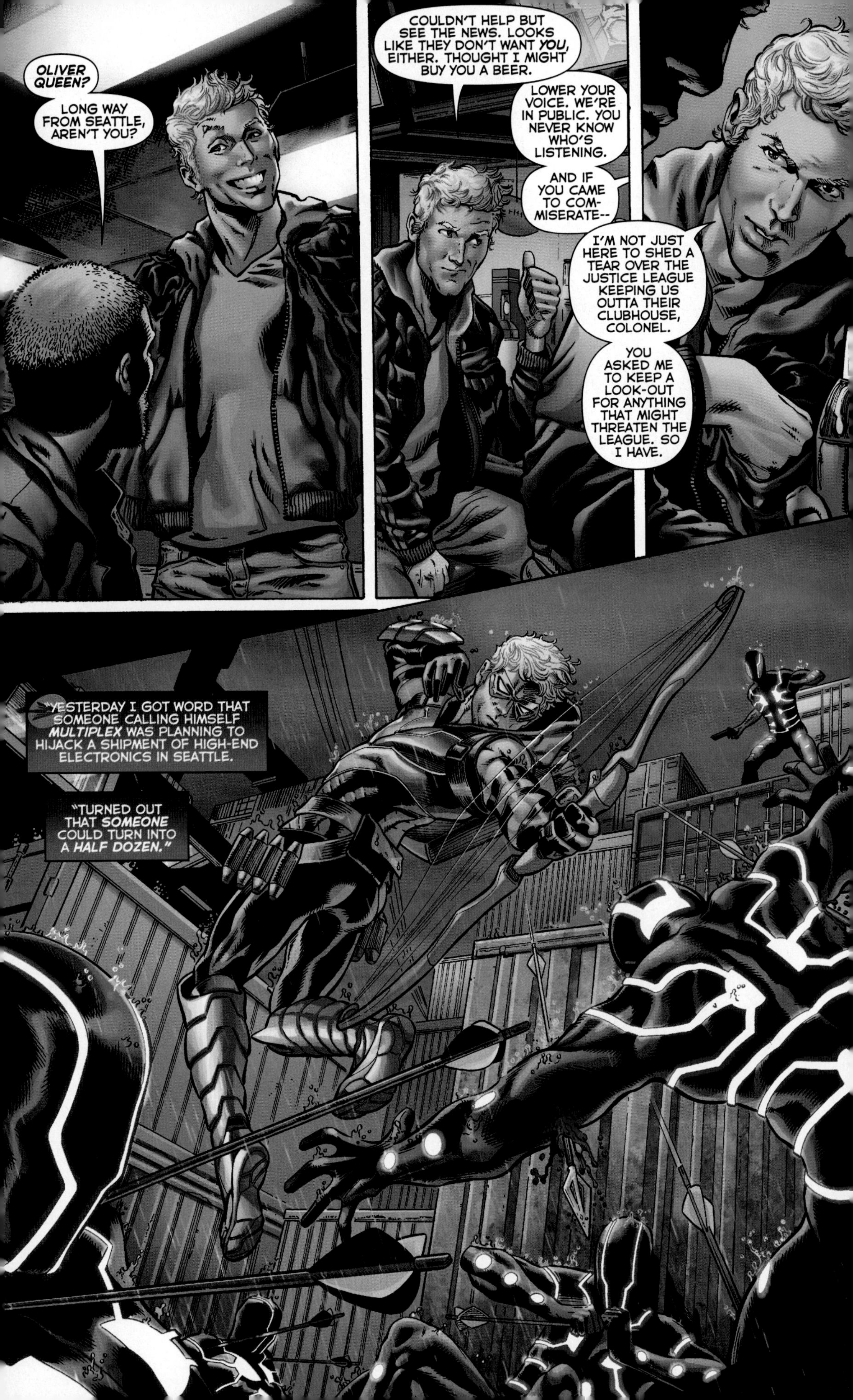

OLIVER QUEEN?
LONG WAY FROM SEATTLE, AREN'T YOU?
COULDN'T HELP BUT SEE THE NEWS. LOOKS LIKE THEY DON'T WANT YOU, EITHER. THOUGHT I MIGHT BUY YOU A BEER.
LOWER YOUR VOICE. WE'RE IN PUBLIC. YOU NEVER KNOW WHO'S LISTENING.
AND IF YOU CAME TO COM-MISERATE--
I'M NOT JUST HERE TO SHED A TEAR OVER THE JUSTICE LEAGUE KEEPING US OUTTA THEIR CLUBHOUSE, COLONEL.
YOU ASKED ME TO KEEP A LOOK-OUT FOR ANYTHING THAT MIGHT THREATEN THE LEAGUE. SO I HAVE.
"YESTERDAY I GOT WORD THAT SOMEONE CALLING HIMSELF MULTIPLEX WAS PLANNING TO HIJACK A SHIPMENT OF HIGH-END ELECTRONICS IN SEATTLE.
"TURNED OUT THAT SOMEONE COULD TURN INTO A HALF DOZEN."

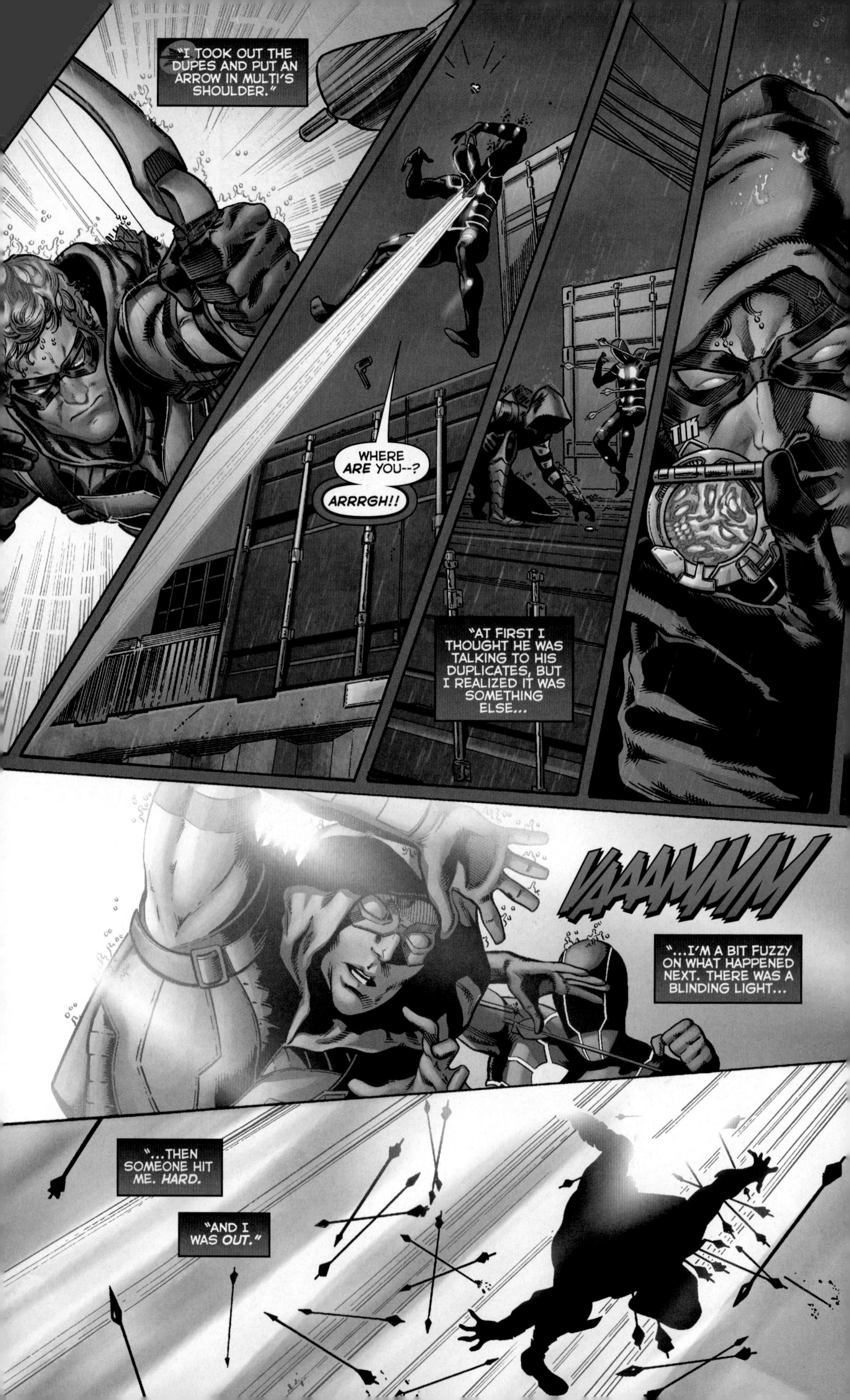
"I TOOK OUT THE DUPES AND PUT AN ARROW IN MULTI'S SHOULDER."
WHERE ARE YOU--?
ARRRGH!!
"AT FIRST I THOUGHT HE WAS TALKING TO HIS DUPLICATES, BUT I REALIZED IT WAS SOMETHING ELSE...
VAAMMM
"...I'M A BIT FUZZY ON WHAT HAPPENED NEXT. THERE WAS A BLINDING LIGHT...
"...THEN SOMEONE HIT ME. HARD.
"AND I WAS OUT."

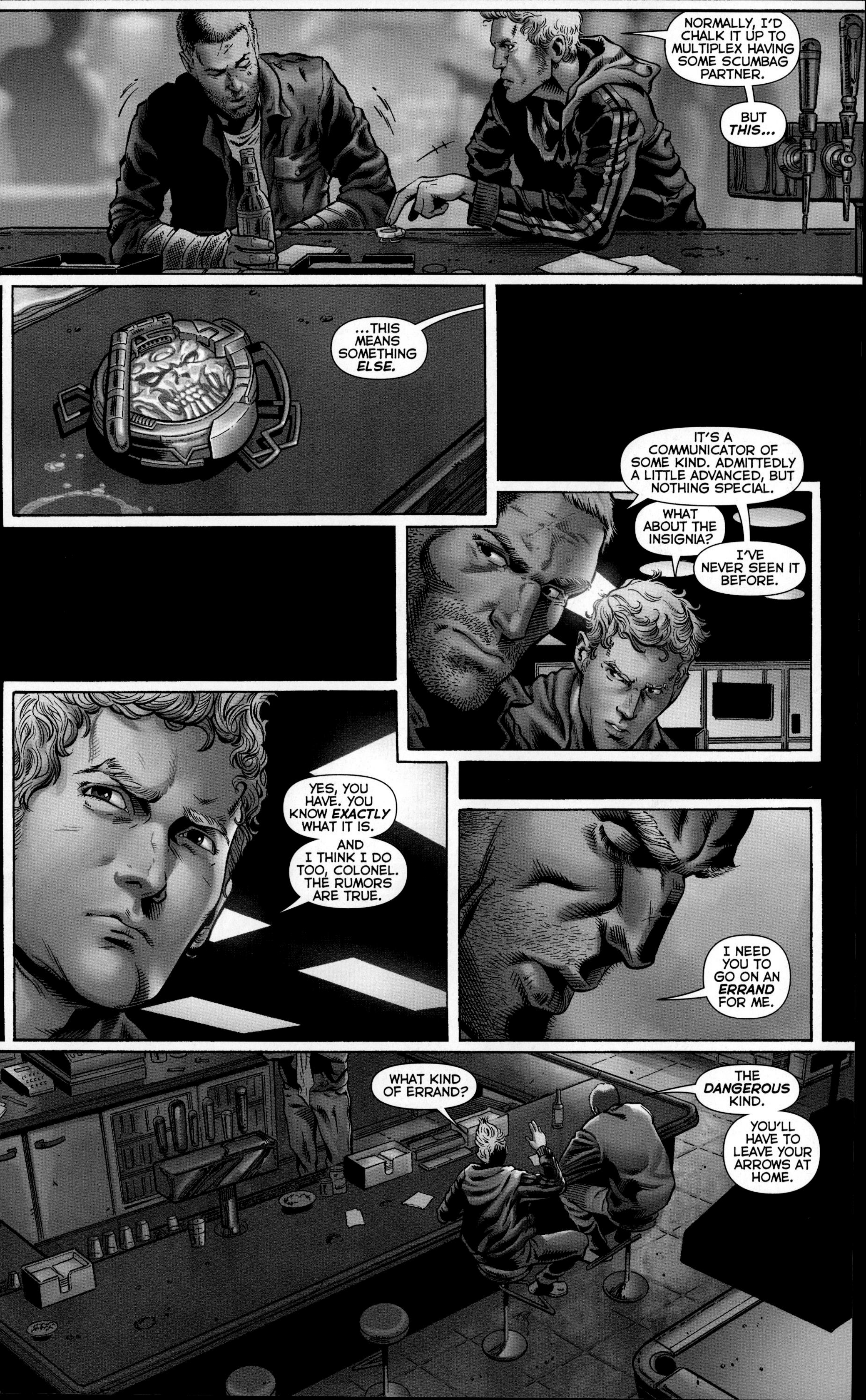
NORMALLY, I'D CHALK IT UP TO MULTIPLEX HAVING SOME SCUMBAG PARTNER.
BUT THIS...
...THIS MEANS SOMETHING ELSE.
IT'S A COMMUNICATOR OF SOME KIND. ADMITTEDLY A LITTLE ADVANCED, BUT NOTHING SPECIAL.
WHAT ABOUT THE INSIGNIA?
I'VE NEVER SEEN IT BEFORE.
YES, YOU HAVE. YOU KNOW EXACTLY WHAT IT IS.
AND I THINK I DO TOO, COLONEL. THE RUMORS ARE TRUE.
I NEED YOU TO GO ON AN ERRAND FOR ME.
WHAT KIND OF ERRAND?
THE DANGEROUS KIND.
YOU'LL HAVE TO LEAVE YOUR ARROWS AT HOME.

MAKE IT RIGHT

JUDD WINICK writer **FREDDIE WILLIAMS II** penciller **ROB HUNTER** inker cover by **IVAN REIS** and **JOE PRADO** with **HI-FI**

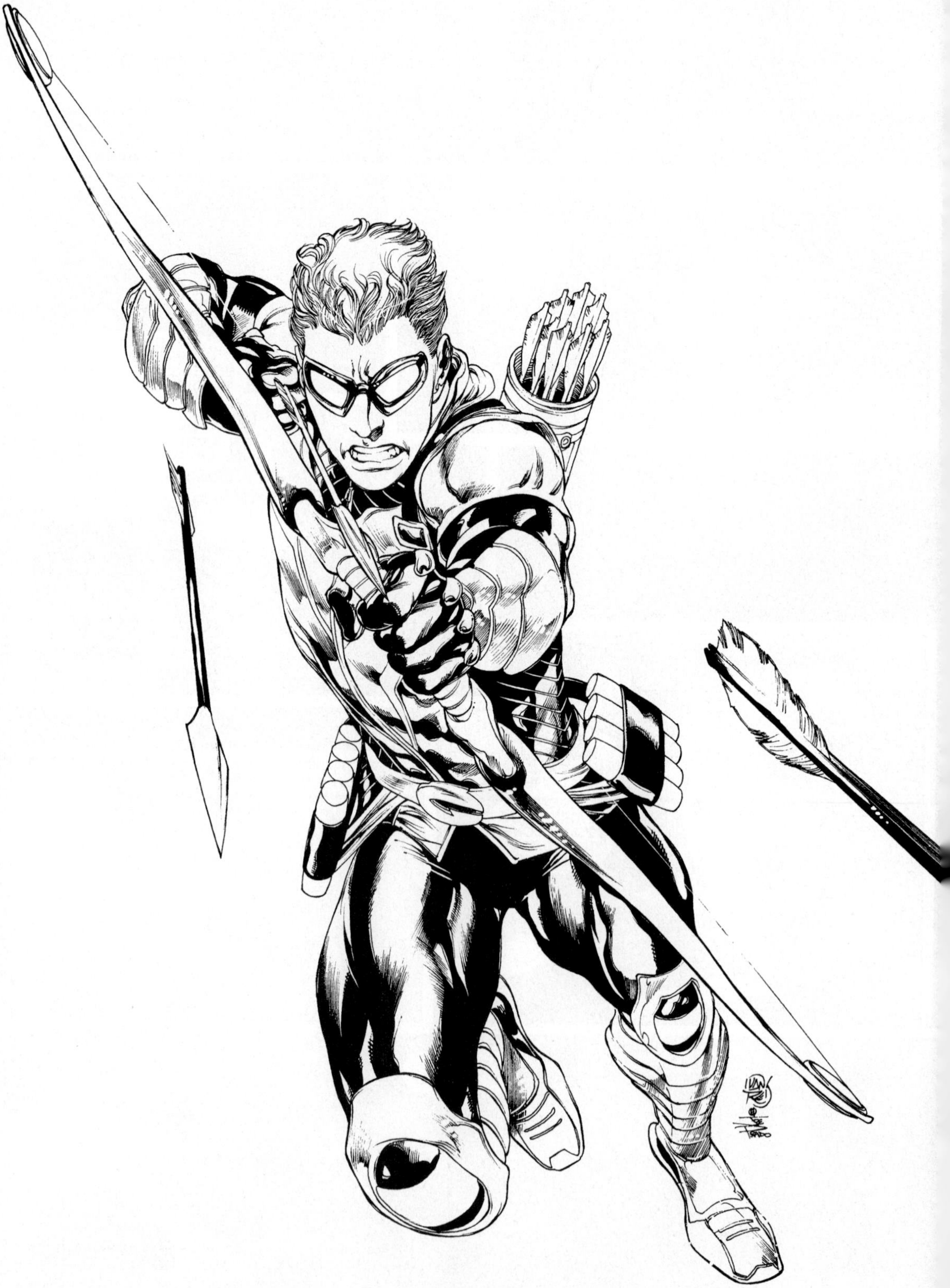

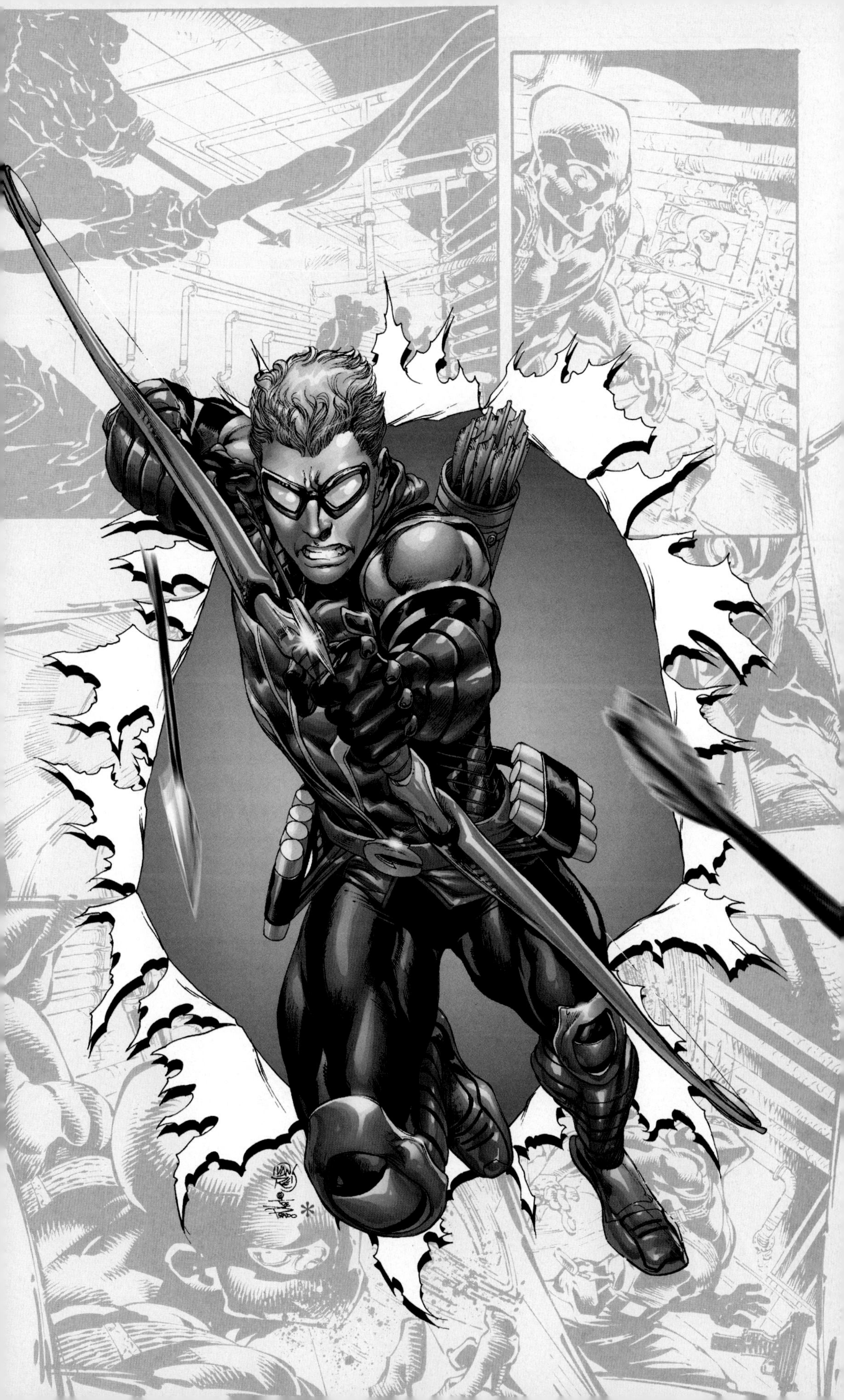

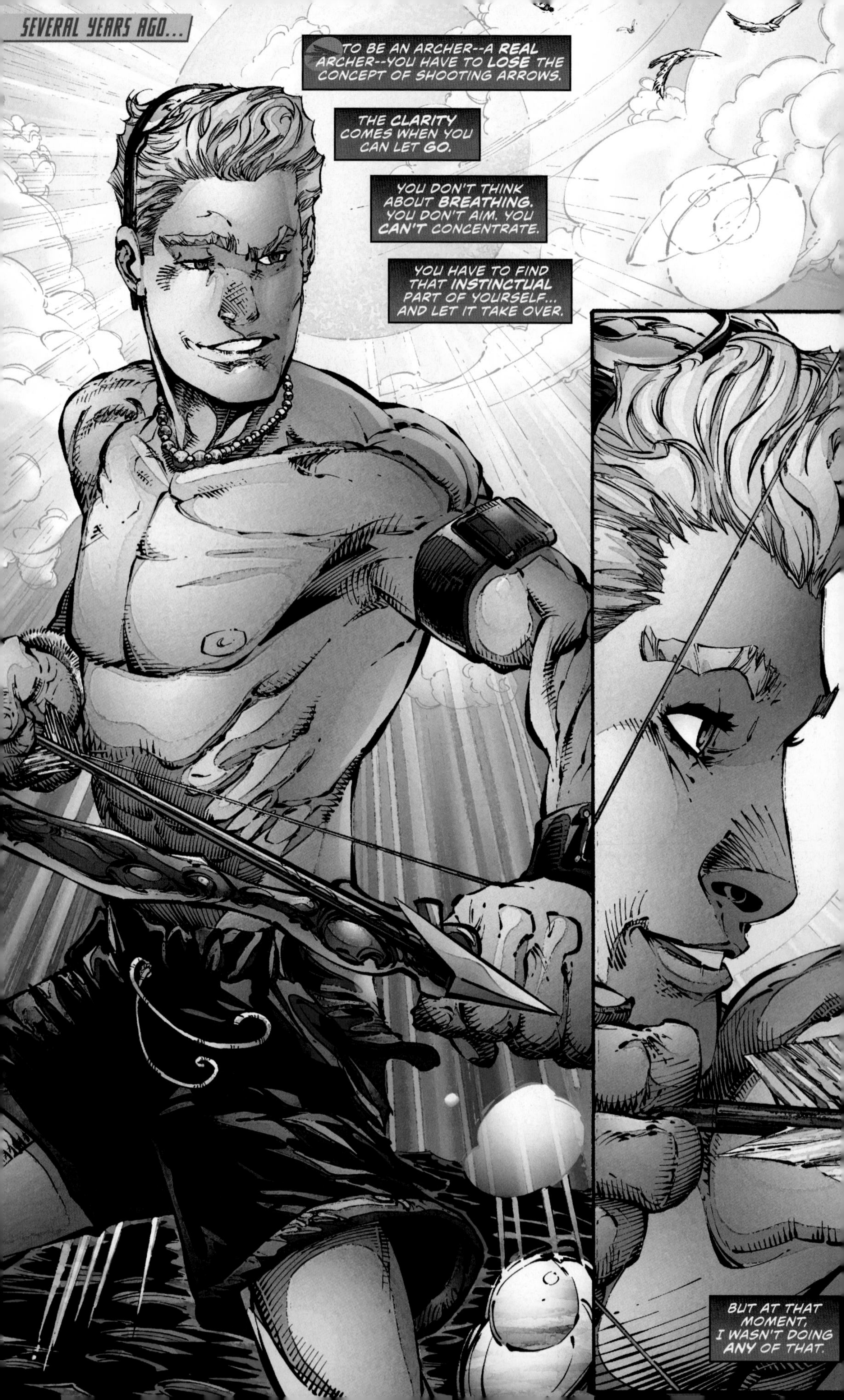
SEVERAL YEARS AGO...
TO BE AN ARCHER--A REAL ARCHER--YOU HAVE TO LOSE THE CONCEPT OF SHOOTING ARROWS.
THE CLARITY COMES WHEN YOU CAN LET GO.
YOU DON'T THINK ABOUT BREATHING. YOU DON'T AIM. YOU CAN'T CONCENTRATE.
YOU HAVE TO FIND THAT INSTINCTUAL PART OF YOURSELF... AND LET IT TAKE OVER.
BUT AT THAT MOMENT, I WASN'T DOING ANY OF THAT.

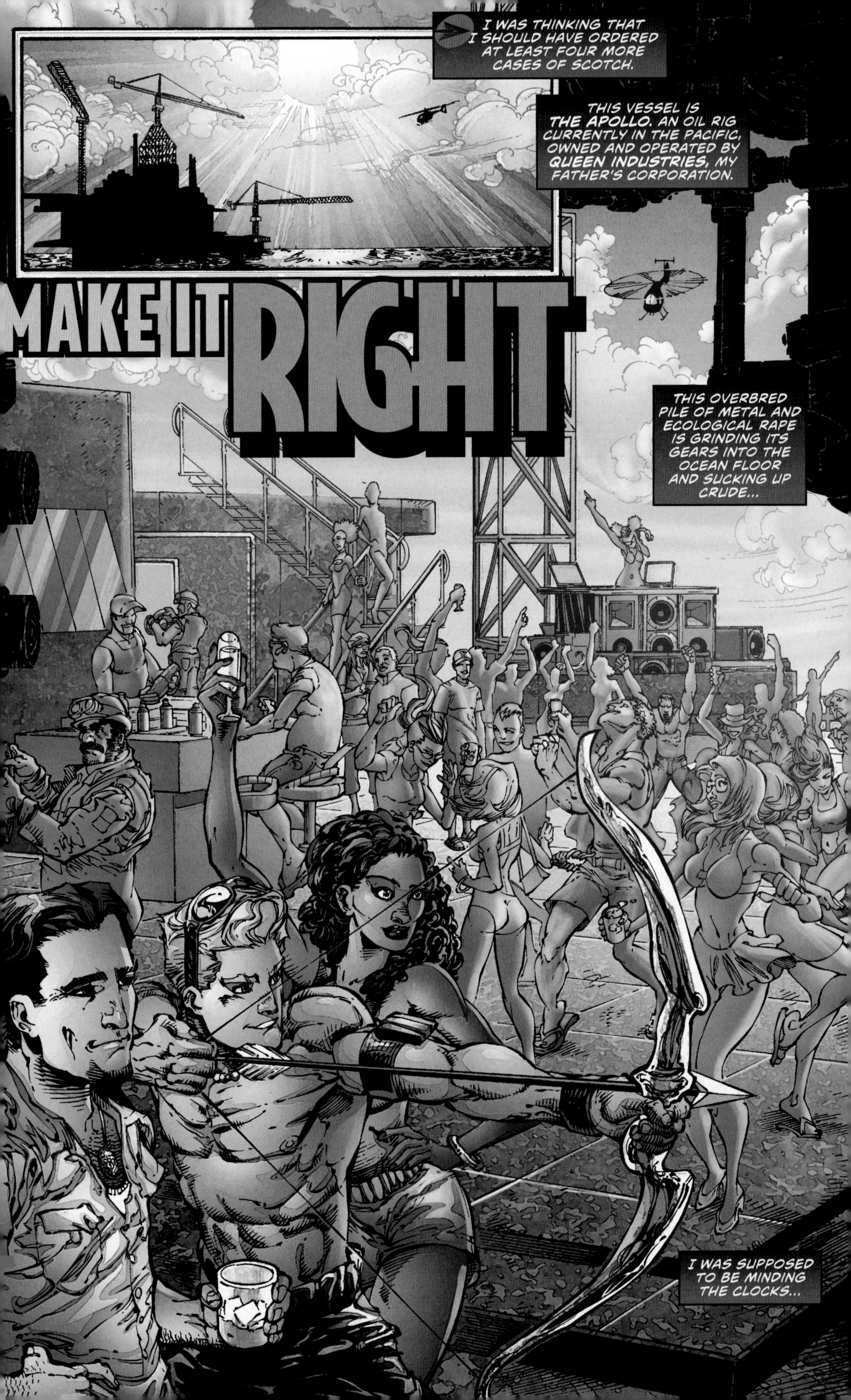
I WAS THINKING THAT I SHOULD HAVE ORDERED AT LEAST FOUR MORE CASES OF SCOTCH.
THIS VESSEL IS THE APOLLO. AN OIL RIG CURRENTLY IN THE PACIFIC, OWNED AND OPERATED BY QUEEN INDUSTRIES, MY FATHER'S CORPORATION.
MAKE IT RIGHT
THIS OVERBRED PILE OF METAL AND ECOLOGICAL RAPE IS GRINDING ITS GEARS INTO THE OCEAN FLOOR AND SUCKING UP CRUDE...
I WAS SUPPOSED TO BE MINDING THE CLOCKS...

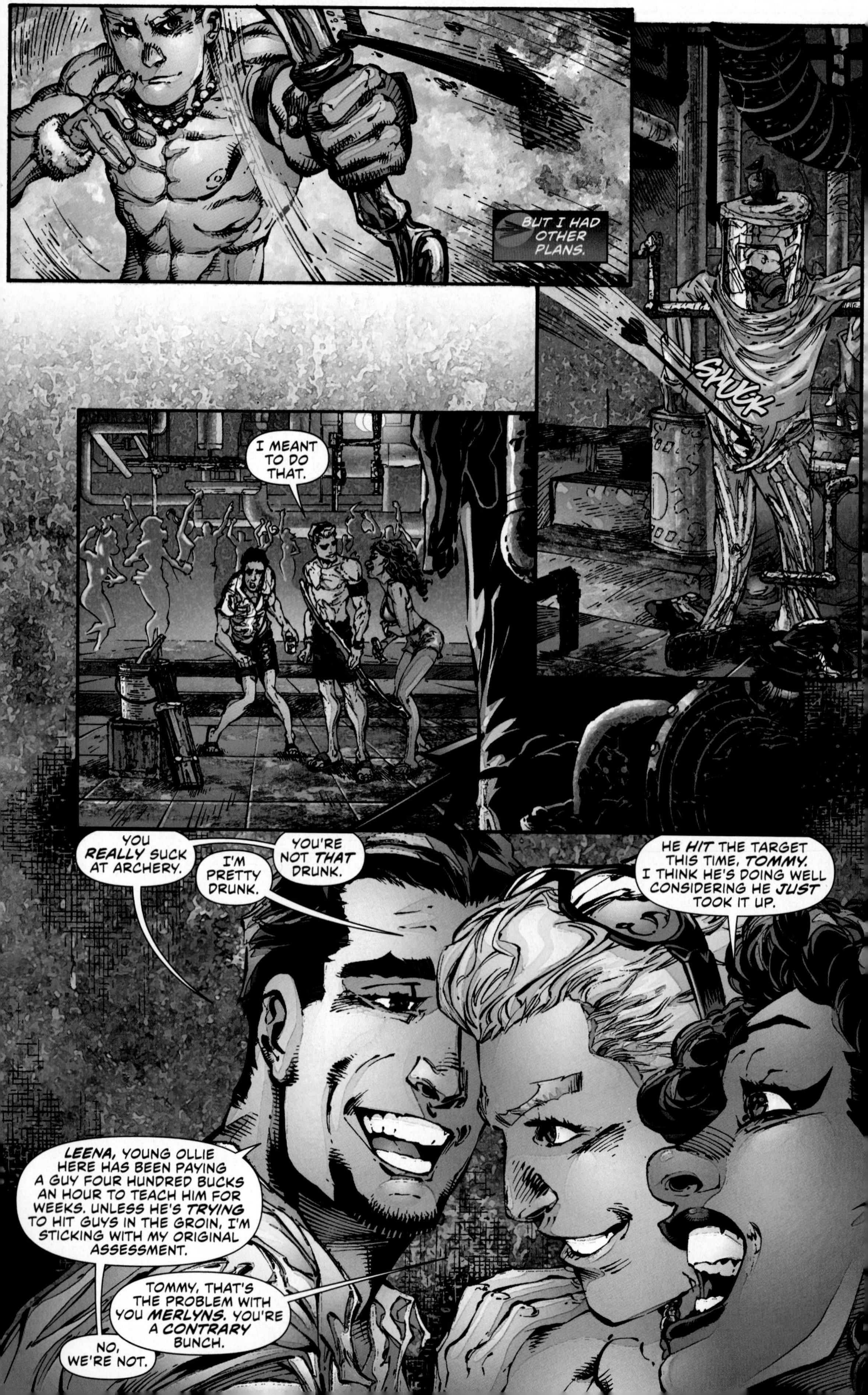
BUT I HAD OTHER PLANS.
SHUCK
I MEANT TO DO THAT.
YOU REALLY SUCK AT ARCHERY.
I'M PRETTY DRUNK.
YOU'RE NOT THAT DRUNK.
HE HIT THE TARGET THIS TIME, TOMMY. I THINK HE'S DOING WELL CONSIDERING HE JUST TOOK IT UP.
LEENA, YOUNG OLLIE HERE HAS BEEN PAYING A GUY FOUR HUNDRED BUCKS AN HOUR TO TEACH HIM FOR WEEKS. UNLESS HE'S TRYING TO HIT GUYS IN THE GROIN, I'M STICKING WITH MY ORIGINAL ASSESSMENT.
TOMMY, THAT'S THE PROBLEM WITH YOU MERLYNS. YOU'RE A CONTRARY BUNCH.
NO, WE'RE NOT.

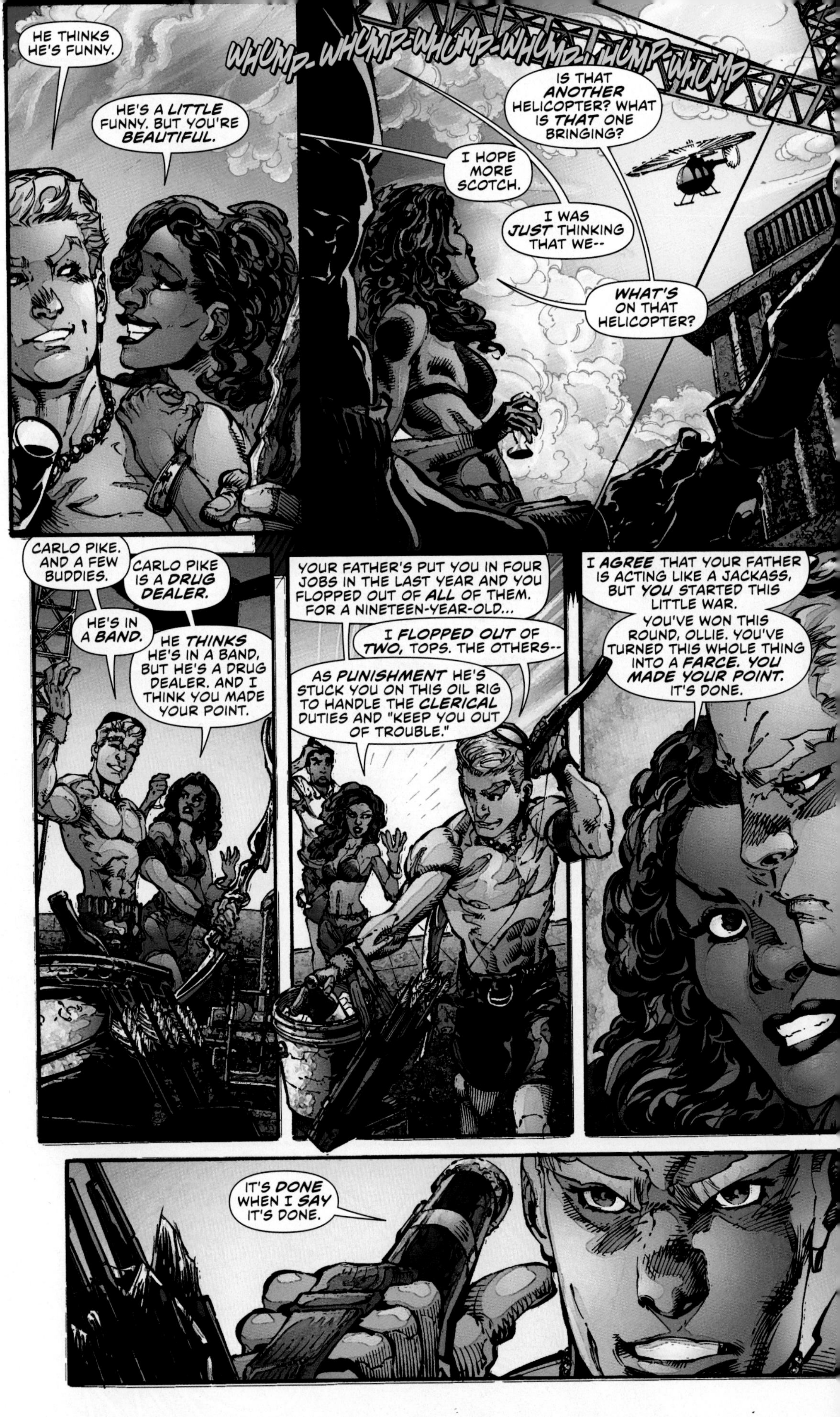
HE THINKS HE'S FUNNY.
HE'S A LITTLE FUNNY. BUT YOU'RE BEAUTIFUL.
WHUMP-WHUMP-WHUMP-WHUMP-THUMP-WHUMP
IS THAT ANOTHER HELICOPTER? WHAT IS THAT ONE BRINGING?
I HOPE MORE SCOTCH.
I WAS JUST THINKING THAT WE--
WHAT'S ON THAT HELICOPTER?
CARLO PIKE. AND A FEW BUDDIES.
CARLO PIKE IS A DRUG DEALER.
HE'S IN A BAND.
HE THINKS HE'S IN A BAND, BUT HE'S A DRUG DEALER. AND I THINK YOU MADE YOUR POINT.
YOUR FATHER'S PUT YOU IN FOUR JOBS IN THE LAST YEAR AND YOU FLOPPED OUT OF ALL OF THEM. FOR A NINETEEN-YEAR-OLD...
I FLOPPED OUT OF TWO, TOPS. THE OTHERS--
AS PUNISHMENT HE'S STUCK YOU ON THIS OIL RIG TO HANDLE THE CLERICAL DUTIES AND "KEEP YOU OUT OF TROUBLE."
I AGREE THAT YOUR FATHER IS ACTING LIKE A JACKASS, BUT YOU STARTED THIS LITTLE WAR.
YOU'VE WON THIS ROUND, OLLIE. YOU'VE TURNED THIS WHOLE THING INTO A FARCE. YOU MADE YOUR POINT. IT'S DONE.
IT'S DONE WHEN I SAY IT'S DONE.

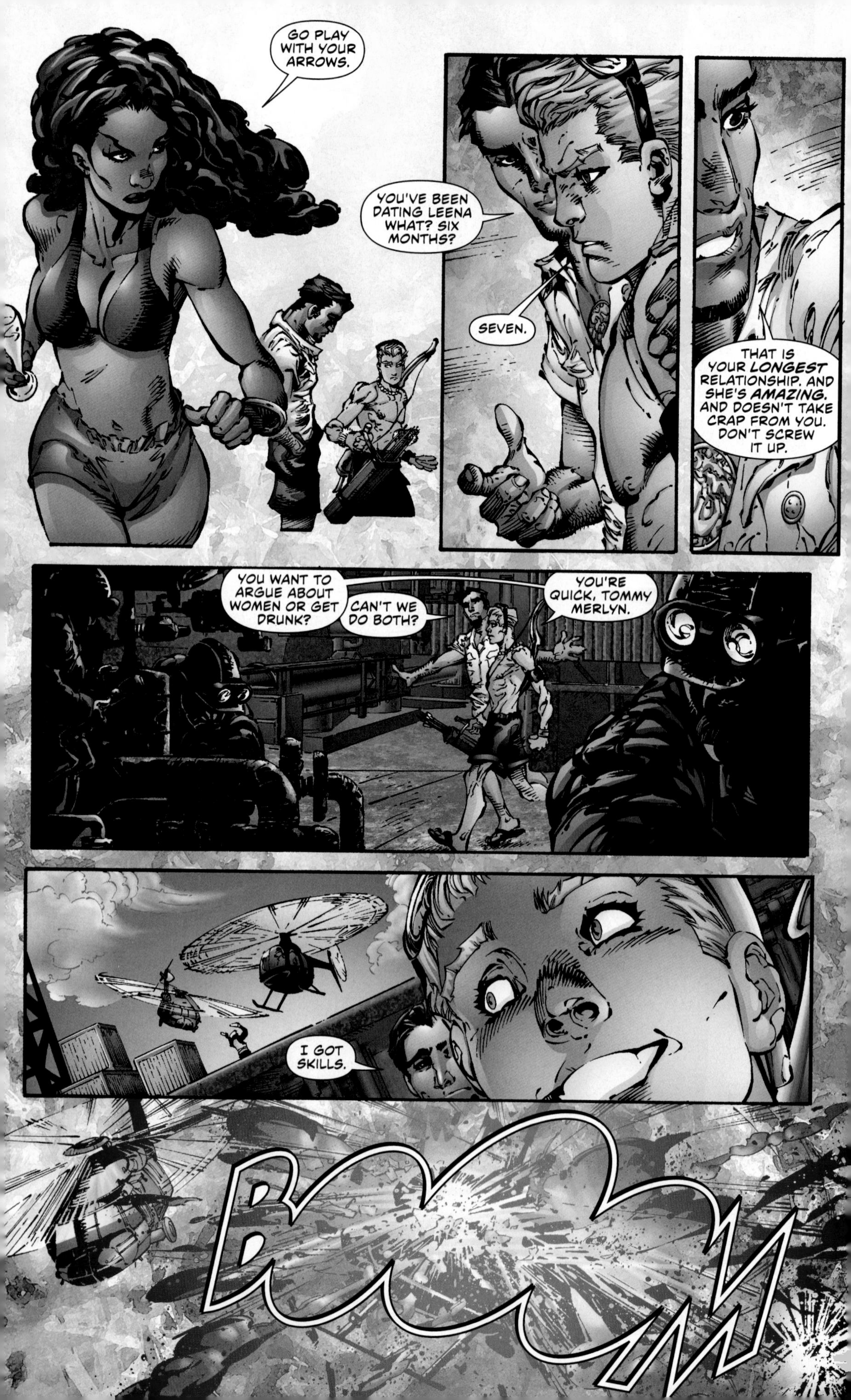
GO PLAY WITH YOUR ARROWS.
YOU'VE BEEN DATING LEENA WHAT? SIX MONTHS?
SEVEN.
THAT IS YOUR LONGEST RELATIONSHIP. AND SHE'S AMAZING. AND DOESN'T TAKE CRAP FROM YOU. DON'T SCREW IT UP.
YOU WANT TO ARGUE ABOUT WOMEN OR GET DRUNK?
CAN'T WE DO BOTH?
YOU'RE QUICK, TOMMY MERLYN.
I GOT SKILLS.
BOOM

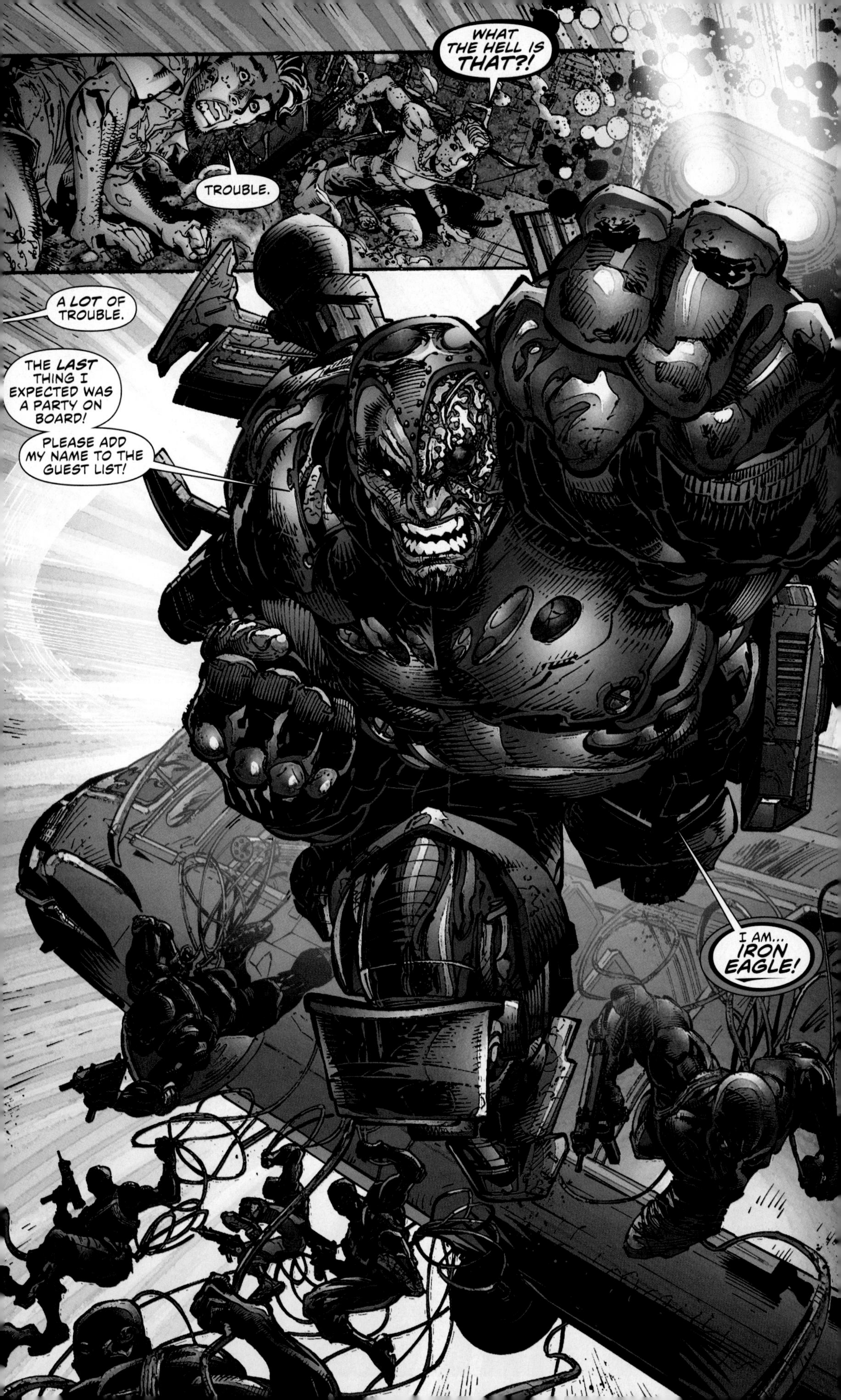

WHAT THE HELL IS THAT?!
TROUBLE.
A LOT OF TROUBLE.
THE LAST THING I EXPECTED WAS A PARTY ON BOARD!
PLEASE ADD MY NAME TO THE GUEST LIST!
I AM... IRON EAGLE!

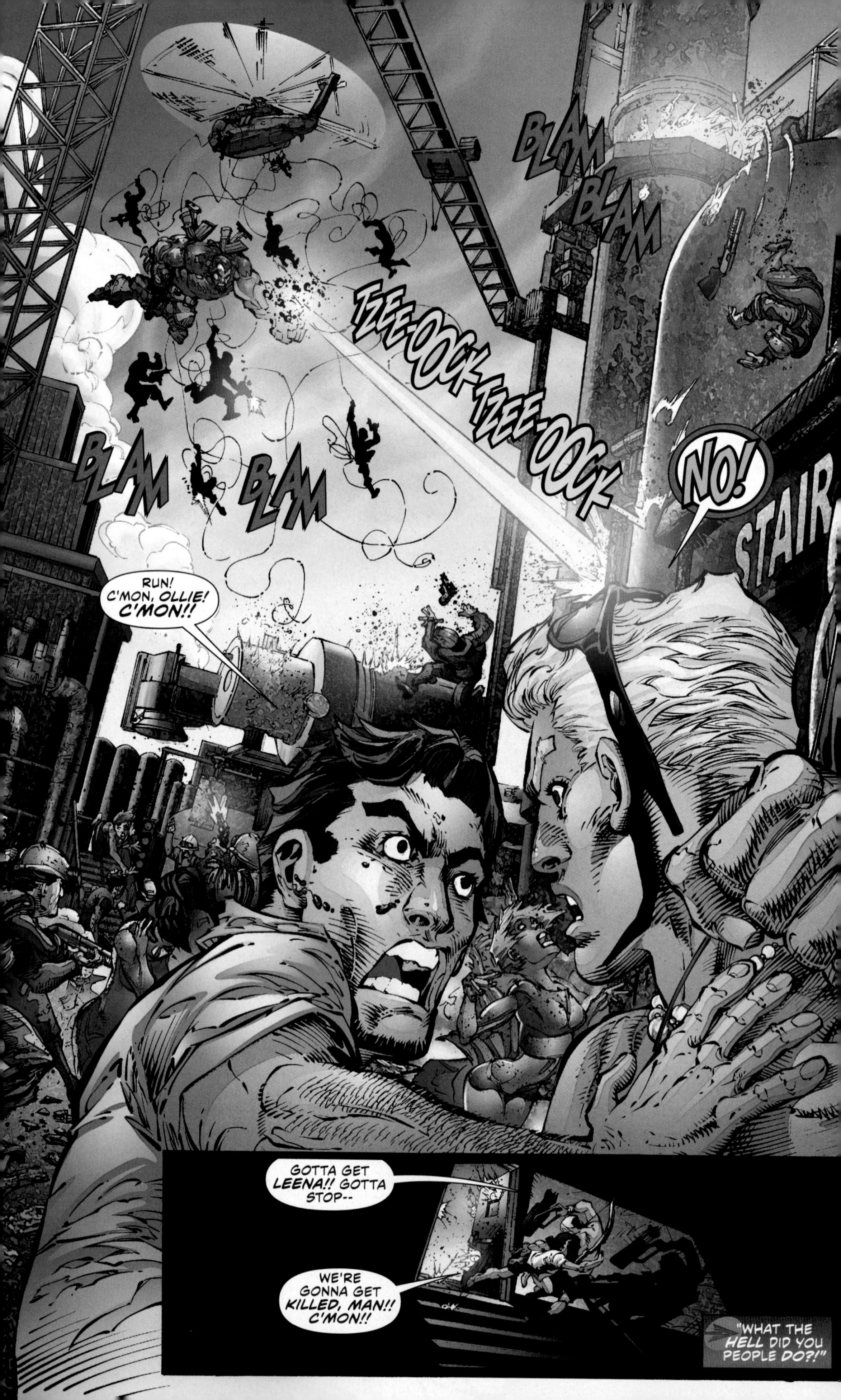

BLAM BLAM
TZEE-OOCK TZEE-OOCK
BLAM BLAM
NO!
STAIR
RUN! C'MON, OLLIE! C'MON!!
GOTTA GET LEENA!! GOTTA STOP--
WE'RE GONNA GET KILLED, MAN!! C'MON!!
"WHAT THE HELL DID YOU PEOPLE DO?!"

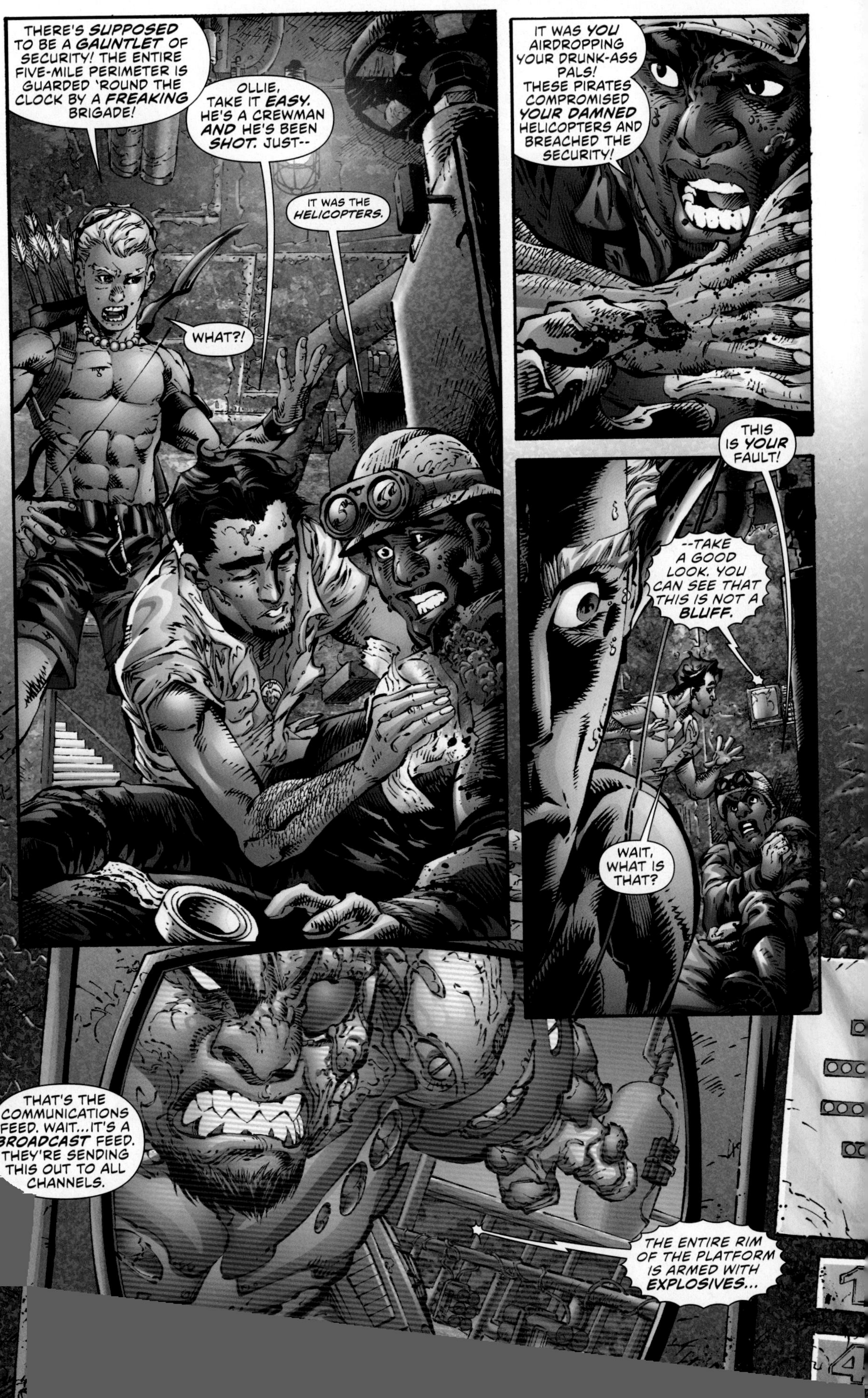
THERE'S SUPPOSED TO BE A GAUNTLET OF SECURITY! THE ENTIRE FIVE-MILE PERIMETER IS GUARDED 'ROUND THE CLOCK BY A FREAKING BRIGADE!
OLLIE, TAKE IT EASY. HE'S A CREWMAN AND HE'S BEEN SHOT. JUST--
IT WAS THE HELICOPTERS.
WHAT?!
IT WAS YOU AIRDROPPING YOUR DRUNK-ASS PALS! THESE PIRATES COMPROMISED YOUR DAMNED HELICOPTERS AND BREACHED THE SECURITY!
THIS IS YOUR FAULT!
--TAKE A GOOD LOOK. YOU CAN SEE THAT THIS IS NOT A BLUFF.
WAIT, WHAT IS THAT?
THAT'S THE COMMUNICATIONS FEED. WAIT...IT'S A BROADCAST FEED. THEY'RE SENDING THIS OUT TO ALL CHANNELS.
THE ENTIRE RIM OF THE PLATFORM IS ARMED WITH EXPLOSIVES...

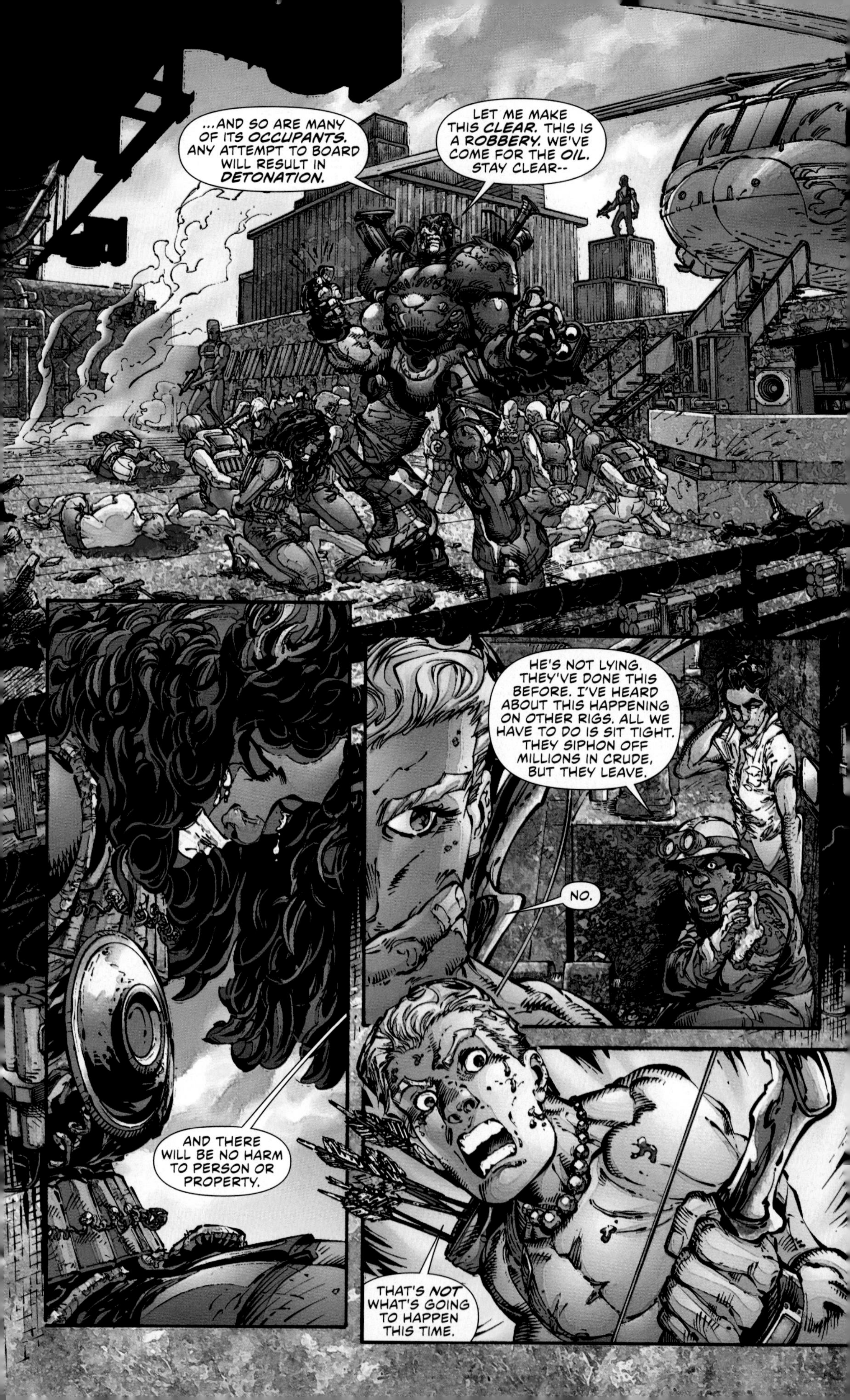
...AND SO ARE MANY OF ITS OCCUPANTS. ANY ATTEMPT TO BOARD WILL RESULT IN DETONATION.
LET ME MAKE THIS CLEAR. THIS IS A ROBBERY. WE'VE COME FOR THE OIL. STAY CLEAR--
HE'S NOT LYING. THEY'VE DONE THIS BEFORE. I'VE HEARD ABOUT THIS HAPPENING ON OTHER RIGS. ALL WE HAVE TO DO IS SIT TIGHT. THEY SIPHON OFF MILLIONS IN CRUDE, BUT THEY LEAVE.
NO.
AND THERE WILL BE NO HARM TO PERSON OR PROPERTY.
THAT'S NOT WHAT'S GOING TO HAPPEN THIS TIME.

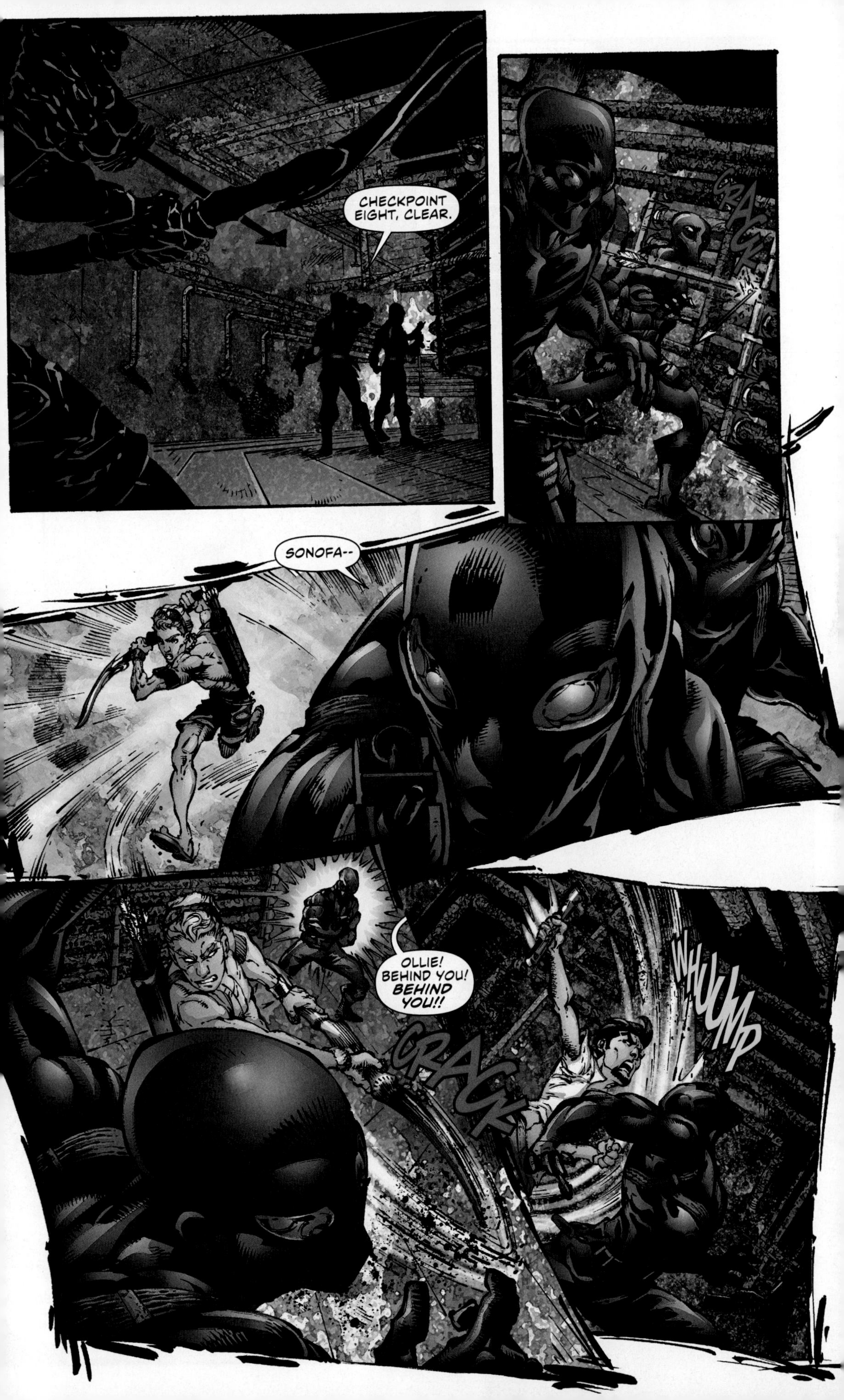
CHECKPOINT EIGHT, CLEAR.
CRACK
SONOFA--
OLLIE! BEHIND YOU! BEHIND YOU!!
CRACK
WHUUMP

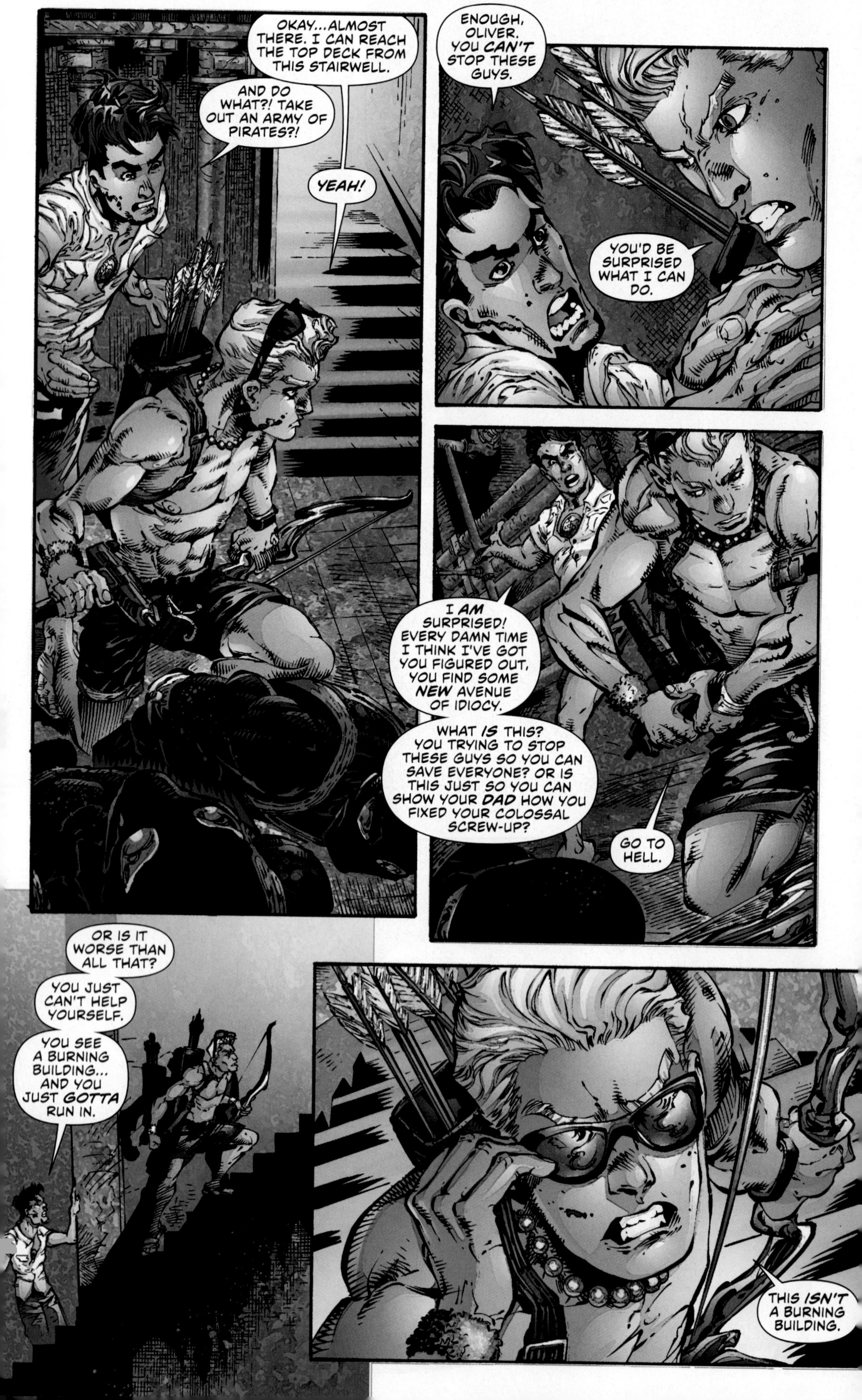
OKAY...ALMOST THERE. I CAN REACH THE TOP DECK FROM THIS STAIRWELL.
AND DO WHAT?! TAKE OUT AN ARMY OF PIRATES?!
YEAH!
ENOUGH, OLIVER. YOU CAN'T STOP THESE GUYS.
YOU'D BE SURPRISED WHAT I CAN DO.
I AM SURPRISED! EVERY DAMN TIME I THINK I'VE GOT YOU FIGURED OUT, YOU FIND SOME NEW AVENUE OF IDIOCY.
WHAT IS THIS? YOU TRYING TO STOP THESE GUYS SO YOU CAN SAVE EVERYONE? OR IS THIS JUST SO YOU CAN SHOW YOUR DAD HOW YOU FIXED YOUR COLOSSAL SCREW-UP?
GO TO HELL.
OR IS IT WORSE THAN ALL THAT?
YOU JUST CAN'T HELP YOURSELF.
YOU SEE A BURNING BUILDING... AND YOU JUST GOTTA RUN IN.
THIS ISN'T A BURNING BUILDING.

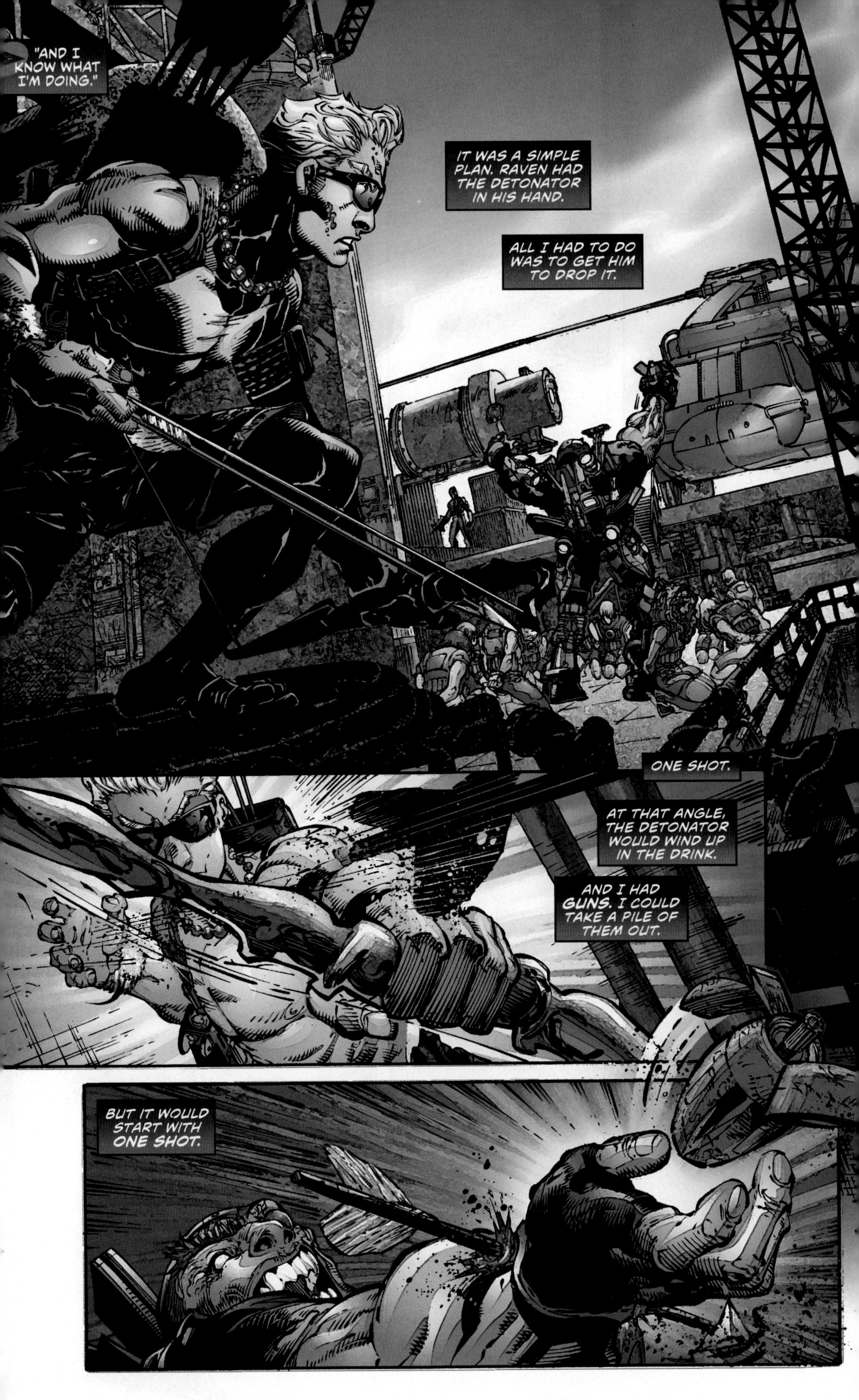
"AND I KNOW WHAT I'M DOING."
IT WAS A SIMPLE PLAN. RAVEN HAD THE DETONATOR IN HIS HAND.
ALL I HAD TO DO WAS TO GET HIM TO DROP IT.
ONE SHOT.
AT THAT ANGLE, THE DETONATOR WOULD WIND UP IN THE DRINK.
AND I HAD GUNS. I COULD TAKE A PILE OF THEM OUT.
BUT IT WOULD START WITH ONE SHOT.

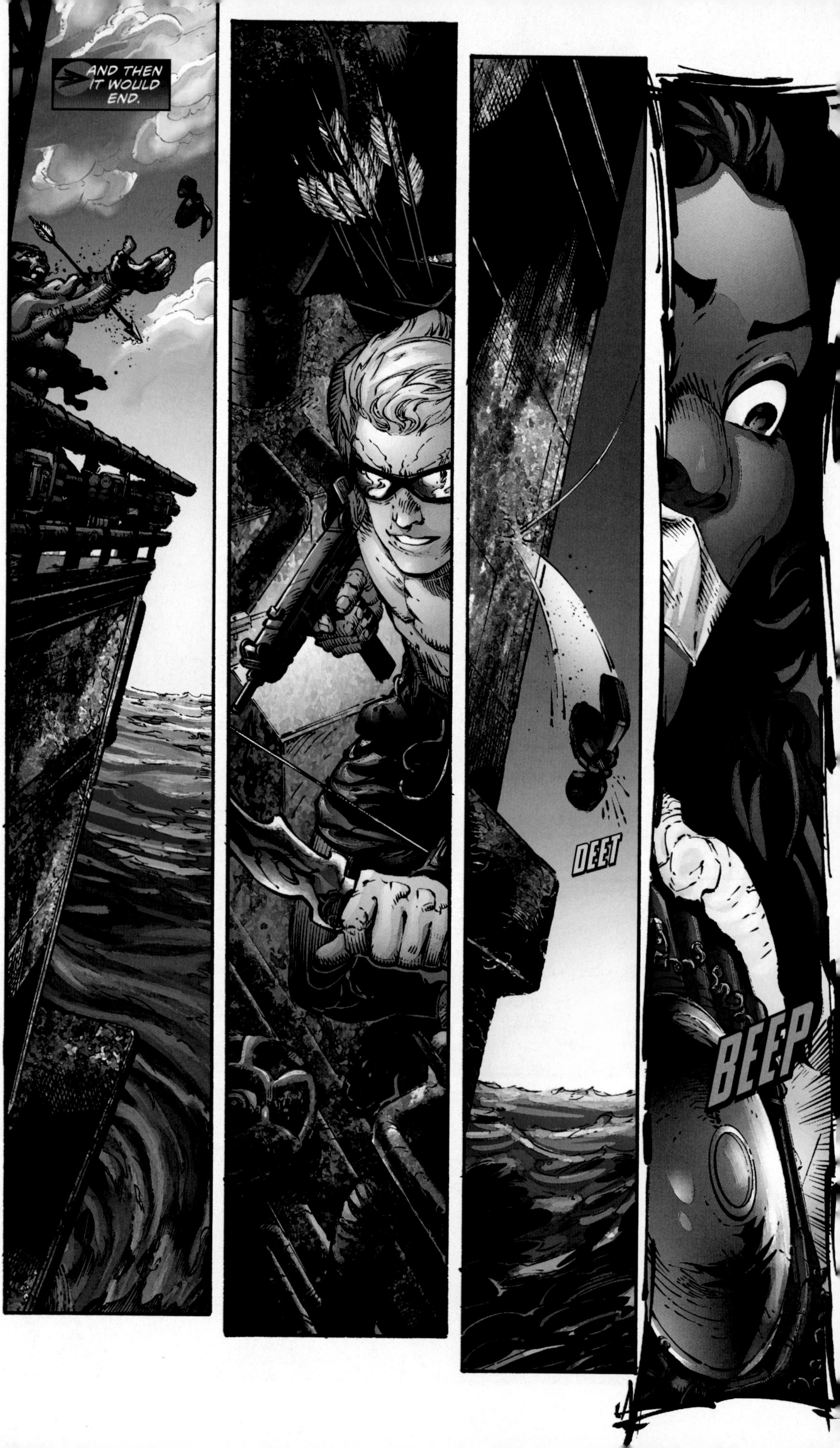
AND THEN IT WOULD END.
DEET
BEEP

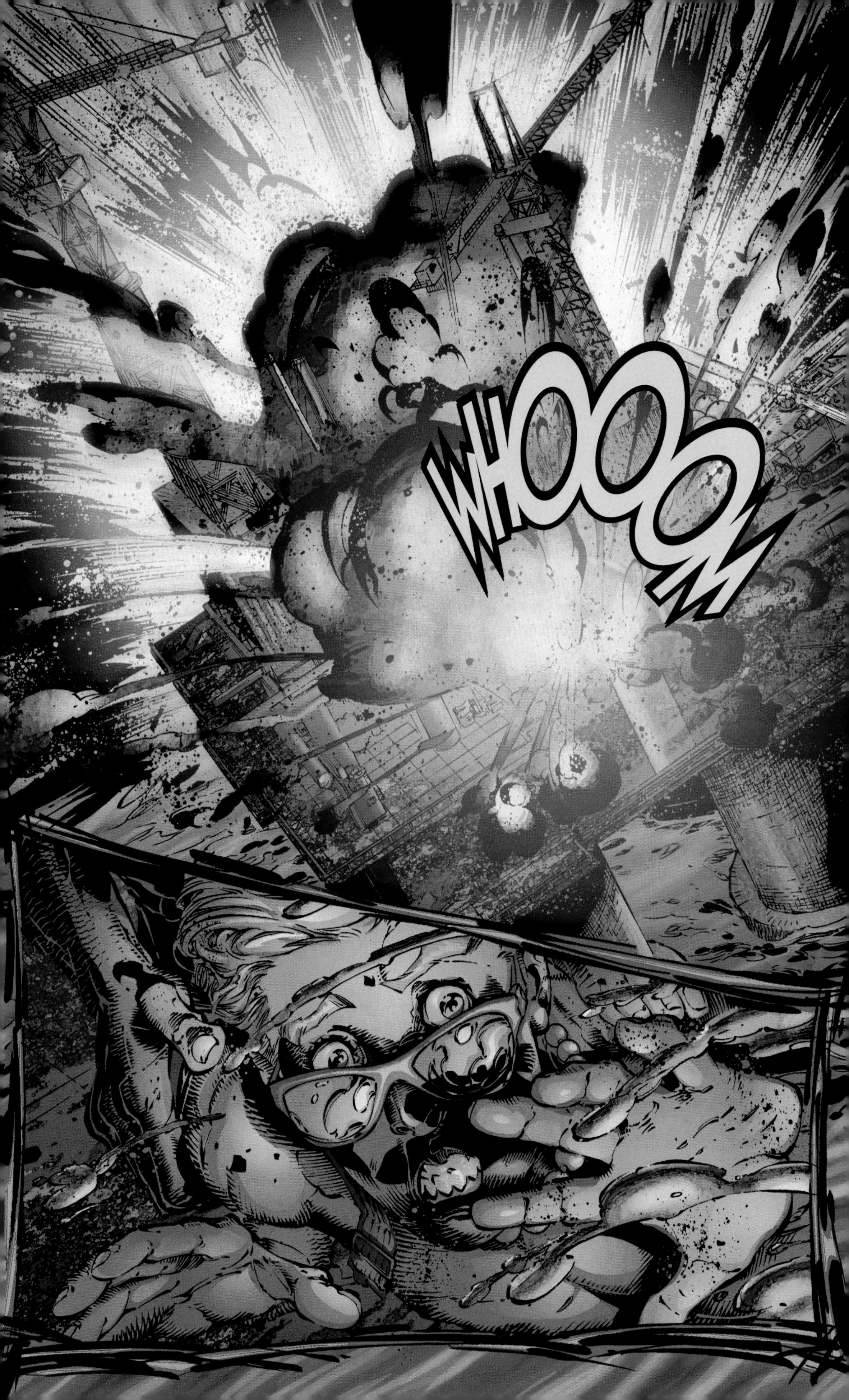
WHOOOM

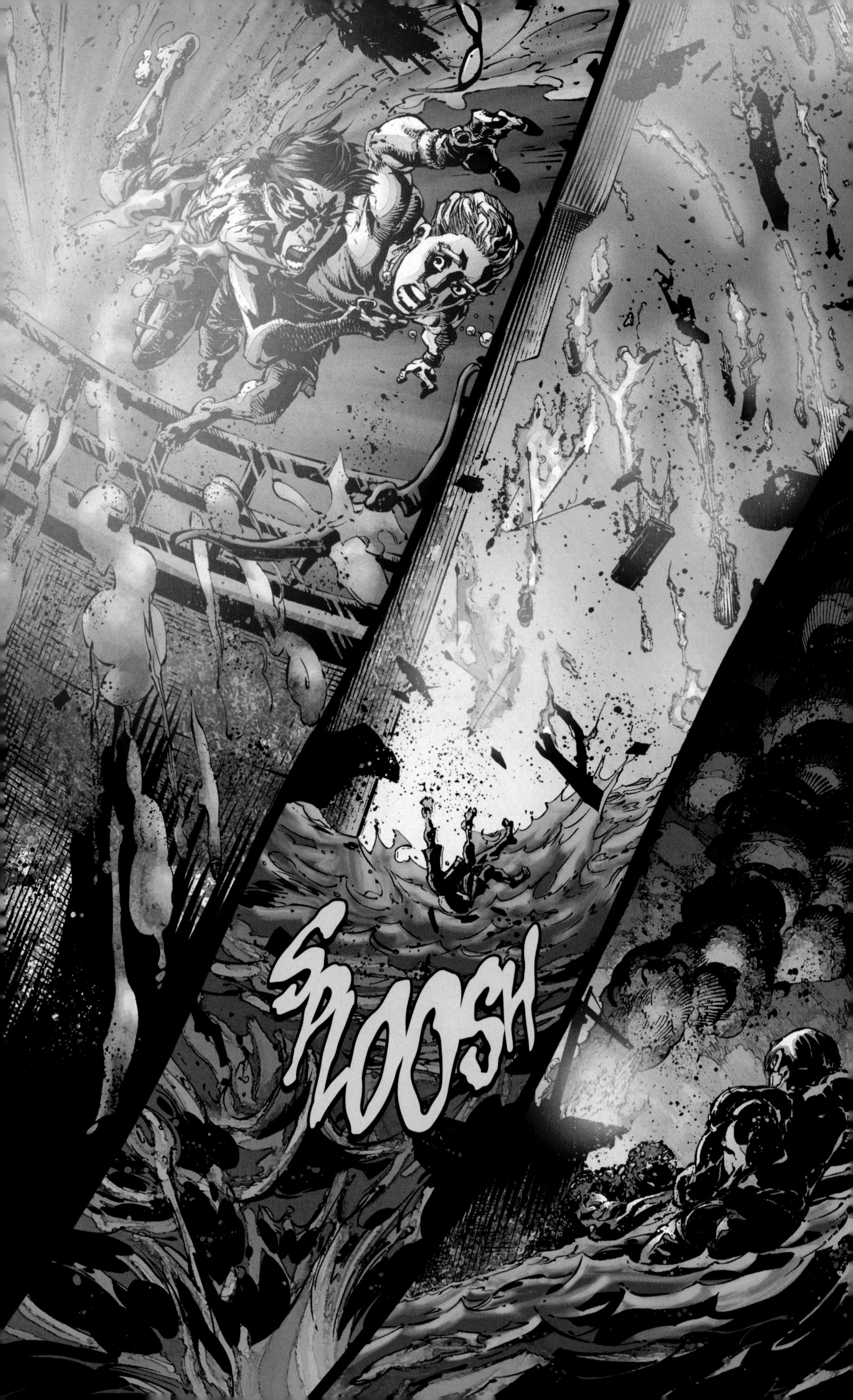
SPLOOSH

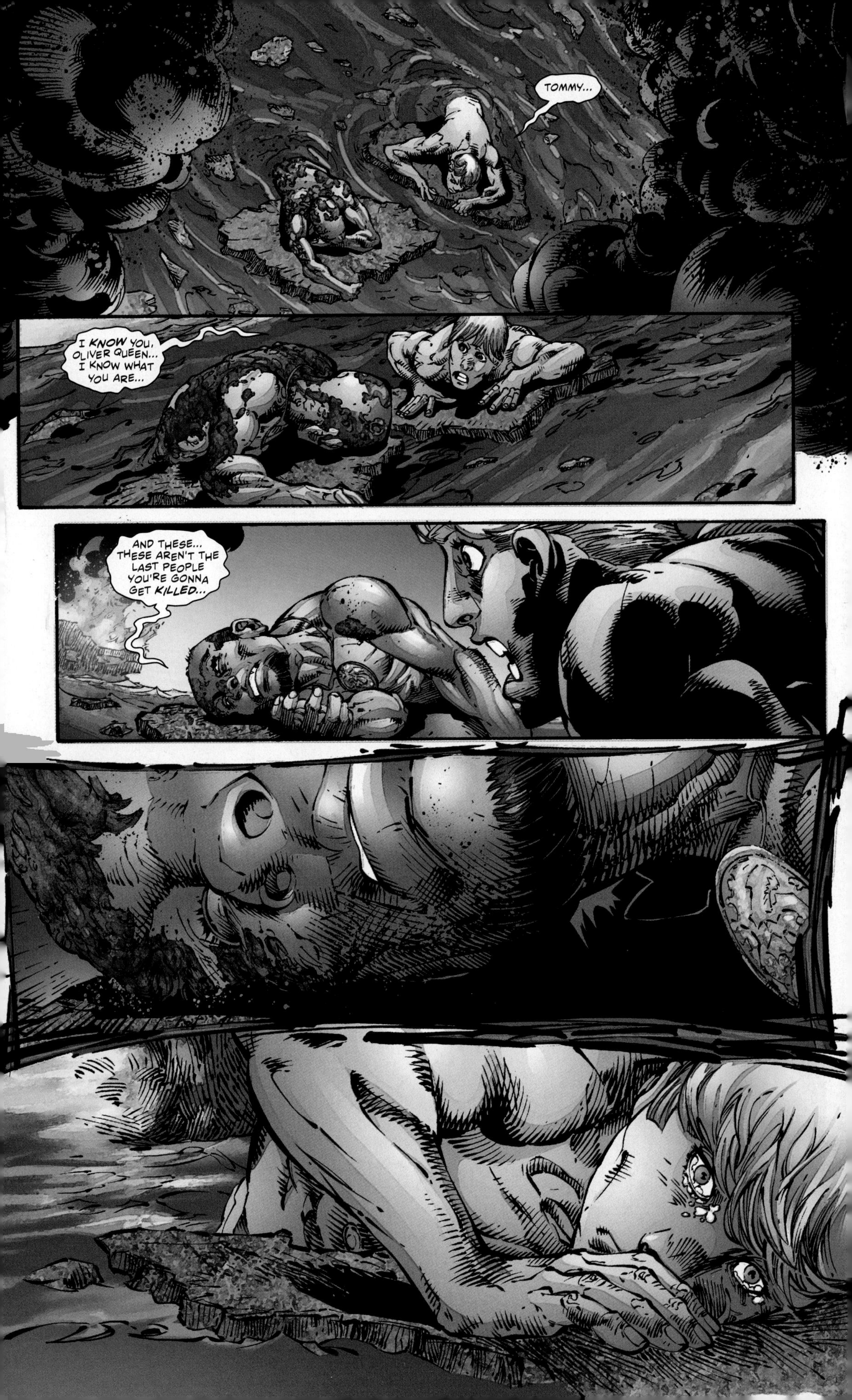
TOMMY...
I KNOW YOU, OLIVER QUEEN... I KNOW WHAT YOU ARE...
AND THESE... THESE AREN'T THE LAST PEOPLE YOU'RE GONNA GET KILLED...

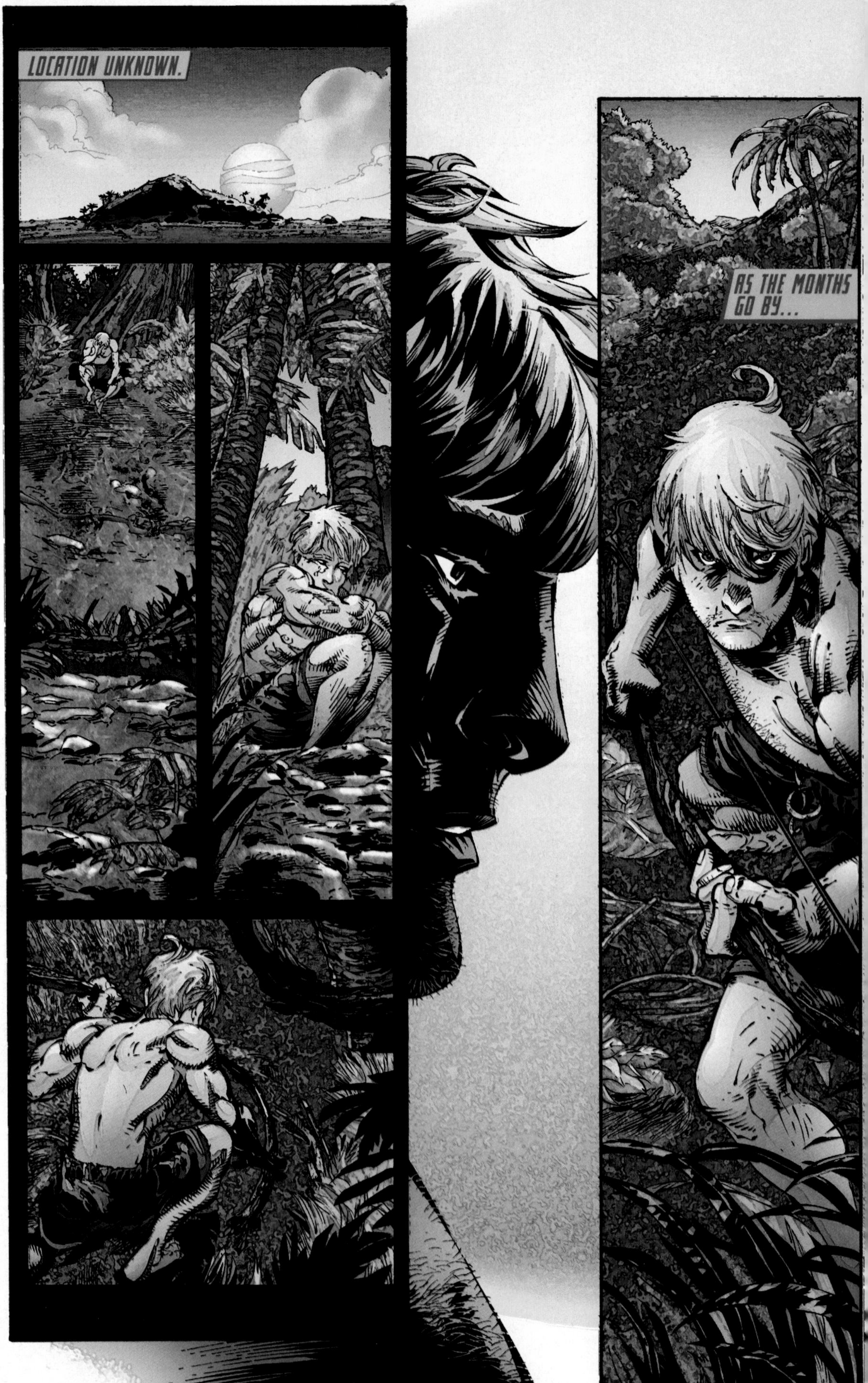
LOCATION UNKNOWN.
AS THE MONTHS GO BY...

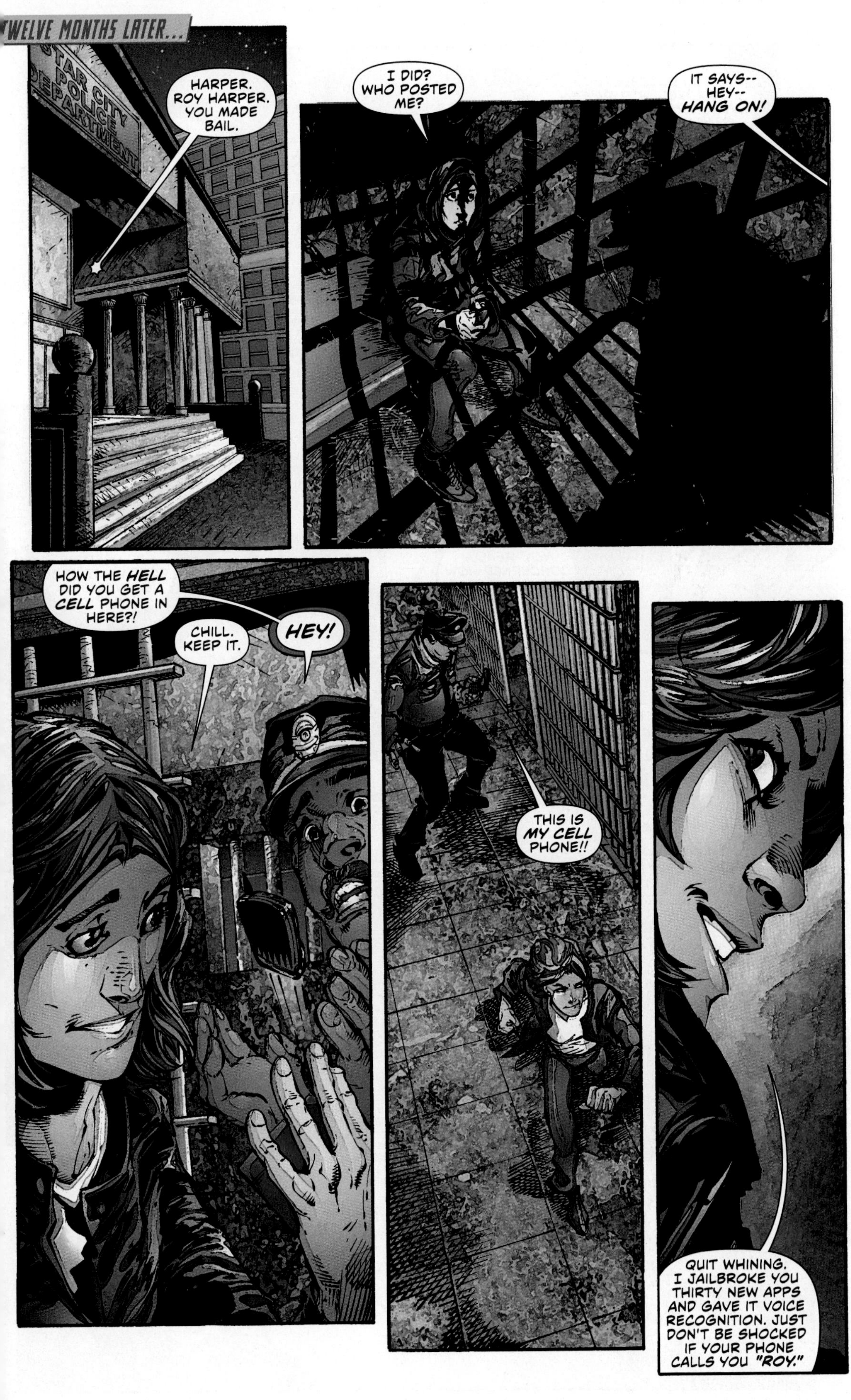
WELVE MONTHS LATER...
STAR CITY POLICE DEPARTMENT
HARPER. ROY HARPER. YOU MADE BAIL.
I DID? WHO POSTED ME?
IT SAYS-- HEY-- HANG ON!
HOW THE HELL DID YOU GET A CELL PHONE IN HERE?!
HEY!
CHILL. KEEP IT.
THIS IS MY CELL PHONE!!
QUIT WHINING. I JAILBROKE YOU THIRTY NEW APPS AND GAVE IT VOICE RECOGNITION. JUST DON'T BE SHOCKED IF YOUR PHONE CALLS YOU "ROY."

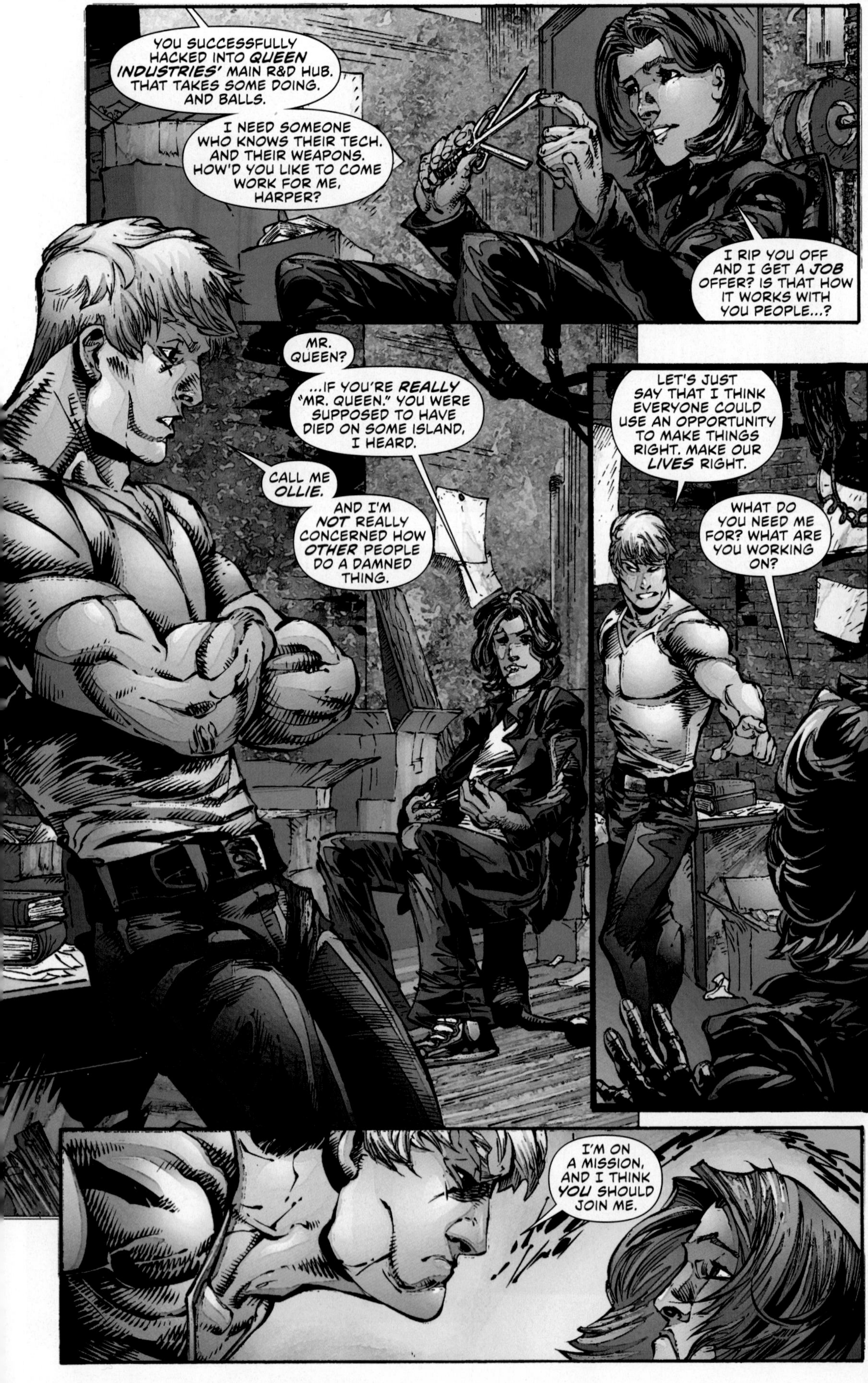
YOU SUCCESSFULLY HACKED INTO QUEEN INDUSTRIES' MAIN R&D HUB. THAT TAKES SOME DOING. AND BALLS.
I NEED SOMEONE WHO KNOWS THEIR TECH. AND THEIR WEAPONS. HOW'D YOU LIKE TO COME WORK FOR ME, HARPER?
I RIP YOU OFF AND I GET A JOB OFFER? IS THAT HOW IT WORKS WITH YOU PEOPLE...?
MR. QUEEN?
...IF YOU'RE REALLY "MR. QUEEN," YOU WERE SUPPOSED TO HAVE DIED ON SOME ISLAND, I HEARD.
CALL ME OLLIE.
AND I'M NOT REALLY CONCERNED HOW OTHER PEOPLE DO A DAMNED THING.
LET'S JUST SAY THAT I THINK EVERYONE COULD USE AN OPPORTUNITY TO MAKE THINGS RIGHT. MAKE OUR LIVES RIGHT.
WHAT DO YOU NEED ME FOR? WHAT ARE YOU WORKING ON?
I'M ON A MISSION, AND I THINK YOU SHOULD JOIN ME.

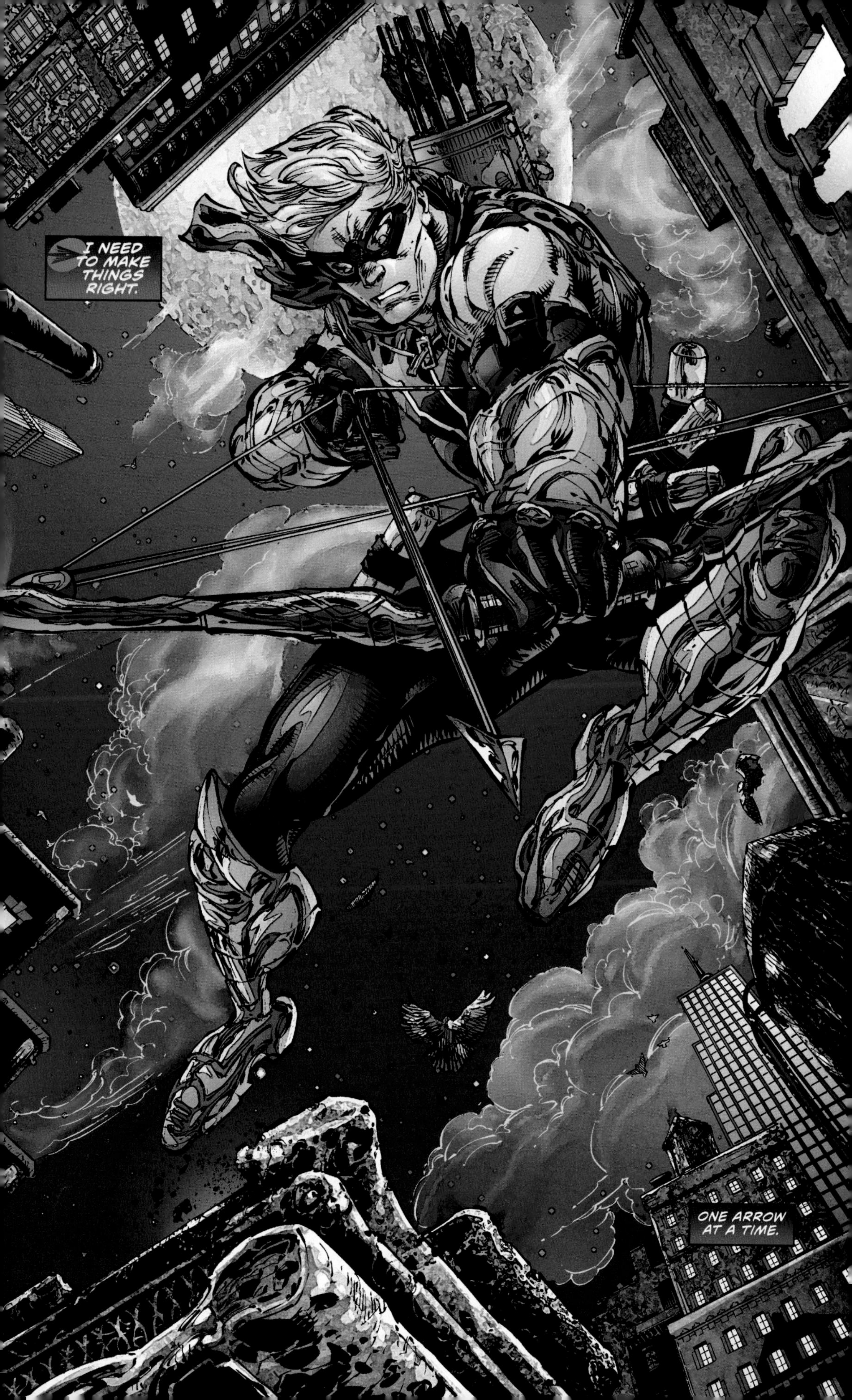
I NEED TO MAKE THINGS RIGHT.
ONE ARROW AT A TIME.

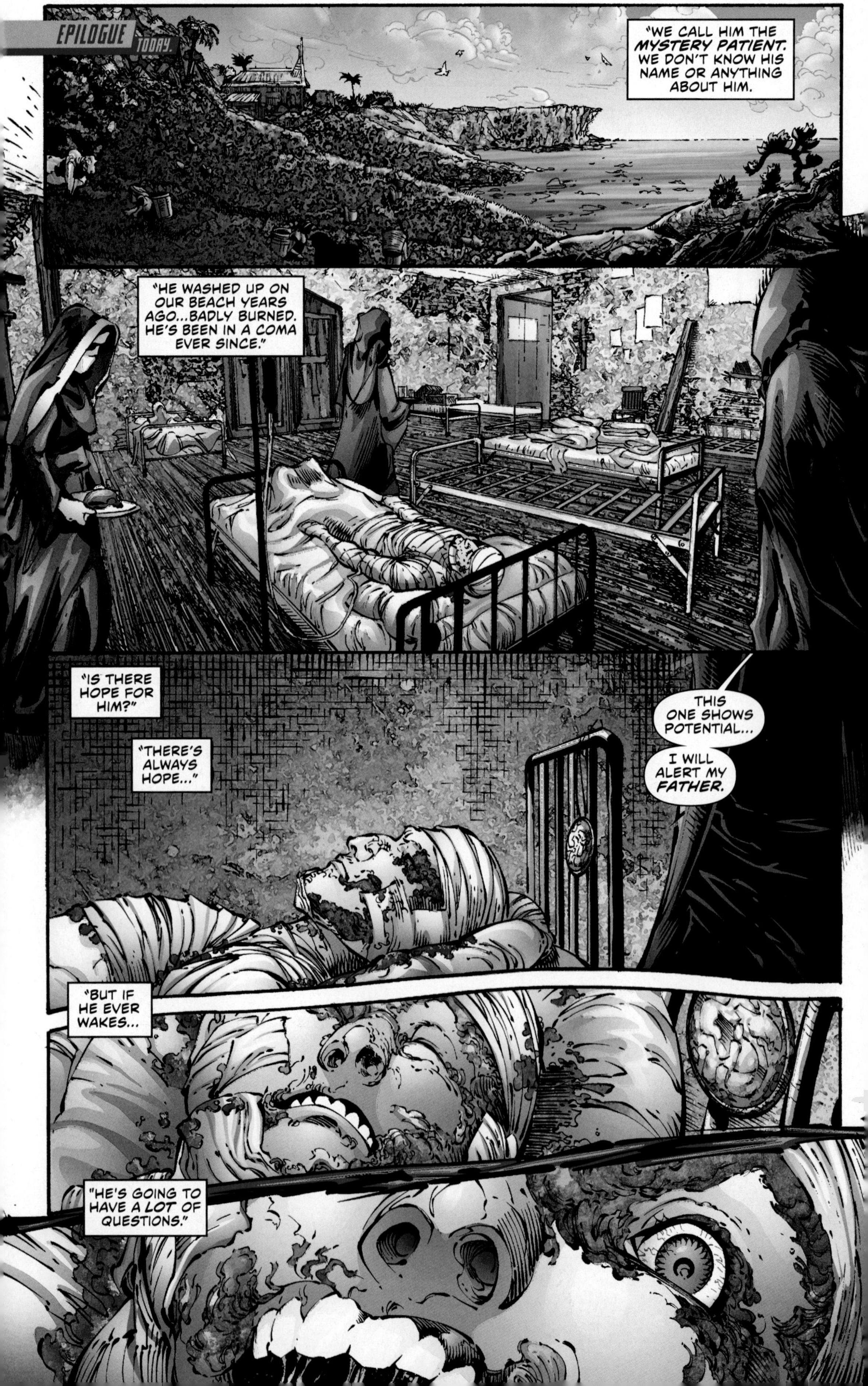
EPILOGUE
TODAY.
"WE CALL HIM THE MYSTERY PATIENT. WE DON'T KNOW HIS NAME OR ANYTHING ABOUT HIM.
"HE WASHED UP ON OUR BEACH YEARS AGO...BADLY BURNED. HE'S BEEN IN A COMA EVER SINCE."
"IS THERE HOPE FOR HIM?"
"THERE'S ALWAYS HOPE..."
THIS ONE SHOWS POTENTIAL...
I WILL ALERT MY FATHER.
"BUT IF HE EVER WAKES...
"HE'S GOING TO HAVE A LOT OF QUESTIONS."

GREEN ARROW

THANAGARIANS CHARACTER DESIGNS BY ROB LIEFELD

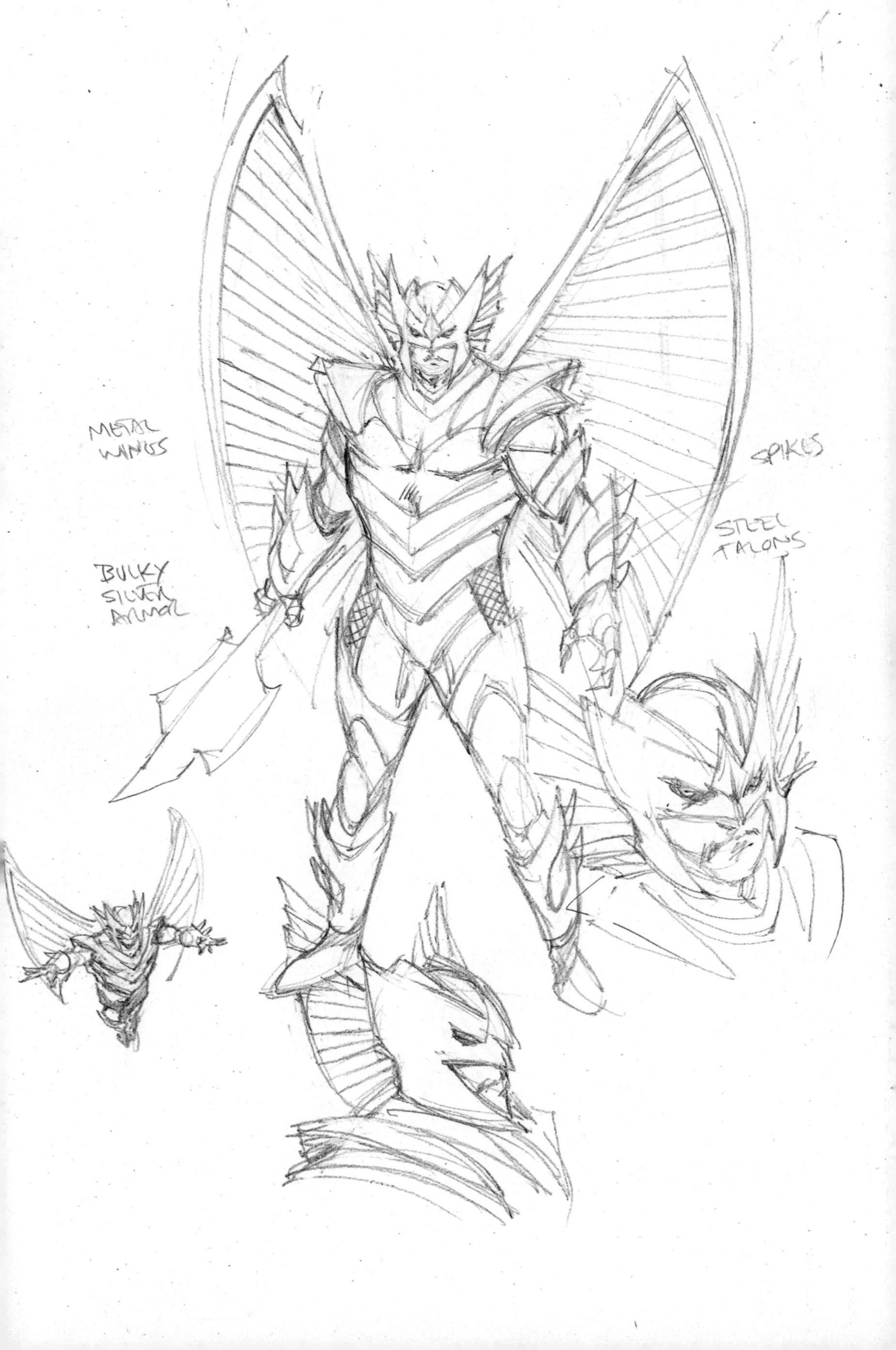

METAL WINGS
SPIKES
STEEL TALONS
BULKY SILVER ARMOR

IRON EAGLE CHARACTER DESIGNS BY FREDDIE WILLIAMS II

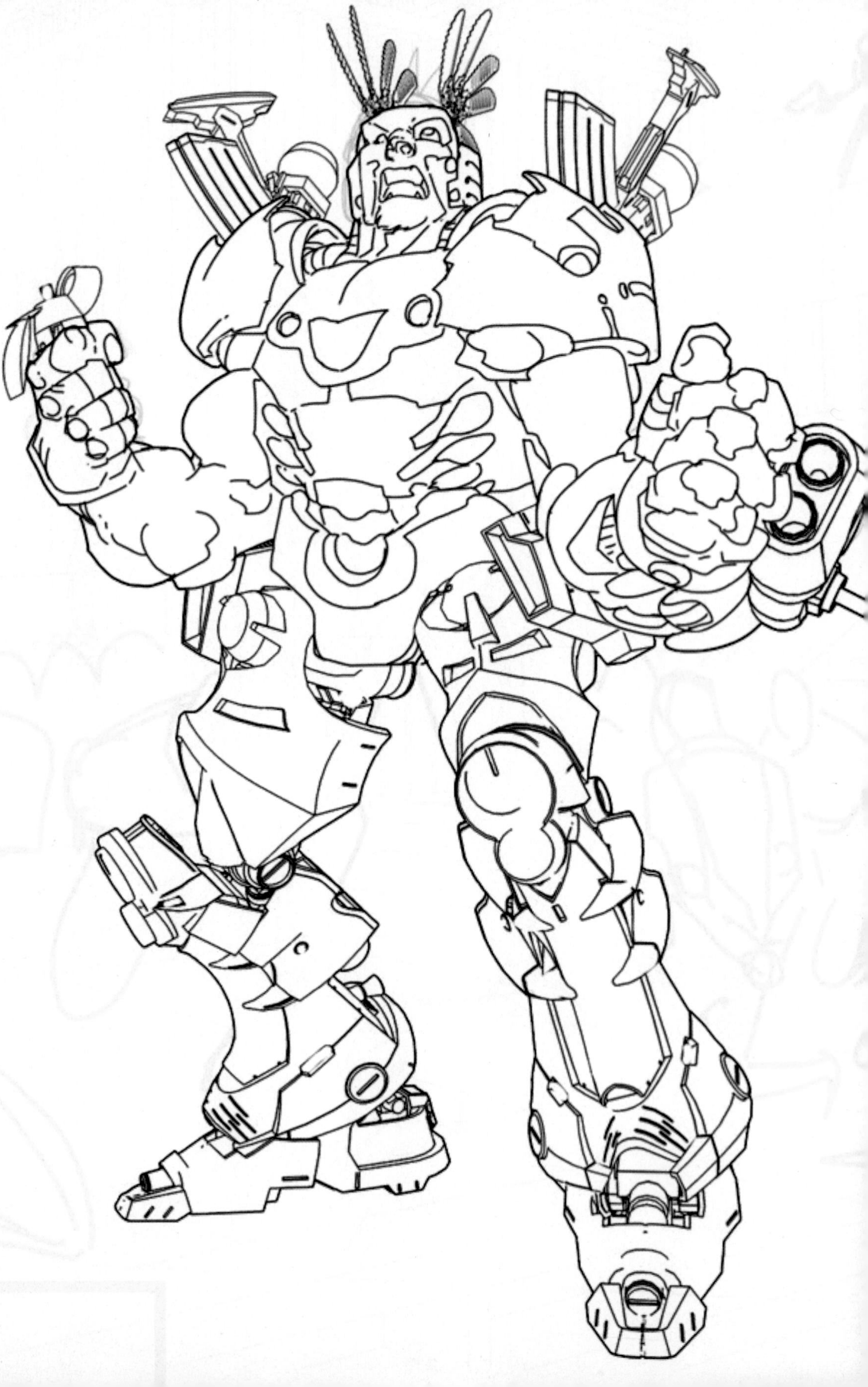